Causes of Action:
Civil Law and Social Justice

Second Edition

**Incorporating findings from the 2004 English and Welsh
Civil and Social Justice Survey**

Pascoe Pleasence

with

Nigel Balmer
and Alexy Buck

(Legal Services Research Centre)

ISBN 13   978 0 11 702284 3
ISBN 10   0 11 702284 5

First edition, 2004
Second edition first published 2006

Printed in the United Kingdom for The Stationery Office
N184712, C12, 2/06

Contents

Foreword by Rt. Hon. Lord Falconer of Thoroton   i

Acknowledgements   iii

Chapter 1.   Introduction: Civil Law and Social Justice   1

Chapter 2.   The Experience and Impact of Justiciable Problems   15

Chapter 3.   Inaction and Action: Responses to Justiciable Problems   79

Chapter 4.   The End: Objectives, and How and When Justiciable Problems   135
                   Conclude

Chapter 5.   An Integrated Approach to Social Justice   153

Appendix A.   Overview   179

Appendix B.   Bibliography   184

Foreword

I am delighted to have been asked to write the foreword to this important and timely publication. It provides an impressive evidence base for assessing the role that advice and legal services can play in tackling social exclusion.

The study demonstrates how people can be excluded from society by problems such as relationship breakdown, homelessness and discrimination. It also shows how many people are denied a resolution to their problems because they don't always know help is available or - if they do - where to go to get it.

For many years it has been argued that the problems people experience have a cost to the individuals concerned, to public services, and to society as a whole. This study allows us to get a clear idea of the extent of those costs. They are substantial. Over the three and a half-year period covered by the 2004 English and Welsh Civil and Social Justice Survey, it is estimated that the cost to individuals, health and other public services was at least £13 billion.

There is now no doubt that solving peoples' problems is – and must remain - a priority across Government.

Left unchecked, problems can escalate, and some problems, such as personal injury, relationship breakdown and employment amongst others, can lead to further problems. These 'trigger' problems can put people at risk of social exclusion.

We also know, from other research, that there are steep costs in providing people with pathways out of exclusion. What is particularly important to me is the role that advice services can play as a means of helping people to resolve their problems.

The most exciting contribution that this study makes to the debate is to give the first clear evidence that advice services improve peoples' chances of resolving their problems. High street advice centres, telephone helplines, solicitors, and the whole civil legal aid system play their part in helping people resolve their problems. Indeed those who are unable to access advice services find their problems persisting. On the other hand advice not only reduces the distress of individuals it also reduces costs for them, for government and for society. Investment in early advice clearly brings benefits for us all.

Reducing social exclusion is a priority across Government. Access to advice services is vital to this. This book helps us understand more about how we can help people with their problems, help them get the advice they need and, critically, help them out of social exclusion. Continued action in this area is vital to enable us to develop our understanding of the problems people face and to assess the impact that advice services make on the resolution of those problems.

The Right Honourable Lord Falconer of Thoroton
Secretary of State for Constitutional Affairs and Lord Chancellor
February 2006

Acknowledgements

The completion of this study would not have been possible but for the contributions of, literally, thousands of people. I could not hope to detail them all here, but I would none the less like to formally acknowledge at least some of them. Specifically, I would like to thank Peter Lynn, Paddy Costigan, Debbie Collins and Kirby Swales, who worked within the National Centre for Social Research (NCSR) to help finalise the questionnaires and manage the fieldwork for the 2001 Legal Services Research Centre (LSRC) national periodic survey of justiciable problems, now known as the English and Welsh Civil and Social Justice Survey, and the simultaneous survey of people living in temporary accommodation, along with the many NCSR fieldworkers who conducted the 2001 survey interviews. I would like to thank Bruce Hayward, Andrew Phelps, Carole Maxwell, Tim Hanson and Eleanor Storey of BMRB, who then expertly prepared and piloted the questionnaires and managed the fieldwork for the 2004 survey, along with the many BMRB fieldworkers who conducted the 2004 survey interviews. Also, most importantly, I would like to thank the 10,823 people who gave up their time for no personal reward to be interviewed about sometimes very personal and life-changing experiences.

I would like to thank the many past and present staff members of the Legal Services Commission and Department for Constitutional Affairs who helped to make this study and this publication a reality, and in particular Clare Dodgson, Richard Collins, Crispin Passmore, Emma Knights, Jill Saville, John Weston, Angela Lake-Carroll, Steve Orchard, Roger Hamilton, Chris Smith, Catherine Max, Helen Perkins, Andrew Frazer, Derek Hill, Robert Gill, Howard Thomson, Alan Cogbill, Phil Staker, Tony Donaldson, Lesley Hopcraft, Penny Innes, Stephen Gascoigne, Colin Myerscough and Kit Opie. I would also like to thank Donald Franklin of H.M. Treasury for contributing ideas during the development of the 2001 survey questionnaire. I am also most grateful for the immense contribution received from the many members of the Legal Services Commission's Regional Partnership and Planning Teams and the many members of Community Legal Service Partnerships throughout England and Wales with whom I discussed provisional findings and from iv

whom I obtained many ideas as to how to best interpret them and develop further analyses.

I would like to thank Kathryn Green, Heather Walker and Cate Fisher of the Legal Services Research Centre for their many helpful comments, literature reviews and diligent checking of the text. Also, I would like to thank Ian Carter of TSO for managing the publication process and Vicky Anning for copy editing the text.

Finally, I would like to thank the Nuffield Foundation for having supported the earlier *Paths to Justice* study, without which this study may never have been undertaken, and Professor Hazel Genn of University College London, Aoife O'Grady of the Department for Transport and Marisol Smith, Vicky Kemp, Ash Patel and, in particular, Alexy Buck and Nigel Balmer of the Legal Services Research Centre for their many contributions to the development of the first and second edition of this book.

Pascoe Pleasence

London, February 2006

1

Introduction: Civil Law and Social Justice

The problems to which the principles of civil law apply are not abstract 'legal problems.' They are not problems familiar only to lawyers, or discussed only in tribunals and civil courts. They are for the most part the problems of 'everyday life'[1] – the problems people face as constituents of a broad civil society. Following the establishment over the last thirty years of an extensive range of rights and obligations related to child support, education, employment, debt, health, housing and welfare benefits, these problems today involve numerous issues of basic social well-being.[2]

This does not mean that legal process provides the best means, or even a sensible means, through which to resolve particular 'justiciable'[3] problems. Many alternative means of resolution exist. Some of these, such as complaint and negotiation, often occur with reference to the law – in the 'shadow of the law.'[4] Others, though, such as Lewis's DIY solution for housing disrepair, invariably occur without any reference to law at all.[5] Also, resolutions may be brought about through governmental or corporate, rather than individual, action. However, the existence of a defining framework of civil law applicable to many problems of everyday social life and social well-being, and the possibilities for utilising legal services and process to

---

[1] 'The bread and butter issues' described by the Consortium on Legal Services and the Public (1996) *Agenda for Access: The American People and Civil Justice,* Chicago: American Bar Association, p.vii.
[2] This is despite a more recent 'backlash against rights,' characterised by internal review and complaints procedures. For a commentary on this and the rise of 'welfare rights,' see T. Goriely (1998) Making the Welfare State Work, in F. Regan, A. Paterson, T. Goriely, and D. Fleming (eds.) *The Transformation of Legal Aid,* Oxford: Oxford University Press.
[3] 'A matter experienced by a respondent which raised legal issues, whether or not it was recognised by the respondent as being "legal" and whether or not any action taken by the respondent to deal with the [matter] involved the use of any part of the civil justice system': H. Genn (1999) *Paths to Justice: What People Do and Think About Going to Law,* Oxford: Hart Publishing, p.12.
[4] R.H. Mnookin and L. Kornhauser (1979) Bargaining in the Shadow of the Law: The Case of Divorce, 88 *Yale Law Journal* 950.
[5] P. Lewis (1973) Unmet Legal Needs, in P. Morris, R. White and P. Lewis (eds.) *Social Needs and Legal Action,* Oxford: Martin Robertson.

reach solutions to such justiciable problems, mean that the infrastructure of *civil* justice today plays an important role in realising *social* justice. Also, especially as those who experience problems 'often experience a problem more than once *and* more than one type of problem,'[6] this infrastructure plays an important role in efforts to tackle 'social exclusion' – the 'shorthand term for what can happen when people or areas suffer from a combination of linked problems such as unemployment, poor skills, low incomes, poor housing, high crime, bad health and family breakdown.'[7]

This link between the infrastructure of civil justice – which comprises courts, tribunals, professional and lay legal and advice services, 'problem noticers,'[8] and professional and public legal education – and social exclusion has become increasingly prominent in government policy. Explicit reference was made to it in the 1998 government white paper *Modernising Justice.*[9] The white paper heralded the Access to Justice Act 1999 and the establishment of a Legal Services Commission with responsibility to develop a Community Legal Service focused on the issues that affect the everyday lives of the 'disadvantaged and socially excluded.'[10] A joint report of the government and Law Centres Federation, published around the time of establishment of the Legal Services Commission, stated that 'lack of access to reliable legal advice can be a contributing factor in creating and maintaining social exclusion.'[11] It explained that 'poor access to advice has meant that many people have suffered because they have been unable to enforce their legal rights effectively, or have even been unaware of their rights and responsibilities in the first place.' In the foreword to a recent follow-up report, David Lammy MP, then Parliamentary Secretary in the Department for Constitutional Affairs, spoke of the 'enormous

---

[6] H. Genn (1999) above, n.3, p.32. See also, for example, American Bar Association (1994) *Legal Needs and Civil Justice: A Survey of Americans – Major Findings from the Comprehensive Legal Needs Study,* Chicago: American Bar Association, p.3.

[7] Social Exclusion Unit (2001) *Preventing Social Exclusion,* London: Cabinet Office, p.10. While the Social Exclusion Unit definition provides a useful indication of the circumstances associated with the concept, it has been criticised for its brevity and for 'implying a passivity on the part of those who are socially excluded': A. Hannah (2004) Exercising Rights as the Way to Social Inclusion, in J. Grieve and R. Howard (eds.) *Communities, Social Inclusion and Crime,* London: Smith Institute. It should also be noted, as Ardill has recently observed, that many definitions of social exclusion exist, and a recent study of European Union policy documents found references to 'at least fifteen different types of social exclusion ... and over fifty ways a person could qualify as "socially excluded"': N. Ardill (2005) The Social Exclusion Trap, in *Legal Action,* August 2005, pp.7-8.

[8] See below, Chapters 3 and 5.

[9] Lord Chancellor's Department (1998) *Modernising Justice,* London: HMSO (Cmd. 4155).

[10] *Ibid.*, p.3.

[11] Lord Chancellor's Department and Law Centres Federation (2001) *Legal and Advice Services: A Pathway out of Social Exclusion,* London: Lord Chancellor's Department, p.11.

potential contribution that legal and advice services can make in tackling social exclusion.'[12] This was echoed by the Director of the Social Exclusion Unit, who was also quoted as asserting that 'independent advice plays an important part in efforts to reduce social exclusion.'[13] Thus, the Legal Services Commission's current corporate plan describes one of its contributions to social justice as enabling people to address problems 'which contribute to their social exclusion or which can help move them out of social exclusion.'[14]

While the language is relatively new, the targeting of social exclusion has long been recognised as a basis for public funding of legal and advice services. In the 1970s, for example, White's report to the Lord Chancellor on the 'unmet need' for such services described them as having three objectives:

> 'The first is to provide equality before the law when matters are dealt with by the courts. The second is directed towards social justice; to leave people who are already economically weak without the means to seek the remedies which the law provides is to emphasise further an existing social imbalance. The third objective is to assist in programmes for community development. Legal services are a means by which confidence can be recreated among deprived and alienated communities so that their members can protect and advance their legitimate interests by the use of the normal legal and administrative machinery.'[15]

The recognition also extends throughout the United Kingdom and beyond government. The Scottish Executive's recent consultation paper *Advice for All* set out, within an overall objective of 'enabling the resolution of justiciable problems,' the three purposes of public funded legal assistance as including 'to contribute to greater social inclusion and help close the opportunity gap in Scotland.'[16] In a report prepared

---

[12] Department for Constitutional Affairs and Law Centres Federation (2004) *Legal and Advice Services: A Pathway to Regeneration,* London: Department for Constitutional Affairs, p.6.

[13] *Ibid.,* p.29.

[14] Legal Services Commission (2005) *Corporate Plan 2005/6-2007/8,* London: Legal Services Commission, p.3. An earlier corporate plan referred more broadly to the Community Legal Service as 'a component of a wider government programme aimed at creating a fair and inclusive society': Legal Services Commission (2002) *Corporate Plan 2002/3-2003/4,* London: Legal Services Commission, p.9.

[15] R. White (1976) *Report to the Lord Chancellor: The Unmet Need for Legal Services,* London: Lord Chancellor's Office, pp.2-3.

[16] Scottish Executive Justice Department (2005) *Advice for All: Public Funded Legal Assistance in Scotland – The Way Forward,* Edinburgh: Scottish Executive, p.6.

for the Northern Ireland Legal Services Commission, Dignan has described how Northern Ireland's overarching Targeting Social Need policy context 'heightens the relevance of legal aid to targeting social need, promoting social inclusion and tackling inequality.'[17] Also, away from government it has been argued that 'legal advocacy and advice for the poor and excluded is an effective engine of social inclusion and fighting poverty through insuring and expanding rights to critical benefits and services, and giving a voice to grievances and empowering people and communities.'[18]

However, despite increased and widespread reference to the link between the civil justice infrastructure and social exclusion, until recently, little research had been undertaken to identify those people most vulnerable to justiciable problems, to determine how such problems impact on people's lives and communities, to ascertain the strategies and objectives people adopt in dealing with problems, or to establish how legal and advice services work to resolve or prevent problems. Prior to the mid-1990s, only a few attempts were made even to assess the prevalence of justiciable problems.[19] In the mid to late 1990s, though, a number of important and innovative studies investigated the prevalence of problems and the strategies used to deal with them. Nevertheless, even Genn's *Paths to Justice* and *Paths to Justice Scotland* surveys, and similar surveys conducted in the United States and New Zealand,[20] left many questions unanswered; particularly around how problems link with each other and broader circumstances, how people navigate the maze of advice services they

---

[17] T. Dignan (2004) *Legal Need in Northern Ireland: Literature Review*, Belfast: Northern Ireland Legal Services Commission, p.iii.

[18] J. Stein (2001) *The Future of Social Justice in Britain: A New Mission for the Community Legal Service*, London: Centre for Analysis of Social Exclusion, London School of Economics, p.48.

[19] See, for example, B. Abel-Smith, M. Zander and R. Brooke (1973) *Legal Problems and the Citizen: A Study in Three London Boroughs,* London: Heinemann; Royal Commission on Legal Services (1979) *Final Report,* London: HMSO (Cmd. 7648). For other jurisdictions see, for example, B. Curran (1977) *The Legal Needs of the Public,* Chicago: American Bar Foundation; M. Cass and R. Sackville (1975) *Legal Needs for the Poor,* Canberra: Australian Government Publishing Service; C. Messier (1975) *Les Mains de la Loi* (In the Hands of the Law), Montreal: Commission des Services Jurisdiques; K. Schuyt, K. Groenendijk and B. Sloot (1976) *De Weg naar Het Recht* (The Road to Justice), Deventer: Klewer. Also, for a more detailed commentary, see P. Pleasence, A. Buck, T. Goriely, J. Taylor, H. Perkins and H. Quirk (2001) *Local Legal Need,* London: Legal Services Research Centre.

[20] H Genn (1999), above, n.3; H. Genn and A. Paterson (2001) *Paths to Justice Scotland: What People in Scotland Do and Think About Going to Law,* Oxford: Hart Publishing; American Bar Association (1994), above, n.6; G. Maxwell, C. Smith, P. Shepherd and A. Morris (1999) *Meeting Legal Service Needs: Research Report Prepared for the Legal Services Board,* Wellington: Legal Services Board. Also see National Consumer Council (1995) *Seeking Civil Justice: A Survey of People's Needs and Experiences,* London: National Consumer Council; and Scottish Consumer Council (1997) *Civil Disputes in Scotland,* Glasgow: Scottish Consumer Council, Report.

utilise and what the infrastructure of civil justice actually 'delivers,'[21] either for individuals or for society at large.

The first edition of this book drew upon the 2001 Legal Services Research Centre (LSRC) national periodic survey of justiciable problems, now known as the English and Welsh Civil and Social Justice Survey. It built upon *Paths to Justice* and set out in some detail the irregular experience and impact of justiciable problems, the pitfalls people face when navigating the advice maze and the degree to which problem resolutions match people's objectives in acting to resolve them. This second edition, drawing on both the 2001 and follow-up 2004 surveys, expands upon the first edition by examining justiciable problems in a broader social and geographical context, setting out more details of the impact of problems, further revealing levels of awareness and understanding of legal and advice services, further depicting the methods and resources used by people to access such services and assessing the degree to which legal and advice services facilitate problem resolution and prevention. In doing so, it again illustrates and underlines the important links between justiciable problems and social exclusion, and between civil law and social justice.

THE ENGLISH AND WELSH CIVIL AND SOCIAL JUSTICE SURVEY

The English and Welsh Civil and Social Justice Survey provides detailed information on the nature, pattern and impact of people's experience of justiciable problems and the use and success of problem resolution strategies. Its purpose is to provide a broad empirical base for civil justice policy development and to allow the impact of government policies to be assessed and progress against Public Service Agreement (PSA) targets to be measured.[22] To date the survey has been conducted twice; first between July and October 2001, then again between July and December 2004. The recurring nature of the survey is intended to overcome the dangers of using different studies to compare changes in experience and processes over time.[23] Since this year the survey, like the British Crime Survey, has become continuous; meaning that

---

[21] H. Genn (1999), above, n.3, p.1.

[22] Legal Services Research Centre (2002) *Summary Technical and Baseline Report on the Lord Chancellor's Department's SR2000 PSA Targets 5 and 6*, London: LSRC; Legal Services Research Centre (2005) *Summary Technical Report on measures for the LCD/DCA SR2000 PSA Targets 5 and 6 / SR2002 PSA Target 6 / SR2004 PSA Target 5*, London: LSRC.

[23] P. Pleasence et al. (2001), above, n.19, p.24; H. Genn (1999), above, n.3, p.25; American Bar Association (1994) *Report on the Legal Needs of the Low- and Moderate-Income Public: Findings of the Comprehensive Legal Needs Study*, Chicago: American Bar Association, p.43.

fieldwork is now conducted every month of every year. This will enable still greater analysis of changes over time.

In terms of detail, the 2001 and 2004 surveys are the most extensive of their kind so far undertaken. They have their origins in a tradition of surveys dating back to the recession at the United States' Bar in the 1930s.[24] The questionnaires that were used share much in common with those used in the *Paths to Justice* surveys; adopting the same approach to identifying problems, including the same 'triviality threshold' for detailed follow-up, and featuring the same limitation to 'private individuals.'[25] However, the 2001 and 2004 surveys have in turn advanced substantially the *Paths to Justice* approach. The 2001 survey addressed problems that arose with the *Paths to Justice* surveys (such as in determining sources of financial assistance for those seeking redress), substantially shifted the focus of questions away from rare events (such as the use of formal process) towards early stage decision-making, and extended a broad range of social and demographic questions to all survey respondents. In addition, the survey reference period was reduced from five-and-a-half to three-and-a-half years to offer a better reflection of government spending review periods. The 2004 survey continued the process of shifting the focus of questions towards early stage decision-making. It introduced questions about people's experiences of crime, as well as additional sets of questions concerning methods of advice delivery and financial assistance. To explore further the complex links between problem experience and underlying vulnerabilities, as well as to further demonstrate the impact of problems, it also introduced additional questions designed to unravel the causes from the consequences of problems.

The basic form of the 2001 and 2004 surveys was the same. All respondents completed a screen interview, in which they were asked if they had experienced 'a problem' since January 1998 or 2001 that had been 'difficult to solve' in each of 18 distinct justiciable problem categories: discrimination; consumer; employment; neighbours; owned housing; rented housing; homelessness; money/debt; welfare benefits; divorce; relationship breakdown; domestic violence; children; personal injury; clinical negligence; mental health; immigration and unfair treatment by the police. To assist recall and to allow some assessment of the relative incidence of the

---

[24] C. Clark and E. Corstvet (1938) The Lawyer and the Public: An A.A.L.S. Survey, 47 *Yale Law Journal,* p.1972. For a history, see P. Pleasence et al. (2001), above, n.19, pp.7-27.
[25] H. Genn (1999), above, n.3, pp.12-14.

different types of problem falling within these categories, respondents were presented with 'show cards' for most of the problem categories (12 in 2001; 14 in 2004). These cards set out detailed lists of constituent problems, and respondents were asked to indicate which of them, if any, matched their own problems.[26] So, for example, constituent problems relating to employment included unfavourable changes being made to terms and conditions of employment, the work environment being unsatisfactory or dangerous, and being sacked or made redundant. Problems relating to rented housing included difficulties in getting a landlord to make repairs, difficulties in obtaining repayment of a deposit and eviction. Problems relating to money/debt included difficulties getting someone to pay money owed, disputes over bills, being threatened with legal action to recover money owed and mismanagement of a pension fund. Problems relating to children included difficulties fostering or adopting children, difficulties with children going to a school for which they are eligible and children being unfairly excluded or suspended from school. Finally, problems relating to mental health included unsatisfactory treatment or care in hospital, unsatisfactory care after release from hospital and difficulties obtaining a discharge from hospital.[27]

---

[26] No constituent problems were presented to respondents regarding the categories of homelessness, divorce, personal injury, clinical negligence and unfair treatment by the police. For these, it was deemed sufficient to refer to 'being homeless or threatened with being homeless,' 'divorce,' 'injuries or health problems ... (caused) by an accident or ... poor working conditions' (recorded separately in 2004), 'suffer(ing) as a result of negligent or wrong medical or dental treatment' (recorded separately in 2004) and being 'unfairly treated by the police ... (by) for example being assaulted by a police officer or being unreasonably arrested.' In 2001, in addition to the above, no constituent problems were presented to respondents in respect of consumer problems and problems with neighbours. The 2004 show cards for these problem types were based on detailed problem descriptions reported in 2001. The detailed problem descriptions for the consumer category were faulty: (a) electrical goods; (b) cars/motorcycles; (c) furniture; (d) clothing/footwear; (e) other goods; (f) major building work; (g) tradespeople's services; (h) garage services; (i) holidays/travel, and (j) other services. The detailed problem descriptions for the neighbours category were: (a) regular or excessive noise; (b) threats or harassment; (c) violence; (d) damage to your property or garden, and (e) other vandalism.

[27] In full, constituent discrimination problems comprised difficulties relating to discrimination because of: (a) race; (b) gender; (c) disability; (d) sexual orientation; (e) age, and (f) religion ((e) and (f) were added in 2004). Constituent employment problems comprised difficulties relating to: (a) being sacked or made redundant; (b) being threatened with the sack; (c) getting pay or a pension to which entitled; (d) other work rights (e.g. maternity pay, sickness pay, holiday entitlement, working hours); (e) changes to terms and conditions; (f) unsatisfactory or dangerous working conditions; (g) unfair disciplinary procedures, and (h) harassment. Constituent owned housing problems comprised difficulties relating to: (a) obtaining planning permission or consent; (b) buying or selling property (e.g. misleading surveys, problems with a lease); (c) communal repairs or maintenance; (d) repossession of the home; (e) being several mortgage payments in arrears; (f) squatters, and (g) boundaries or rights of way or access to property ((e) and (f) were recorded separately in 2004). Constituent rented housing problems comprised difficulties relating to: (a) unsafe living conditions; (b) otherwise unsuitable living conditions; (c) getting a deposit back; (d) being several rent payments in arrears; (e) getting a landlord to make repairs; (f) getting a landlord to provide other services; (g) agreeing with a landlord on rent,

The 18 problem categories used in the 2001 and 2004 surveys are very similar to those used in the *Paths to Justice* surveys, but with the inclusion of mental health and homelessness categories and the exclusion of a renting out property category. Also, no *separate* categories regarding neighbours, welfare benefits, domestic violence, clinical negligence, immigration or unfair treatment by the police were included in the *Paths to Justice* surveys.

In the 2001 survey, respondents were asked additionally whether, apart from anything they had already reported, they had had legal action taken against them, had been threatened with legal action or had started, or considered starting, any court proceedings. Respondents to the 2004 survey were not asked about these additional matters, as they were unnecessary to PSA target measurement and introduced

---

council tax, housing benefit payments or other terms of a tenancy agreement; (h) getting a written tenancy agreement; (i) transfer of tenancy on death or separation; (j) harassment by a landlord; (k) eviction or threat of eviction; (l) flatmates (non-relatives) not paying the rent or behaving in an antisocial manner; (m) renting out rooms to lodgers or sub-letting, and (n) boundaries or rights of way or access to property ((d) and (k) were recorded separately in 2004). Constituent money/debt problems comprised difficulties relating to: (a) getting someone to pay money they owed; (b) insurance companies unfairly rejecting claims; (c) incorrect or disputed bills (excluding rent/mortgage payments); (d) incorrect or unfair tax demands; (e) incorrect information or advice that led to the purchase of financial products; (f) mismanagement of a pension fund; (g) unfair refusal of credit as a result of incorrect information; (h) disputed (repeated) penalty charges by banks or utilities; (i) unreasonable harassment by creditors; (j) division of the content of a will or property after the death of a family member; (k) severe difficulties managing money; (l) being threatened with legal action to recover money owed, and (m) being the subject of a county court judgment. Constituent welfare benefits problems comprised difficulties relating to: (a) entitlement to welfare benefits; (b) entitlement to state pension/pension credits; (c) entitlement to student loans; (d) entitlement to grants; (e) the amount of welfare benefits; (f) the amount of state pension/pension credits; (g) the amount of student loans, and (h) the amount of grants ((a), (b), (c) and (d) were recorded separately in 2004, as were (e), (f), (g) and (h)). Constituent relationship breakdown problems comprised difficulties relating to: (a) the division of money, pensions or property on divorce or separation; (b) obtaining maintenance for self; (c) agreeing to pay maintenance to a former partner (other than for children); (d) obtaining child support payments; (e) agreeing to pay child support payments; (f) residence (custody) arrangements for children, and (g) access (contact) arrangements for children ((f) and (g) were recorded separately in 2004). Constituent domestic violence problems comprised: (a) suffering violence or abuse from a partner, ex-partner or other family member, and (b) children suffering violence or abuse from a partner, ex-partner or other family member. The additional constituent problem of 'being violent or abusive to a partner, ex-partner or other family member' was removed in 2004. Constituent children problems comprised difficulties relating to: (a) fostering or adopting children, or becoming a legal guardian; (b) children being taken into care or being on the Child Protection Register; (c) abduction or threatened abduction of children by a parent or family member; (d) children going to a school for which they are eligible; (e) children receiving an appropriate education (e.g. special needs); (f) children being unfairly excluded or suspended from school, and (g) children's safety at school or on school trips. Constituent mental health problems comprised difficulties relating to: (a) treatment or care received in hospital; (b) treatment or care received after leaving hospital; (c) other treatment or care; (d) admission to hospital; (e) obtaining discharge from hospital, and (f) restrictions or conditions of discharge ((e) and (f) were recorded separately and (c) and (d) added in 2004). Constituent immigration problems included difficulties relating to: (a) obtaining UK citizenship; (b) disputes over nationality; (c) obtaining authority to remain in the UK; (d) change of conditions under which it is possible to remain in the UK; (e) a partner or children entering the UK, and (f) asylum.

ambiguity to the scope of the survey. Instead, respondents were asked whether they had been a victim or perpetrator of crime during the reference period.[28]

For the two most recent problems identified in each category (other than crime), respondents were asked what help they had tried to obtain to resolve them, whether any formal dispute resolution processes had been utilised and what these were, whether and when the problems concluded, and if nothing was done to deal with problems, why this was so. In addition, in 2004, respondents were asked about the impact problems had had on their lives. All respondents were also asked for a range of details about themselves and the household in which they resided.

If respondents reported at least one problem in the screen interview (excluding problems with neighbours in 2001[29] and consumer problems and crime in 2004[30]), they progressed to a main interview, which addressed *a single problem* in more depth.[31] Areas covered by the main interview included: sources of advice that respondents considered; awareness and prior use of advice services; obstacles faced in obtaining advice; the nature and extent of assistance provided by advisers; respondents' objectives in taking action; the impact and outcome of problems and resolution strategies; respondents' regrets about resolution strategies; sources of financial assistance; and general attitudes to the civil justice system.

All interviews were conducted face-to-face in respondents' own homes and were arranged and conducted by the National Centre for Social Research (2001) and BMRB (2004). In 2001, the 5,611 survey respondents were drawn from a random selection of 3,348 residential household addresses across 73 postcode sectors of England and Wales.[32] Ninety-two per cent of adult household members (over 18 years of age) were interviewed.[33] The household response rate was 57 per cent (66 per cent where successful contact was made with an adult occupant), and the cumulative eligible adult response rate was 52 per cent. In 2004, the 5,015 survey respondents were drawn from a random selection of 3,832 residential addresses across 250

---

[28] The victim and perpetrator questions used the same categories of crime: (a) theft, (b) burglary, (c) robbery/mugging, (d) criminal damage/vandalism, (e) assault or threat of assault and (f) other.

[29] This was because they were not defined as 'priority' problems by the Lord Chancellor's Department at that time.

[30] This was to offset the following-up of problems with neighbours in 2004.

[31] The one problem was selected on an otherwise random weighted basis, to ensure the main section questions were asked of a reasonable number of all the main problem categories, and as many of the smaller categories as possible.

[32] The small user Postcode Address File (PAF) was used as the sampling frame.

[33] All adults were screened in 2,971 households. Some adults were screened in 377 households.

10

postcode sectors.[34] Seventy-two per cent of adult household members (over 18 years of age) were interviewed. The household response rate was 79 per cent (89 per cent where successful contact was made with an adult occupant), and the cumulative eligible adult response rate was 57 per cent. These response rates compare with other large-scale social surveys, such as the Expenditure and Food Survey,[35] Family Resources Survey and General Household Survey.[36]

Twenty-nine per cent of respondents to the 2001 survey and 22 per cent of respondents to the 2004 survey completed both a screen interview and a main interview. In part, the lower percentage for 2004 reflects the ineligibility for main interviews of consumer problems, which were the most frequently reported problem type. This lower percentage, though, also reflects a decrease in reported problem incidence.

Eighteen per cent of 2001 survey households contained just one adult, 66 per cent contained two adults and the remainder contained three or more. Households in 2004 were broadly similar, with 20 per cent containing one adult and 58 per cent containing two. The average number of adults in each household was 1.8 in both 2001 and 2004. Overall, the average survey household size was 2.4 in 2001, the same as the 2001 census estimate, and 2.7 in 2004. Also, 25 per cent of both 2001 and 2004 respondents aged between 25 and 74 years old reported a long-term limiting illness or disability, compared to the 2001 census estimate of 24 per cent.

Full technical reports of both surveys have been published elsewhere.[37]

---

[34] As with the 2001 survey, the small user Postcode Address File (PAF) was used as the sampling frame.

[35] This survey replaced the Family Expenditure Survey and the National Food Survey in 2001.

[36] The reported response rates for these household surveys are not directly comparable. Calculations differ between them. They are provided for indicative purposes. The response rates of the surveys in 2000/2001 were 59 per cent, 65 per cent and 67 per cent respectively: D. Down (2002) *Family Spending: A Report on the 2000-01 Family Expenditure Survey,* London: The Stationery Office; M. Rowland (2002) *Family Resources Survey: Annual Technical Report: 2000-01,* London: Office for National Statistics; A. Walker, J. Maher, M. Coulthard, E. Goddard and M. Thomas (2001) *Living in Britain: Results from the 2000-01 General Household Survey,* London: The Stationery Office. The reported response rates for 2003/4 were 58 per cent, 65 per cent and 72 per cent respectively: C. Gibbins (2004) *Family Spending: A Report on the 2003-04 Expenditure and Food Survey,* London: The Stationery Office; R. Chung, D. Donaldson, I. Herring, H. McColl, J. Snow, J. Cockerham, S. Ellerd-Elliott, B. Hirani and J. Shome (2004) *Family Resources Survey,* London: Department for Work and Pensions; National Statistics (2004) *General Household Survey 2003 Technical Appendix B*, London: Office for National Statistics.

[37] K. Swales (2001) *Measuring Legal Needs: Technical Report*, London: National Centre for Social Research; A. Phelps, B. Hayward and T. Hanson (2005) *2004 English and Welsh Civil and Social Justice Survey: Technical Report*, London: BMRB.

Unless indicated otherwise, all figures and analyses reported below are weighted for non-response using 2001 census data, so that the information can be generalised to the adult population of England and Wales.[38]

SURVEY OF PEOPLE LIVING IN TEMPORARY ACCOMMODATION

In parallel with the 2001 survey, a separate one-off survey was conducted of 197 adults in 170 households living at 47 temporary accommodation addresses (i.e. hostels, boarding houses, bed and breakfast lodgings and hotels) in seven local authority areas. This parallel 'temporary accommodation' survey was not intended to be representative of all adults living in this type of temporary accommodation. Instead, it was intended to provide an indication of the particular experience of one group of people normally excluded from national surveys – due to the difficulty of constructing an inclusive sample frame – and contrast it with the experience of 'national' survey populations. Living in such temporary accommodation is not only symptomatic of a broad range of social (and justiciable) problems, it can also have 'a hugely negative effect on the health, educational, welfare and social development of children,'[39] and consequently increases the likelihood of further problems. In light of this, the current government made the reduction of families living in Bed and Breakfast accommodation a priority, establishing a Bed and Breakfast Unit in November 2001, and in May 2004 reported a 99 per cent reduction of homeless

---

[38] Weighting of 2001 survey data also included a factor to reverse the effect of oversampling in three postcode sectors. Three 'case study' areas (Cumbria (rural), Kirklees (urban/rural) and Birmingham (dense urban)) were oversampled to allow for comparative analysis between the three. The general profile of 2001 and 2004 survey respondents was similar to that of the general population. Unweighted, 2001 survey respondents were 47 per cent male and 53 per cent female. 2004 respondents were 48 per cent male and 52 per cent female. This compares to 48 per cent and 52 per cent respectively across the general population (2001 census). Eight per cent of 2001 respondents were aged between 18 and 24 years, 39 per cent between 25 and 44 years, 27 per cent between 45 and 59 years, and 26 per cent 60 years or older. Nine per cent of 2004 respondents were between 18 and 24 years, 35 per cent between 25 and 44 years, 27 per cent between 45 and 59 years, and 29 per cent 60 years or older. This compares to 11 per cent, 38 per cent, 25 per cent and 27 per cent respectively across the general population (2001 census). Sixty-four per cent of 2001 respondents were in households with a weekly income of less than £500, 27 per cent in households with a weekly income of between £500 and £999, and 9 per cent in households with a weekly income of £1,000 or more. This compares to 62 per cent, 28 per cent and 10 per cent respectively across the general population at that time: Rowland M. (2002) *Family Resources Survey: Annual Technical Report: 2000-01*, London: Office for National Statistics. Around 51 per cent of 2004 respondents were in households with a weekly income of less than £500, 34 per cent in households with a weekly income of between £500 and £999, and 15 per cent in households with a weekly income of £1,000 or more. This compares to 60 per cent, 29 per cent and 11 per cent respectively across the general population at that time: R. Chung, et al. (2004), above, n.36, p.58
[39] Bed and Breakfast Unit (2001) *Targets and Action for Reducing B&B – The Way Forward,* London: Department for Transport, Local Government and the Regions.

families with children in long-term bed and breakfast accommodation.[40] The 2001 census estimated that, of the 934,263 people living in 'communal establishments,' 38,366 were living in hotels and hostels (excluding medical and care establishments).[41] This represents just one-tenth of one per cent of the adult population of England and Wales;[42] a small percentage, but nonetheless a considerable number.

As with the 2001 general population survey, all interviews for this separate survey were conducted face-to-face and were arranged and conducted by the National Centre for Social Research.

STRUCTURE OF THE BOOK

Chapter 2 sets out the pattern of experience of justiciable problems across England and Wales. It provides a detailed analysis of how differences in life circumstances entail differences in vulnerability to problems, and why different rates of problem incidence are therefore associated with differently constituted population groups, both in general terms and within individual problem categories. In doing so, it describes the vulnerability of certain population groups to problems that can be constituent elements of social exclusion, and the particular vulnerability of socially excluded groups to the experience of justiciable problems. It then explains how some types of justiciable problem are commonly experienced in combination, and how certain problems are more likely to lead to others, or to other social, economic and health problems; at great cost to the public purse. As a part of this, it is revealed how, reinforcing the disadvantage of those who are vulnerable to justiciable problems, the experience of problems has an additive effect – meaning that each time a person experiences a problem, they become increasingly likely to experience additional problems. Moreover, it demonstrates how people who experience multiple problems

---

[40] Statement by Lord Rooker, Minister for Homelessness, 4 May 2004.

[41] Table S126 ('Type of communal establishment and sex by resident type and age'), available for download at http://www.nationalstatistics.gov.uk. The total number of people living in all forms of temporary accommodation is much higher than this. For example, the Office of the Deputy Prime Minister reports that, at the end of March 2003, the total number of households accommodated in temporary accommodation by local authorities was 90,680: Table 623 ('Social housing: homeless households in temporary accommodation, by type of accommodation'), available for download at http://www.odpm.gov.uk.

[42] The census adult population estimate was 40,246,780.

become disproportionately more likely to experience the problems that play a direct role in social exclusion.

Chapter 3 sets out the ways in which people deal with justiciable problems. It highlights the sense of powerlessness and helplessness often experienced by those who face problems, and confirms there is a general lack of knowledge about obligations, rights and procedures on the part of the general public. It reveals that inaction is common in relation to some serious problem types, and also more likely among some disadvantaged population groups. In describing the problems about which people most often obtain advice, it demonstrates that advice is more likely to be sought in relation to more serious problems, but also explains how decisions on whether or not to obtain advice influence the way subsequent problems are resolved. Further, it explains how decisions on whether or not to obtain advice influence the conduct of other household members. The chapter then details the many sources from which people attempt to obtain advice, the difficulties they experience in doing so, and the nature of the advice and additional help received by those who are successful in doing so. Through this, it illustrates how certain advisers tend to be used in combination and how people's choices of advisers, although often logical and apposite, can be uncertain and unpromising. It also shows how people's choices can be undermined by the provision of services in manners that do not fit with their lives. Next, it exposes the phenomenon of referral fatigue, whereby the more times people are referred on by one adviser to another, the less likely they become to act on referrals. The chapter thus highlights the importance of equipping those to whom people initially turn for advice with the means to quickly and effectively refer them on to the most appropriate adviser when necessary. The chapter also demonstrates the relatively infrequent use of court, tribunal and, particularly, alternative dispute resolution processes in problem resolution. Lastly, it details how people pay for advice, confirms that most advice is provided free at the point of delivery, and explores the funding of advice services by third parties, such as the government, trade unions and insurers.

Chapter 4 sets out the range of objectives that motivate people to act to resolve justiciable problems. It illustrates the different objectives associated with different problem types, problem resolution strategies, advisers and population groups. In doing so, it describes how objectives vary along with the consequences of problems. It then details the ways in which problems conclude, and the extent to which people obtain their objectives. It points to evidence that resolutions are more favourable for those who obtain advice. It also suggests that those who are represented before courts and tribunals fare better than those who are not, and that objectives are more often met in relation to more important problems. The chapter then explains how the duration of problems varies by problem and adviser type, and also, seemingly, by seriousness. Lastly, it shows that, although people can benefit greatly from taking action to resolve justiciable problems, the resolution process can itself be stressful and even bring about ill-health.

Chapter 5 highlights the principal findings of the 2001 and 2004 surveys, along with those of the parallel 2001 survey of people living in temporary accommodation, and draws together the various threads running through the discussion in previous chapters. It also sets out the implications of our improved understanding of the nature and experience of justiciable problems, the impact of problems, people's strategies and difficulties in dealing with them, the reach of public funding of legal services, the manner in which problems are resolved and the impact of advice.

2

The Experience and Impact of Justiciable Problems

This chapter sets out the pattern of experience of justiciable problems across England and Wales. It provides a detailed analysis of the different rates of problem incidence associated with differently constituted population groups, both in general terms and within individual problem categories. In so doing, it describes the vulnerability of particular population groups to problems that can be constituent elements of social exclusion, and the particular vulnerability of socially excluded groups to the experience of justiciable problems. Building upon previous analyses, it also illustrates how vulnerability to justiciable problems is linked to geography and crime. The chapter then describes the distribution of justiciable problems among those respondents who reported having experienced one or more of them. It shows how the experience of problems has an additive effect; meaning that each time a person experiences one problem, they become increasingly likely to experience another. It illustrates how this additive effect can act to reinforce social exclusion. It explains how certain justiciable problems are more likely to lead to others, and then demonstrates the extent to which justiciable problems also lead to broader social, economic and health problems. Finally, it sets out a series of problem clusters and reveals the population groups most vulnerable to them.

THE INCIDENCE OF JUSTICIABLE PROBLEMS

Thirty-six per cent of respondents to the 2001 survey and 33 per cent of respondents to the 2004 survey reported having experienced one or more justiciable problems in the three-and-a-half year survey reference period (excluding the three residual problem categories included in 2001).[43] The decrease is significant,[44] reflects in part differences in the social and demographic profile of the 2001 and 2004 samples,[45] and mirrors the decrease in crime victimisation recorded through the British Crime Survey in recent years.[46] The 2001 survey's reported incidence rate is in turn down on the earlier *Paths to Justice* survey (40 per cent),[47] although the longer reference period of the *Paths to Justice* survey and differences in problems surveyed mean that incidence is more likely equivalent between the two surveys.[48]

All three English and Welsh surveys indicated substantially higher incidence rates than the *Paths to Justice Scotland* survey (24 per cent[49]) and three more recent derivative surveys conducted in Scotland (25 per cent and 29 per cent[50]) and Japan (19 per cent[51]). In contrast, they indicated substantially lower incidence rates than recent surveys in the United States (49 per cent[52]), New Zealand (51 per cent[53]), the

---

[43] This equates to 2,031 of 5,611 and 1,674 of 5,015 respondents respectively. Including the three residual problem categories (see above, Chapter 1, p.8), 37 per cent of respondents to the 2001 survey reported problems. The 2001 percentage reduces to 35 per cent (36 per cent including residual categories) if 'trivial' (H. Genn (1999), above, n.3, p.13) problems are excluded. The 2004 percentage remains at 33 per cent, as few of the problems reported fell within the Genn definition.

[44] $\chi^2_1 = 9.25$, $p < 0.01$

[45] Given the social and demographic profile of the 2004 sample, on the basis of the general incidence models set out in the first edition of this book, reported problem incidence would have been expected to decrease, but only marginally.

[46] The British Crime Survey indicates that the risk of being a victim of crime has fallen significantly in recent years from 40 per cent in 1995 to 26 per cent in 2003/04 and 24 per cent in 2004/05: T. Dodd, S. Nicholas, D. Povey and A. Walker (2004) *Crime in England and Wales 2003/2004,* London: Home Office (Home Office Statistical Bulletin 10/04); S. Nicholas, D. Povey, A. Walker and C. Kershaw (2005) *Crime in England and Wales 2004/2005,* London: Home Office (Home Office Statistical Bulletin 11/05).

[47] Thirty-four per cent if trivial problems are excluded.

[48] H. Genn (1999), above, n.3, p.23 and p.271. The steep decline in respondents' recall of problems going back over time suggests that the longer reference period of the *Paths to Justice* survey is likely to have inflated the incidence rate by no more than a few per cent. Given also that the differences in problems surveys was slight, the incidence rates appear broadly similar. See P. Pleasence, H. Genn, N.J. Balmer, A. Buck and A. O'Grady (2003) Causes of Action: First Findings of the LSRC Periodic Survey, 30(1) *Journal of Law and Society,* p.11.

[49] Twenty-three per cent if trivial problems are excluded. H. Genn and A. Paterson (2001), above, n.20, p.34 and p.275.

[50] The lower incidence rate was reported in C. Palmer and C. Monaghan (2001) *The Public Perspective on Accessing Legal Advice and Information: Key Findings from a Microcosm Study,* Edinburgh: Scottish Executive Central Research Unit. The higher rate was reported in J. Law, S. Assenti, G. Barton, K. McKissock, D. Baker, S. Ballow and D. Cookson (2004) *Community Legal Service: Assessing Need for Legal Advice in Scotland,* Edinburgh: The Stationery Office.

[51] M. Murayama, S. Minamikata, R. Hamano, K. Ageishi, I. Ozaki and I. Sugino (2005) *Legal Problems and their Resolution – Disputing Behaviour in Japan,* paper presented at the Annual Meeting of the Research Committee of Sociology of Law, International Sociological Association, Paris, France, 11-13 July 2005, p.5.

[52] American Bar Association (1994), above, n.6. The ABA sample was comprised of 1,782 low-income and 1,305 moderate-income households. The reported incidence rates were 47 per cent and 52 per cent respectively.

[53] G. Maxwell, C. Smith, P. Shepherd and A. Morris (1999) above, n.20.

Netherlands (67 per cent[54]), Canada (48 per cent[55]) and Australia (69 per cent[56]). However, the higher incidence rates in the surveys conducted in the United States, New Zealand and Australia are at least in part attributable to the inclusion of a broader range of problem categories.[57] Additionally, the American survey was of households, rather than individuals, thus entailing a greater chance of problems being reported in each instance. The American survey was also based on 'disadvantaged rather than general population samples,'[58] as were the Canadian and Australian surveys. As detailed below, this may provide a further explanation of differences.

Although the problem categories included in the Dutch and Canadian surveys were broadly similar to those included within the English and Welsh surveys, the methods used to conduct the surveys were markedly different. The Dutch survey was conducted via the internet, while the Canadian survey, like the American and Australian surveys, was conducted over the telephone. This, as Currie has observed, raises the possibility that people responding to internet and telephone surveys 'are more likely to have problems and be willing to talk about them.'[59] This is consistent with the lower rates of problem incidence indicated by the Scottish and Japanese surveys, which were conducted face-to-face.

However, neither focus nor method can account for the much lower reporting rate in Scotland relative to England and Wales. The *Paths to Justice Scotland* survey used the same methodology and questionnaire as the earlier *Paths to Justice* survey and therefore shares the earlier survey's great similarities to the 2001 and 2004 surveys.

---

[54] B.C.J. van Velthoven and M. ter Voert (2005) *Paths to Justice in the Netherlands*, paper presented at the ILAG conference, Killarney, Ireland, 8-10 June 2005.

[55] A. Currie (2005) *A National Survey of the Civil Justice Problems of Low And Moderate Income Canadians: Incidence and Patterns*, paper presented at the ILAG conference, Killarney, Ireland, 8-10 June 2005.

[56] C. Coumarelos, Z. Wei and A. Zhou (2006) *Multiple Pathways to Justice in Disadvantaged Communities: NSW Legal Needs Survey 2003*, Sydney: Law and Justice Foundation of New South Wales.

[57] The United States survey included 67 problem categories, extending to concerns about the community/regional environment and problems connected with small businesses: American Bar Association (1994), above, n.6, Appendix B. The New Zealand survey included 27 problem categories, extending to crime, carer problems and disagreements with public bodies. It also provided an opportunity to report on problems or disagreements not included within the 27 categories: G. Maxwell, C. Smith, P. Shepherd and A. Morris (1999) above, n.20, p.30. The Australia survey included 101 different legal events, extending to problems encountered in the running of a business, wills and estates, general crime and traffic offences. The incidence rate of civil justice problems alone was also in excess of 60 per cent: C. Coumarelos, Z. Wei and A. Zhou (2006), above, n.56.

[58] C. Coumarelos, Z. Wei and A. Zhou (2006), above, n.56.

[59] A. Currie (2005), above, n.55, p.5.

In *Paths to Justice Scotland,* Genn and Paterson 'discounted the possibility that there is actually a lower incidence of justiciable problems in Scotland, and instead suggested explanations for a substantial reporting difference between the population of England and Wales and that of Scotland.' The lower rate in Scotland was ascribed to a 'greater sense of fatalism' and more 'community-orientation' on the part of the Scottish population. These factors would lead, it was argued, to systematic under-reporting of problems and a lesser likelihood of them being perceived as 'individual matters rather than collective problems.'[60] Certainly, attitude may in part explain the difference. However, other factors cannot be discounted. The number and type of problems people experience will be affected by the form and 'adequacy'[61] of law governing people's lives, as well as the adequacy of public services. As a distinct legal jurisdiction and with different forms and levels of public service provision to England and Wales – perhaps an aspect of greater community-orientation – Scotland is certainly no mirror of England and Wales. Moreover, there are undoubtedly real differences in people's underlying circumstances north and south of the English-Scottish border. There are significant geographical and demographic dissimilarities between Scotland, England and Wales,[62] and these dissimilarities will be reflected in real differences in life experience. In turn, as is illustrated in later sections, differences in life experience entail differences in vulnerability to justiciable problems.[63]

THE DISTRIBUTION OF JUSTICIABLE PROBLEMS

Although around one-third of 2001 and 2004 survey respondents reported one or more justiciable problems, the experience of problems was far from randomly distributed across the survey populations. Multi-level binary logistic regression was used to test the influence of a range of social and demographic predictors on the likelihood of reporting one or more justiciable problems.[64] A number of predictors were found to be

---

[60] H. Genn and A. Paterson (2001), above, n.20, p.251.

[61] C. Coumarelos, Z. Wei and A. Zhou (2006), above, n.56.

[62] P. Pleasence, H. Genn, N.J. Balmer, A. Buck and A. O'Grady (2003), above, n.48, p.18.

[63] Genn and Paterson themselves observed a substantial difference in reporting rates between 'urban' (28 per cent) and 'rural' (23 per cent) Scottish regions (H. Genn and A. Paterson (2001), above, n.20, p.41) though this was not reflected in the findings of the more recent Scotland survey (J. Law et al. (2004), above, n.50, p.17) nor to any great extent by the findings set out below.

[64] The analysis was reworked from the first edition of this book to enable improved analytical techniques to be used, to remove some problems of multicolinearity and to provide directly comparable findings. The independent variables used in the analysis were: gender, ethnicity (white, black, Asian, other), house type (detached, semi-detached, terrace, flat), availability of private motorised transport,

influential in relation to both surveys: health/disability status; family type; housing type; means tested benefits status; age; availability of private transport and qualifications. In addition, economic activity and tenure type were both found to be significantly influential in relation to the 2001 survey and income in relation to the 2004 survey.

Long-standing ill-health or disability was a strongly influential predictor of justiciable problems reported in both surveys. So, whereas 43 per cent of respondents to the 2001 survey who reported long-standing ill-health or disability also reported having experienced one or more justiciable problems,[65] only 35 per cent of the remaining respondents did so. In 2004 the figures were 38 per cent and 32 per cent respectively.[66]

The type of family in which respondents lived was also an important influence on whether justiciable problems were reported. In both 2001 and 2004, respondents in relationships reported problems on fewer occasions than others. However, the form of relationships and the presence of children in families appeared to be the most important factors. There was, for example, a significant difference between those who were married and those who were cohabiting, with the latter much more likely to report problems. Thus, whereas 45 per cent of cohabitees reported problems in the 2001 survey, just 34 per cent of those who were married did. In 2004, the difference was even greater, with 44 per cent of cohabitees reporting problems, compared to 30 per cent of those who were married. However, while in both surveys cohabitees reported problems more often than single people without children, lone parents were by far the most likely to report problems, with 66 per cent doing so in 2001 and 57 per cent in 2004.[67]

---

family type (married with children, married with no children, cohabiting with children, cohabiting without children, lone parent, single without children), tenure type (own, mortgage, rent public, rent private, rent free), economic activity (active, inactive), long-standing illness/disability status, qualifications, means tested welfare benefit status, income (<£10,000 p.a., >£50,000 p.a., other), age and age[2]. We also looked at between-household variance. Not all variables were included in all analyses, as incidence was sometimes too rare to allow the full set to be included. Further technical details and output tables are available for download from www.lsrc.org.uk.

[65] Six hundred of 1395. Also, 54 per cent (133/246) of respondents who were economically inactive as a result of 'sickness' reported problems. This is echoed by the Canadian findings relating to disability pension status. See, further, A. Currie (2005), above, n.55, p.6.

[66] Four hundred and eighty of 1275 respondents to the 2004 survey who reported long-standing ill-health or disability also reported one or more justiciable problems. Also, 52 per cent (124/240) of respondents who were economically inactive as a result of 'sickness' reported problems.

[67] One hundred and forty-seven of 223 (2001) and 108 of 189 (2004). See, further, A. Buck, P. Pleasence, N.J. Balmer, A. O'Grady and H. Genn (2004) Lone Parents and Civil Law: Their Experience of Problems and Their Advice Seeking Behaviour, in *Social Policy and Administration*,

As with type of family, the type of home in which respondents lived had a strong influence on whether justiciable problems were reported, both in terms of tenure and physical structure. Those living in high-density housing – flats in particular – appeared more likely than others to report problems. As a result, whereas 52 per cent of respondents living in flats and 40 per cent of respondents living in terraced houses reported one or more problems in 2001, only 34 per cent of those living in detached or semi-detached houses did. Likewise, in 2004, whereas 41 per cent of respondents living in flats reported a problem, only 28 per cent of those living in detached houses did. In 2001, respondents who lived in rented accommodation were also significantly more likely than others to report problems, and those with mortgages were more likely to report problems than those who owned their own homes outright. While this significant difference in likelihood was not seen in 2004, the proportion of those 2004 respondents who lived in rented accommodation who reported problems was still higher, particularly in relation to those who owned their own homes outright.[68]

The reporting rate of justiciable problems also varied with age. Problems were most frequently reported by respondents in their mid-thirties, with a peak at 41 years of age in 2001 and 37 in 2004. As with other surveys, the reporting of problems then declined consistently as age increased.[69] So, in 2001 whereas 45 per cent of respondents aged between 25 and 44 reported one or more problems, just 18 per cent of respondents aged 75 or over did so. Younger respondents were also less likely to report problems, with only 34 per cent of respondents aged between 18 and 24 doing so in 2001. The pattern in 2004 was much the same.[70] However, as Kenrick has observed, respondents aged between 18 and 24 reported more problems in 2001,

Vol.38, No.3 and R. Moorhead, M. Sefton, G. Douglas (2004) *The Advice Needs of Lone Parents,* London: National Council for One Parent Families. This finding also echoes the recent findings of Currie and van Velthoven and ter Voert: A. Currie (2005), above, n.55, p.6; B.C.J. van Velthoven and M. ter Voert (2005), above, n.54, p.5.

[68] Accordingly, whereas 46 per cent of respondents who were renting in the private or public rented sector reported one or more problems, 40 per cent of those with mortgages and just 25 per cent of those who owned their home outright did so. This is a similar finding to that of G. Maxwell, C. Smith, P. Shepherd and A. Morris (1999) above, n.20, p.47.

[69] See H. Genn (1999), above, n.3, H. Genn and A. Paterson (2001), above, n.20, American Bar Association (1994), above, n.6, National Consumer Council (1995), above, n.20, and Scottish Consumer Council (1997), above, n.20, G. Maxwell, C. Smith, P. Shepherd and A. Morris (1999) above, n.20, A. Currie (1995), above, n.55 and B.C.J. van Velthoven and M. ter Voert (2005), above, n.54.

[70] In 2004, just under 35 per cent of those aged 18 to 24, 41 per cent of those aged 25 to 44 and 15 per cent of those aged 75 or over reported problems.

proportionately, than the population as a whole in 10 out of 18 problem categories.[71] The same was the case in 2004. Furthermore, as is shown below, 'these problem types include many of the key areas of social welfare law.'[72]

Also, respondents in different economic circumstances reported problems at different rates. Economically inactive respondents to the 2001 survey were significantly more likely to report problems. While this was not so generally in 2004, in both 2001 and 2004 unemployed respondents and those unable to work through sickness reported problems more often than others. So, in 2001, whereas 54 per cent of unemployed respondents reported one or more justiciable problems, 39 per cent of the remainder of respondents of working age did so. The figures were 55 per cent and 37 per cent respectively in 2004. In addition, reflecting the findings of the Dutch and Canadian surveys,[73] respondents in receipt of welfare benefits were more likely than others to report problems. However, demonstrating the complexity of patterns of vulnerability, those at either end of the income spectrum were found to report problems more often than others. In 2001, respondents on exceptionally low incomes (less than £4,000 per annum) were the most likely to report problems.[74] Forty-eight per cent of these exceptionally low-income respondents reported one or more problems in 2001, compared to 37 per cent of other respondents. The picture was less clear in 2004, though, with figures of 37 per cent and 33 per cent respectively.[75]

In addition, in both 2001 and 2004, respondents who owned or had regular use of a motor vehicle were significantly more likely to report problems.

Finally, as the surveys in New Zealand, the Netherlands and Canada also found, respondents with academic qualifications were more likely to report justiciable problems than those without.[76] To some extent, though, this reflected a link between academic qualifications and age, with older respondents less likely to hold qualifications. Thus, if age was standardised for those with or without academic qualifications, to produce similar age profiles, the difference between those with or without academic qualifications became less pronounced.[77]

---

[71] J. Kenrick (2005) Young People Need Advice Too, in *Legal Action*, July 2005.
[72] *Ibid.*, p.6.
[73] B.C.J. van Velthoven and M. ter Voert (2005), above, n.54, p.5; A. Currie (2005), above, n.55, p.6.
[74] Forty-eight per cent of this group reported problems. $\chi^2_1 = 9.5$, p = 0.002. 101 of 210.
[75] $\chi^2_1 = 1.9$, p = 0.17. 132 of 360.
[76] G. Maxwell, C. Smith, P. Shepherd and A. Morris (1999) above, n.20, p.43; B.C.J. van Velthoven and M. ter Voert (2005), above, n.54, p.5; A. Currie (2005), above, n.55, p.5.
[77] In 2004, 37 per cent of those with academic qualifications had one or more problem, compared to 25 per cent of others. Following age standardisation, these figures changed to 36 per cent and 29 per cent.

22

By using multi-level models, it was possible to explore whether the experience of problems by individuals within a household had an impact on the problem experience of others within the household. The models indicated that household effects explained around 30 per cent of the residual variability of overall problem experience,[78] meaning that there was indeed such an impact. Thus, if others in a respondent's household reported no problems, the likelihood of a respondent reporting problems was significantly lower. However, if respondents reported one or more problems, then the likelihood of someone living in the same household reporting problems was significantly higher.

As with the *Paths to Justice* surveys,[79] no differences were found in the overall problem reporting rates of male or female respondents, or white or black and minority ethnic respondents.[80] These results contrast with those of the New Zealand and Canadian surveys, which found that indigenous respondents reported problems more often than others.[81] They also contrast with those of the Australian survey, which found that respondents 'born in an English-speaking country' reported problems more often.[82] However, as is illustrated below, there were significant differences, in both 2001 and 2004, in the types of problems reported by men and women and respondents in different ethnic groups.

Certainly, in part the above findings reflect differences in understanding, perception and attitude towards what constitutes 'a problem' that is 'difficult to solve.' It would be unrealistic to believe surveys such as the English and Welsh Civil and Social Justice Survey could completely bypass 'socially stratified differences in lay perceptions'[83] of justiciable problems. Also, the findings will reflect the nature of

---

[78] Using a simple threshold model where the intra-household correlation was not dependent upon covariates. See T.A.B. Snijders and R.J. Boskers (1999) *Multilevel Analysis,* Newbury Park, California: Sage.
[79] H. Genn (1999), above, n.3, p.28. H. Genn and A. Paterson (2001), above, n.20, pp.37-38.
[80] In 2001, 38 per cent of female respondents reported one or more problems, compared to 37 per cent of male respondents. In 2004, the figures were 33 per cent and 34 per cent respectively. In 2001, 38 per cent of black and minority ethnic respondents reported one or more problems, compared to 37 per cent of white respondents. In 2004, the figures were 36 per cent and 33 per cent respectively. A recent study for Citizens Advice, however, did find differences in the rate at which black and Asian respondents reported 'a difficulty over the last year that they would have liked free advice on' (MORI (2004) *Unmet Demand for Citizens Advice Bureaux,* London: Citizens Advice). Fifty-two per cent of black respondents reported such a difficulty, compared to 39 per cent of Asian respondents.
[81] G. Maxwell, C. Smith, P. Shepherd and A. Morris (1999) above, n.20, p.40; A. Currie (2005), above, n.55, p.6.
[82] C. Coumarelos, Z. Wei and A. Zhou (2006), above, n.56.
[83] M. Noble, M. Lloyd, M. Sigala, G. Wright, M. Cox, C. Dibben, H. Perkins and N. Strudwick (2002) *Predictive Legal Needs Models Development Project: Report to the Legal Services Research Centre,*

the sampling frames used for the 2001 and 2004 surveys. For example, homeless people and people living in institutions, such as prisoners or those in residential care, were excluded. The findings of surveys that focus on these excluded groups, such as the temporary accommodation survey reported on below, are therefore a vital element of our understanding.

Lastly, since the social and demographic data used in the models relate only to the time of interview, differences in propensities to report problems reflect in part vulnerability to problems and in part their social, economic and health impact. In the sections that follow, it will be illustrated clearly how reporting patterns of different types of problem reflect both real underlying patterns of vulnerability and also the far-reaching consequences that follow from some problems.

INCIDENCE AND GEOGRAPHY

In both 2001 and 2004, respondents in Wales reported significantly fewer problems than their counterparts in England, mirroring the differences reported between Scotland and England.[84] In 2001, whereas 32 per cent of Welsh respondents reported one or more problems, 38 per cent of English respondents did so. In 2004, the figures were 28 per cent and 34 per cent respectively.[85] Moreover, in both 2001 and 2004 there were differences in the incidence rate of problems between the different regions of England, with the highest rates in London.[86] Outside of London, though, there was no discernable pattern. Also, there was no difference in incidence between urban and rural areas, although there was some suggestion that incidence was lower in areas of lowest population density.[87]

Oxford: Social Disadvantage Research Centre, Department of Social Policy and Social Work, University of Oxford.

[84] H. Genn and A. Paterson (2001), above, n.20.

[85] $\chi^2_1 = 5.25$, p<0.05 (2001); $\chi^2_1 = 3.69$, p<0.1 (2004). It should be noted, though, that the nature of the sampling frames used in the 2001 and 2004 surveys does not provide for Welsh respondents being representative of the population of Wales as a whole. Further, 2001 and 2004 Welsh respondents may not be representative of each other.

[86] $\chi^2_9 = 67.97$, p<0.001 (2001); $\chi^2_9 = 35.42$, p<0.001 (2004). The incidence rate in London was 47 per cent in 2001 and 40 per cent in 2004.

[87] The results of both the *Paths to Justice Scotland* and follow-up Palmer and Monaghan surveys suggested 'that members of the public in rural areas experienced fewer civil problems than those in urban areas.' However, the report of the latter also warned that there was an 'uneven and complex' distribution of problems, which prevented any clear conclusions from being drawn: C. Palmer and C. Monaghan (2001), above, n.50, p.13. See, also, H. Genn and A. Paterson (2001), above, n.20, p.41. However, the results of the later Law et al. survey indicated no such difference: J. Law et al. (2004), above, n.50.

JUSTICIABLE PROBLEMS AND THE EXPERIENCE OF CRIME

The 2004 survey included questions concerning not only people's experience of justiciable problems, but also their experience of crime. Overall, 20 per cent of respondents reported having been a victim of crime during the survey reference period. Eight per cent reported having been a victim of theft, 7 per cent reported criminal damage, 5 per cent reported burglary, 2 per cent reported assault, 2 per cent reported robbery and 1 per cent reported some other offence. This is comparable to the findings of the 2004/05 British Crime Survey, in which 24 per cent of respondents aged 16 or over reported having been a victim of one or more of a broad range of crimes in the preceding year. The 2004/05 British Crime Survey also revealed a similar pattern of offences, with the great majority concerning property.[88]

When being a victim of crime during the survey reference period was added to the regression model outlined above, it was found to be the most significant predictor of justiciable problems. In fact, of those people who reported having been a victim of crime, 47 per cent also reported one or more justiciable problems. This echoes the experience of crime itself, which has attracted the observation that 'victimisation is the best single predictor of victimisation.'[89]

Of course, as Young has noted, 'the people who suffer most from crime tend to suffer most from other social problems,'[90] and there is evident coincidence between the demographics and geography of crime and of justiciable problems. Although, as Zedner has commented, the British Crime Survey 'tends to gloss over major geographical, social and economic differences' in regard to the risk of crime victimisation, clear and significant differences are apparent.[91] So, for example, people living in 'hard pressed'[92] areas are more likely to report having been victims of crime, especially if they are single (particularly lone parents) and young.[93] There is also a

---

[88] S. Nicholas et al. (2005), above, n.46.

[89] K. Pease (1998) *Repeat Victimisation: Taking Stock,* London: Home Office, Crime Detection and Prevention Paper 90, p. v.

[90] J. Young (1994) Recent Paradigms in Criminology, in M. Maguire, R. Morgan and R. Reiner (eds.) *The Oxford Handbook of Criminology* (first edition), Oxford: Clarendon Press, p.113. He goes on in the same sentence to give the examples of physical and mental illness and bad housing and states: 'the effect of crime thus *compounds* with other problems' (emphasis in the original).

[91] L. Zedner (2002) Victims, in M. Maguire, R. Morgan and R. Reiner (eds.) *The Oxford Handbook of Criminology,* third edition, Oxford: Clarendon Press, p. 422.

[92] As defined by ACORN.

[93] S. Nicholas et al. (2005), above, n.46.

difference in the proportion of people who report having been victims of crime in urban and rural areas.[94]

The extent of the overlap between crime victimisation and experience of justiciable problems varied considerably by offence type (see Table 2.1). Whereas 42 per cent of respondents who reported having been burgled also reported one or more justiciable problems, the figure rose to 69 per cent for those who had been assaulted. Linked to this, as is further illustrated below, different offence types were associated with different categories of justiciable problem.

Table 2.1

Incidence of Crime Victimisation and Justiciable Problems

Offence Type	% of respondents who reported being victims	% of respondents who reported being victims and justiciable problems	% of victims who also reported justiciable problems
Theft	7.7	3.6	46.9
Criminal damage	6.8	3.7	54.2
Burglary	5.3	2.2	41.7
Assault	2.1	1.5	69.1
Robbery	1.5	0.7	44.0

Weighted base = 5,015

Although few respondents to the 2004 survey admitted to having committed one of the crimes asked about,[95] it is evident that there is a great deal of commonality between people who are victims of crime and offenders.[96] Thus, 64 per cent of those respondents who reported having been offenders also reported having been victims. In addition, 57 per cent reported having experienced one or more justiciable problems. As Williams has argued, victims and offenders should therefore not be thought of as

---

[94] S. Nicholas et al. (2005), above, n.46, pp97-98. For example, violence and vehicle theft were reported around twice as often by people living in urban areas, while burglary was reported 50 per cent more often. The 2004 English and Welsh Civil and Social Justice Survey also suggested that the risk of victimisation was greater in urban areas. So, while 21 per cent of respondents in urban areas reported having been a victim of crime, the figure was 18 per cent for others. Moreover, just 13 per cent of those living in 'coastal and countryside' areas reported having been the victim of a crime, as opposed to 20 per cent of others.

[95] Two per cent of respondents said they had committed an offence during the survey reference period.

[96] D. Deadman and Z. MacDonald (2004) Offenders as victims of crime? An Investigation into the Relationship Between Criminal Behaviour and Victimization, in the *Journal of the Royal Statistical Society*, Vol. 167, Part 1, pp. 35-67.

discrete, but as intricately interwoven categories,[97] both closely associated with social adversity and exclusion.

INCIDENCE AMONG THOSE IN TEMPORARY ACCOMMODATION

Respondents to the 2001 survey of people living in temporary accommodation were far more likely to be lone parents (30 per cent, compared to 4 per cent in both the 2001 and 2004 surveys).[98] They were also substantially younger than the general population survey respondents (43 per cent aged under 25, compared to 8 per cent in 2001 and 11 per cent in 2004).[99] They were less economically active (25 per cent in employment, compared to 60 per cent in 2001 and 58 per cent in 2004).[100] They also tended to be on very low incomes (with a median income of less than £6,000 per annum, compared to more than £20,000 for the general population survey respondents, in both 2001 and 2004),[101] and they were not living in their own homes. Temporary accommodation survey respondents unsurprisingly, therefore, also reported justiciable problems much more often than general population survey respondents. Overall, 84 per cent of temporary accommodation survey respondents reported one or more justiciable problems.[102]

THE INCIDENCE OF PROBLEMS OF DIFFERENT TYPES

The reported incidence of problems of different types varied greatly in both the 2001 and 2004 surveys. As with the surveys carried out in the United States, New Zealand, the Netherlands and first *Paths to Justice* survey, consumer problems were reported most frequently (13 per cent of respondents in 2001 and 10 per cent in 2004), and immigration and nationality problems least frequently (one-third of 1 per cent of

---

[97] B. Williams (1999) *Working with Victims of Crime: Policies, Politics and Practice.* London: Jessica Kingsley Publishers.

[98] This compares to $6^1/_2$ per cent of the population of England and Wales, as estimated by the 2001 Census.

[99] The mean age of temporary accommodation survey respondents was 30 years old, compared to 46 for 2001 survey respondents and 47 for 2004 survey respondents.

[100] Also, 18 per cent were unemployed, compared to 3 per cent of 2001 survey respondents and just over 2 per cent for 2004 survey respondents.

[101] Thirty-two per cent of temporary accommodation survey respondents had an income below £4,000, compared to 4 per cent of 2001 survey respondents. Seven per cent of 2004 respondents had an income below £5,000.

[102] One hundred and sixty-five of 197. If 'trivial' problems are excluded, the percentage reduces slightly to 83 per cent.

respondents in 2001 and one-fifth of 1 per cent of respondents in 2004).[103] Other
commonly reported problems were those relating to noisy or anti-social neighbours,
money and debt, employment, housing (owned or rented),[104] personal injury, and
family breakdown.[105] Other rarely reported problems were those relating to unfair
treatment by the police, homelessness, and mental health.

Table 2.2

Reported Incidence of Problem Types

Problem Type	2001 N	2001 %	2004 N	2004 %
Consumer	748	13.3	503	10.0
Neighbours	471	8.4	329	6.6
Money/debt	465	8.3	279	5.6
Employment	344	6.1	260	5.2
Personal injury	217	3.9	244	4.9
Rented housing	215	3.8	137	2.7
Owned housing	135	2.4	121	2.4
Welfare benefits	127	2.3	98	1.9
Relationship breakdown	124	2.2	84	1.7
Divorce	122	2.2	106	2.1
Children	108	1.9	75	1.5
Clinical negligence	92	1.6	79	1.6
Domestic violence	88	1.6	42	0.8
Discrimination	80	1.4	111	2.2
Unfair treatment by the police	38	0.7	40	0.8
Homelessness	36	0.6	61	1.2
Mental health	26	0.5	11	0.2
Immigration	18	0.3	16	0.3

Weighted base: 5,611 (2001), 5,015 (2004)

Reflecting the significant decrease in general reporting of problems between
2001 and 2004, reported incidence decreased in 11 problem categories and increased
in just four (see Table 2.2). Of those categories that saw an increase in incidence,

---

[103] American Bar Association (1994), above, n.6, G. Maxwell, C. Smith, P. Shepherd and A. Morris (1999) above, n.20, H. Genn (1999), above, n.3. In *Paths to Justice Scotland*, consumer problems were the second most frequently reported type of problem, and immigration problems the second least frequently reported: H. Genn and A. Paterson (2001), above, n.20.
[104] Six per cent in 2001 and 5 per cent in 2004.
[105] Four per cent in 2001 and 3 per cent in 2004. Family breakdown problems include divorces and problems ancillary to the breakdown of any relationship. For more details see P. Pleasence, N.J. Balmer, A. Buck, A. O'Grady, M. Maclean and H. Genn (2003) Family Problems – What Happens and to Whom, 33 *Family Law,* p.497.

discrimination included additional constituent problems to reflect the evolving law,[106] homelessness was enquired into within the context of other problems as well as on its own,[107] personal injury increased from an unexplained low level in 2001 (as compared to the *Paths to Justice* survey),[108] and unfair police treatment increased only very slightly.[109] Thus, the four observed increases were each understandable. Of the categories that saw a decrease in incidence, the changes were significant in relation to consumer, neighbours, money/debt, employment, rented housing, welfare benefits, relationship breakdown, domestic violence and mental health. This decrease in the reported incidence of domestic violence is also reflected by the British Crime Survey, which has seen a steady decline since 1995.[110]

The frequency of reporting of different problem types in large part reflects the frequency of experience of the 'defining circumstances' from which they can arise. The most common problems arise from circumstances routinely experienced across the adult population. Consumer problems arise from transactions for goods and services. Problems with noisy or anti-social neighbours arise where people live in close proximity to one another. Money and debt problems arise from financial dealings. Employment problems arise from being employed. Rare problems, on the other hand, arise from circumstances that people experience much less frequently. Immigration problems arise from people changing their country of abode, residence status or citizenship. Mental health problems arise from people suffering or appearing to suffer from mental illness. Clinical negligence problems arise from people receiving clinical treatment.[111]

---

[106] Looking only at the 2001 constituent problems, the 2004 incidence rate was 1.7 per cent.

[107] Burrows has reported that 4 per cent of respondents to the Survey of English Housing in 1994-5 had experienced homelessness in the preceding 10 years: R. Burrows (1997) The Social Distribution of the Experience of Homelessness, in R. Burrows, N. Pleace and D. Quilgars (eds.) *Homelessness and Social Policy,* London: Routledge.

[108] A recent analysis of personal injury claims has indicated that while the number of accident claims has reduced in recent years, the number of disease claims has risen strongly: Datamonitor (2005) *UK Personal Injury Litigation 2004,* London: Datamonitor.

[109] The increase was not significant.

[110] S. Walby and J. Allen (2004) Domestic Violence, Sexual Assault and Stalking: Findings from the British Crime Survey, London: Home Office (Home Office Research Study 276), p.112. For details of government initiatives that have been aimed at reducing the incidence of domestic violence and assisting victims see, for example, Home Office (2003) *Safety and Justice: The Government's Proposals on Domestic Violence,* London: The Stationery Office, and Home Office (2005) *Domestic Violence: A National Report,* London: Home Office.

[111] Thus, general exposure to disputes, as Van Velthoven and Ter Voert have suggested, drawing on 'participation theory,' might be expected to increase along with greater participation in social and economic life. For example, the risk of many types of disputes might be expected to increase with, for

Of course, the reporting rates of different problem types also reflect other things. The likelihood of justiciable problems arising from defining circumstances varies between problem types, as does the likelihood of problems arising that are 'difficult to solve.' Accordingly, reporting rates in part reflect these likelihoods. This explains why, despite the fact that many more respondents owned their homes, as opposed to renting them, more people reported problems relating to rented housing than reported problems relating to owned housing.

In addition, the reporting rates of different problem types in part reflect the propensity of respondents to recall and then disclose details of them. The similarity, frequency and salience of problems all influence the propensity of respondents to recall them.[112] Beyond recall, though, disclosure of the details of some problems may involve social embarrassment or shame, and may also raise concerns of privacy, confidentiality, and personal safety. As a consequence, problems relating to domestic violence, mental health and debt might all be expected to be underreported to some degree.[113]

PATTERNS OF VULNERABILITY AND THE IMPACT OF JUSTICIABLE PROBLEMS

The fact that justiciable problems arise from defining circumstances entails that experience of them varies between different population groups. Those people who most often experience the defining circumstances of a particular type of problem will also, all else being equal, most often experience problems of that type. However, all

---

example, education, employment and income: B.C.J. van Velthoven and M. ter Voert (2005), above, n.54, p.2.

[112] See, for example, B.J. Reiser (1988) Predictive Inferencing in Autobiographical Memory Retrieval, in M.M. Gruneberg, P.E. Morris and R.N. Sykes (eds.) *Practical Aspects of Memory, Volume 1: Memory in Everyday Life,* New York: Wiley; B. Means and E. Loftus (1991) When Personal History Repeats Itself: Decomposing Memories for Recurring Events, 5 *Applied Cognitive Psychology,* p.297; A. Baddeley, V.J. Lewis and I. Nemo-Smith (1978) When Did You Last …? In M.M. Gruneberg, P.E. Morris and R.N. Sykes (eds.) *Practical Aspects of Memory. Volume 1: Memory in Everyday Life,* New York: Wiley; U. Neisser (1986) Nested Structure in Autobiographical Memory, in D.C. Rubin (ed.) *Autobiographical Memory,* Cambridge: Cambridge University Press; D.C. Rubin and M. Kozin (1984) Vivid Memories, 16 *Cognition;* p.81, W.A. Wagenaar (1986) My Memory: A Study of Autobiographical Memory Over Six Years, 18 *Cognitive Psychology,* pp.225-252; P. Chapman and G. Underwood (2000) Forgetting Near-Accidents: The Roles of Severity, Culpability and Experience in the Poor Recall of Dangerous Driving Situations, 14(1) *Applied Cognitive Psychology,* p.31.

[113] See, for example, A.G. Turner (1982) What Subjects of Survey Research Believe About Confidentiality, in J.E. Sieber (ed.) *The Ethics of Social Research: Surveys and Experiments,* New York: Springer Verlag; C. Mirrlees-Black (1999) *Domestic Violence: Findings From a New British Crime Survey Self-Completion Questionnaire,* London: Home Office (Home Office Research Study 191); M. Ellsberg, A. Winkvist, L. Heise, R. Peña, S. Agurto (2001) Researching Domestic Violence Against Women: Methodological and Ethical Considerations, 32(1) *Studies In Family Planning,* p.116.

else is not always equal. People's physical make-up, experience, resources and disposition will also affect their vulnerability to experiencing problems – especially problems that are 'difficult to solve.' Justiciable problems, and particularly those that are difficult to solve and are the subject of this study, do not therefore strike indiscriminately.

Multi-level binary logistic regression was used to test the influence of a range of social and demographic predictors on the likelihood of individual problem types being reported in each of the 2001 and 2004 surveys.[114] Drawing on those predictors found to be significantly influential, it was possible to map out broad patterns of vulnerability to the problems studied. Some of the predictors also give an indication of the substantial impact that problems can have on people's lives. To facilitate analysis of the links between the experience of problems and stages of life, two continuous age-related variables were included in regressions; age and age squared. By including both of these variables, it was possible to identify both general increases and decreases, as well as peaks in age where respondents were most likely to report problems.

The social and demographic data collected through the 2001 survey related only to the time of interview, making it difficult sometimes to establish whether particular situations contribute to, or follow on from, individual problems. In 2004, data relating to economic activity, family type and long-standing illness and disability over the survey reference period was also collected. This allowed changes preceding, accompanying, or following problem experience to be identified.

Stages of Life

As people move through life, their circumstances change and expose them to different types of justiciable problem.

The youngest respondents to both surveys were most likely to report problems relating to rented housing, unfair treatment by the police and homelessness. This reflects the fact that younger people are less economically independent, more

---

[114] See above, n.64, for a list of variables. Not all variables were included in all analyses, as incidence was sometimes too rare to allow the full set to be included. Further technical details and output tables are available for download from www.lsrc.org.uk.

mobile,[115] live in lower standard accommodation,[116] and are most likely to be involved in criminal activity (and therefore most likely to have contact with the police).[117] The difference in simple numerical reporting rates of rented housing and homelessness problems between 18 to 24 year old respondents and older respondents was compounded by the fact that around twice as many respondents in the youngest age group lived in the rented housing sector. Whereas in 2001, 11 per cent of 18 to 24 year old respondents reported rented housing problems, just 3 per cent of older respondents did so. In 2004, the figures were 6 per cent and 2 per cent respectively. Likewise, in both 2001 and 2004, whereas 3 per cent of 18 to 24 year old respondents reported homelessness problems, fewer than 1 per cent of older respondents did so.[118] Moreover, the likelihood of respondents having reported homelessness problems increased further still for the youngest respondents within the 18 to 24 year old range (Figure 2.1).

All else being equal, 25 to 34 year old respondents were most likely to report problems with employment, money/debt and domestic violence.[119] The likelihood of reporting employment problems peaked in the early thirties, although there was not a great deal of variation between age groups in actual reporting rates until retirement age. Money/debt problems peaked in the mid-thirties, echoing increasing personal expenditure as people become economically independent and start acquiring major assets − such as houses. However, there were clear differences in the ages at which respondents reported different types of money/debt problems. Thus, whereas the

---

[115] See, for example, Statistics New Zealand (1998) *Young New Zealanders,* Wellington: Statistics New Zealand.

[116] Office of the Deputy Prime Minister (2003) English House Condition Survey, London: HMSO.

[117] T. Newburn (2002) *Young People, Crime and Youth Justice,* in M. Maguire, R. Morgan and R. Reiner (eds.), *The Oxford Handbook of Criminology* (third edition), Oxford: Oxford University Press. Also, National Statistics (2003) *Social Trends 33,* London: The Stationery Office.

[118] The link between age and homelessness has also been observed from the Survey of English Housing. See R. Burrows (1997), above, n.107. The prevalence of homelessness among younger people has been exacerbated by low priority status for social housing: J. Bradshaw, P. Kemp, S. Baldwin and A. Rowe (2004) *The Drivers of Social Exclusion: A Review of the Literature for the Social Exclusion Unit in the Breaking the Cycle Series,* London: Office of the Deputy Prime Minister, p.73.

[119] The finding relating to money/debt problems is consistent with those of the MORI Financial Services Survey 2004, commissioned by the Department of Trade and Industry. That survey found debt problems to be most common among 25-44 year olds: Department of Trade and Industry (2004) *Over-Indebtedness in Britain: A DTI Report on the MORI Financial Services Survey 2004,* London: Department of Trade and Industry. See also, Department of Trade and Industry (2005) *Tackling Over-Indebtedness: Annual Report 2005,* London: HMSO. As regards domestic violence, it appears to be a worldwide phenomenon that it tends to affect younger people. See, for example, World Health Organisation (2005) *WHO Multi-Country Study on Women's Health and Domestic Violence Against Women: Initial Report on Prevalence, Health Outcomes and Women's Responses,* Geneva: World Health Organisation.

likelihood of reporting problems with debt generally decreased as age increased, problems relating to recovering money and financial services did not peak until the early to mid-forties. Domestic violence problems also peaked in the mid-thirties, with increasing numbers of people living with partners while still at an age where violent conduct is prevalent.

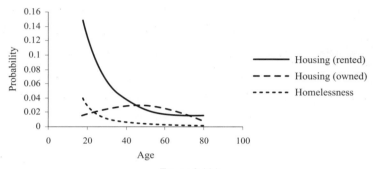

Figure 2.1(a)
Probability of Experiencing Problems by Age (2001)

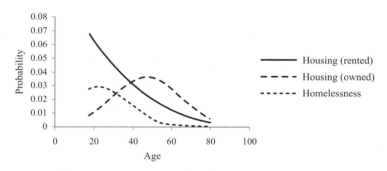

Figure 2.1(b)
Probability of Experiencing Problems by Age (2004)

As people move on through their thirties and forties, the great majority will live with a partner, and the number of households containing children will peak and then fall. Thus, this is an age associated with divorce, problems ancillary to relationship breakdown and problems relating to children.[120] So, those between 35 and 44 reported twice as many divorces as others. However, while problems ancillary to relationship breakdown were most common for those in their late thirties and early forties, there were important differences observed between problems relating to children and problems relating to assets. Whereas disputes over assets peaked in the late thirties and early forties, disputes over residence and contact peaked earlier, in the late twenties and early thirties, reflecting an interaction between the age of children and the accumulation of equity.

Problems relating to consumer transactions, neighbours and welfare benefits also peaked in the late thirties and early forties.[121]

In 2001, discrimination on the basis of race, gender or disability peaked in the mid-forties. However, in 2004, with the inclusion of the further bases of discrimination of sexual orientation, age and religion, the peak dropped to the mid-twenties. There was also an increase in the proportion of discrimination problems concerning race in 2004; problems that tended to be associated with younger respondents. The peak for such problems was 22 years of age.

As people move into their late forties and fifties, their children start to leave home and the number of family problems subsides appreciably. By this age, rented housing problems are also in steep decline, and problems relating to homelessness and unfair police treatment are very rarely experienced. Homelessness problems, for example, were reported by only one-quarter of 1 per cent of respondents aged over 44 across the two surveys. Evidently, though, those people who become homeless later in life may be less able to escape from the predicament, which would result in underreporting by people in standard residential accommodation.[122] In contrast, all else being equal, owned housing problems peaked at this stage of life. Also, economic

---

[120] In 2001, the peak ages derived from the models were 44, 40 and 40 respectively. In 2004, they were 46, 25 and 40 respectively. Although the peak age for problems ancillary to relationship breakdown was just 25 in 2004, age was not significant in the model and the simple percentage of people reporting problems was highest in the 35 to 44 years old range.

[121] Consumer problems peaked at 38 in 2001 and 44 in 2004; problems with neighbours at 48 and 35, and welfare benefits problems at 37 and 36.

[122] For more details relating to older people rough sleeping and experiencing homelessness, see M.Crane and A.M. Warnes (2000) Policy and Service Responses to Rough Sleeping Among Older People, in 29 *Journal of Social Policy,* p.645.

problems (those related to consumer transactions, employment, money/debt and welfare benefits) continued to be reported frequently.[123]

However, respondents aged over 59 reported fewer occurrences of most types of problems. The only exceptions were problems related to neighbours, personal injury, clinical negligence and mental health. Indeed, age did not appear to play a significant role in the distribution of personal injury, clinical negligence or mental health problems. Given the increasing frailty of older people, their use of health services and the increasing risk of depression, anxiety disorder and dementia among this age group, a reduction in related problems would not be expected.[124] Also, although in general rented housing problems were much less frequently reported by older respondents, problems with unsafe or unsatisfactory rented housing were frequently reported by retired respondents, perhaps reflecting a greater reliance on others to maintain the upkeep of their accommodation, in both physical and economic terms.

Decreasing reporting rates of problems among older respondents do not necessarily reflect an equal decline in the prevalence of the defining circumstances of problems. As already suggested, people will find problems easier to deal with as they become more familiar with them. People's sensitivities and priorities will also change over time. In addition, the decreased reporting rates of respondents of retirement age may in part reflect ignorance of circumstances, compounded by the frequent growing isolation of old age. For example, the decrease in welfare benefits problems reported by those aged 75 or over may reflect lack of knowledge of the availability of benefits. It may also reflect a reluctance to engage with the benefits system.[125]

In addition, as Ellison et al. have recently described, there are specific types of justiciable problem that impact on older people, not all of which fall within the scope of the 2001 and 2004 surveys. This is particularly so in relation to 'the diverse

---

[123] The incidence rates were 14 per cent, 7 per cent, 8 per cent and 2 per cent respectively in 2001 and 11 per cent, 6 per cent, 7 per cent and 2 per cent in 2004.
[124] See, for example, L. Bird (1999) *Fundamental Facts: All the Latest Facts and Figures on Mental Illness*, London: The Mental Health Foundation. There is also, though, evidence that older people with mental health problems disproportionately under use available services. See, for example, J.A. Yang and C.L. Jackson (1998) Overcoming Obstacles in Providing Mental Health Treatment to Older Adults: Getting in the Door, in 35(4) *Psychotherapy*, p.498.
[125] Craig et al. suggested that the complexity of the benefits system and also attitudes towards claiming benefits both reduce the numbers of older people who claim benefits: G. Craig, P. Dornan, J. Bradshaw, R. Garbutt, S. Mumtaz, A. Syed and A. Ward (2002) *Understanding Citizenship for Older People: The Impact of Additional Benefit Income for Older People*, London: National Audit Office.

accommodation-related issues confronted by older people.'[126] For example, many potential problems relating to nursing homes do not fall within the 106 categories included within the English and Welsh Civil and Social Justice Survey. Indeed, people living in such types of accommodation will fall outside of the sampling frame used for the survey. Other distinct problems older people may encounter include problems concerning access to health services, levels of health care, abuse,[127] substitute decision making, wills and grandparenting.[128]

Gender

Although men and women were equally likely to report one or more justiciable problems in both 2001 and 2004, the two surveys reveal significant differences in the types of problems reported by male and female respondents.

Female respondents were more likely than male respondents to report being victims of domestic violence.[129] In both 2001 and 2004, fewer than one-quarter of reported victims of domestic violence were men. This is in keeping with most survey findings, although the 1996 and 2001 British Crime Surveys – using a computer assisted self-interviewing (CASI) method – suggested that there may be a particular issue of underreporting of domestic violence by men.[130] The 1996 British Crime Survey found there was no difference in the reporting rates of domestic assault (4 per cent) between female and male respondents, though female respondents more often reported threats.[131] However, just 32 per cent of female and 9 per cent of male respondents who reported domestic violence through the 1996 British Crime Survey CASI questionnaire also reported it through standard face-to-face interviews. The 2001 British Crime Survey CASI interviews revealed a significant difference in reporting rates between women and men (3 per cent versus 2 per cent),[132] but it was much narrower than indicated by face-to-face interviews. Thus, on the basis of both the 1996 and 2001 British Crime Survey findings, fewer male than female

---

[126] S. Ellison, L. Schetzer, J. Mullins, J. Perry and K. Wong (2004) *Access to Justice and Legal Needs: The Legal Needs of Older People in New South Wales*, Sydney: Law and Justice Foundation of New South Wales, p.13.
[127] Other than by family members.
[128] S. Ellison et al. (2004), above, n.126, p.14.
[129] This finding was just slightly short of being significant in 2001.
[130] C. Mirrlees-Black (1999), above, n.113 and S. Walby and J. Allen (2004), above, n.110.
[131] The percentages were 6 per cent and 5 per cent if threats were included.
[132] The percentages were 4 per cent and 2 per cent if threats were included.

respondents would be expected to report domestic violence through the 2001 and 2004 face-to-face surveys. Also, the 2001 and 2004 surveys included only problems that were 'difficult to solve.' As the 1996 and 2001 British Crime Surveys also found that male respondents were far less likely to report violence that resulted in injury, and also far less likely to report having been upset or frightened by it, this would again suggest that fewer male respondents would report domestic violence through the 2001 and 2004 surveys.[133]

Involvement in and attitudes to violence may also be a factor in female respondents having reported problems with neighbours more often than male respondents in both 2001 and 2004.[134] Another factor may be the greater proportion of women acting as carers in the home, leading to greater exposure to activity in the neighbourhood.[135]

Although the number of problems reported was small, the 2001 survey also indicated that female respondents were more likely than male respondents to report clinical negligence problems. This perhaps reflects the greater use of health services by women and the unique risks associated with childbirth.[136] In 2004, however, no difference was observed.

Male respondents to both the 2001 and 2004 surveys were much more likely than female respondents to report unfair treatment by the police, accounting for three-quarters of all such problems. As was the case with young respondents, this reflects the greater male involvement in criminal activity and proportion of men therefore becoming the subject of police interest.[137]

There were also indications from the 2004 survey that male respondents were more likely to report money/debt and employment problems. This was consistent with higher incidence rates for men in the 2001 survey. The types of such problems reported by men and women also differed. For example, male respondents were

---

[133] C. Mirrlees-Black (1999), above, n.113, p.77 and S. Walby and J. Allen (2004), above, n.110, p.19 and p.33. There is also evidence elsewhere that men are less likely to be seriously injured by domestic violence, less likely to suffer repeat violence and less likely to be scared by domestic violence. See, for example, D. Gadd, S. Farrall, D. Dallimore and N. Lombard (2002) *Domestic Abuse Against Men in Scotland,* Edinburgh: Scottish Executive Central Research Unit.

[134] Gender was a significant predictor of problems with neighbours in 2004 only. However, in simple frequency terms, more male than female respondents reported neighbours problems in 2001 ($\chi^2_1 = 4.05$, $p < 0.05$).

[135] J. Maher and H. Green (2002) *Carers 2000,* London: The Stationery Office.

[136] National Statistics (2001) *Social Trends 31,* London: The Stationery Office.

[137] M. Maguire, R. Morgan and R. Reiner (eds.), *The Oxford Handbook of Criminology* (third edition), Oxford: Oxford University Press.

typically more likely than female respondents to be sacked or threatened with the sack, to face problems with obtaining pay or pensions, and negotiating terms and conditions. Female respondents, on the other hand, were more likely to report unsafe/unsatisfactory conditions and harassment.

Gender was also found to be a significant influence in predicting more narrowly defined problems relating to obtaining maintenance payments, a continuing symptom of the economic imbalance between women and men in this country. In fact, in the 2004 survey, all respondents reporting difficulties obtaining maintenance or child support payments were female.

Ethnicity

As with gender, the 2001 and 2004 surveys indicated significant differences in the types of problems experienced by white and black and minority ethnic people. Ethnicity was particularly influential in predicting problems relating to discrimination and immigration. In both surveys, white respondents were found to be less than one-quarter as likely as black and minority ethnic respondents to report discrimination and less than one-tenth as likely to report an immigration problem. Indeed, in 2004, not a single white respondent reported such a problem.

In addition, while problems with rented housing were reported equally by white and black and minority ethnic respondents, white respondents were far less likely to report problems relating to unsafe or unsatisfactory rented housing. This perhaps reflects the reduced likelihood of white respondents living in a high-density urban environment.[138] The 2004 survey also indicated that ethnicity may influence the experience of problems relating to clinical negligence, consumer transactions and owned housing. However, no difference was found in 2001.

---

[138] See, for example, Welsh Assembly (2003) *The Housing and Socio-Economic Circumstances of Black and Minority Ethnic People Living in Wales*, Cardiff: Welsh Assembly (Housing Research Report HR 1/03), and G. Netto, R. Arshad, P. de Lima, F.A. Diniz, M. MacEwen, V. Patel and R. Syed (2001) *Audit of Research on Minority Ethnic Issues in Scotland from a 'Race' Perspective*, Edinburgh: Central Research Unit. Interestingly, the model indicated that black and 'other' ethnicity respondents were the most likely to report such problems. This is consistent with the MORI survey finding that black respondents were more likely than others to report difficulties with housing about which they would have liked free advice. The MORI survey also found that minority ethnic respondents were generally more likely to report housing difficulties: MORI (2004), above, n.80, p.13.

Echoing Smith's findings in relation to the criminal justice system,[139] analysis revealed that it is inadequate to distinguish merely between white and black and minority ethnic respondents in an investigation into differences in the experience of diverse ethnic populations. There are important differences in the experience of different black and minority ethnic groups, and these are masked when black and minority ethnic groups are amalgamated. For example, Asian respondents appeared less likely to report problems ancillary to relationship breakdown than other respondents.[140] They also appeared less likely to report problems with their children's education, consistent with the differing patterns of educational attainment associated with different ethnic groups in the United Kingdom.[141] On the other hand, black respondents (and, in 2001, 'other' ethnicity respondents) were more likely to report immigration problems than either white or Asian respondents, reflecting changing patterns of immigration to the United Kingdom. For example, the number of people immigrating from outside of the old and new Commonwealth countries and the European Union more than doubled between 1997 and 1999.[142] However, the numbers of respondents within specific ethnic categories were relatively small in the 2001 and 2004 surveys, and the composition of respondents within those categories could easily have varied between the surveys as a consequence of including different geographical areas within the samples. Thus, the picture was not as clear as it might have been, and the results were not as decisive.

---

[139] D.J. Smith (1997) Ethnic Origins, Crime and Criminal Justice in England and Wales, in M. Tonry (ed.) *Ethnicity, Crime and Immigration: Comparative and Cross-National Perspectives*, Chicago: University of Chicago Press.

[140] See also A. O'Grady, N.J. Balmer, B. Carter, P. Pleasence, A. Buck and H. Genn (2005) Institutional Racism and Civil Justice, in 28(4) *Ethnic and Racial Studies*, p.620. There were also indications that Asian respondents were less likely to report domestic violence, in line with the findings of the 1996 British Crime Survey: C. Mirrlees-Black (1999), above, n.113, p.72. However, there may also have been underreporting of domestic violence problems by Asian respondents as a consequence of cultural and religious attitudes to problems occurring within the family See, for example, J. Bindel (1994) *The Hidden Figure: Domestic Violence in North London,* report prepared for Islington Council, London, and Asian and Pacific Islander Institute on Domestic Violence (2002) *Fact Sheet: Domestic Violence in Asian and Pacific Islander Communities,* San Francisco: Asian and Pacific Islander Institute on Domestic Violence, available for download at www.apiahf.org.

[141] R.M. Blackburn, A. Dale, and J. Jarman (1997) Ethnic Differences in Attainment in Education, Occupation and Lifestyle, in V. Karn (ed.) *Employment, Education and Housing among Ethnic Minorities in Britain*, London: HMSO. The suggested higher reporting rate of education problems by black respondents also concords with these patterns of educational attainment.

[142] J. Dobson, K. Koser, G. Mclaughlan and J. Salt (2001) *International Migration and the United Kingdom: Recent Patterns and Trends,* London: Home Office (RDS Occasional Paper No.75), p.42. See also, S. Kyambi (2005) *Beyond Black and White: Mapping New Immigrant Communities,* London: Institute for Public Policy Research.

Economic Circumstances

Aspects of respondents' economic circumstances[143] had a significant influence in predicting most types of justiciable problem studied. Unlike age, gender and ethnicity, though, economic circumstances can change as a result of the experience of justiciable problems. To some extent, therefore, we are looking here not only at patterns of vulnerability to problems, but also their impact.

Respondents on higher incomes were more likely than those lower down the income scale to report consumer problems, presumably in consequence of their greater consumer activity.[144] For example, in both 2001 and 2004, respondents earning in excess of £50,000 per annum reported consumer problems twice as often as those earning less than £10,000, and problems with builders and holidays more than three times as often. Respondents receiving welfare benefits were also, though, more likely than others to report consumer problems,[145] a finding perhaps explained by the greater relative value to them of routine consumer transactions. This explanation is consistent with the 2001 finding that respondents receiving welfare benefits reported a disproportionate number of low value consumer problems, including, for example, problems relating to unfit food products and small electrical purchases.

Respondents on higher incomes were more likely to report problems with investment services, such as mismanagement of pensions, problems to do with owned housing (although this difference was not observed in 2004) and clinical negligence, echoing their greater opportunities to purchase pensions, homes and clinical interventions.[146]

Respondents on lower incomes, on the other hand, were more likely than those higher up the income scale to report problems relating to unsafe or unsatisfactory rented housing and homelessness. Indeed, respondents earning less than £10,000

---

[143] Economic circumstances here include income, benefits status and economic activity.

[144] This finding was short of being significant at the 95 per cent confidence level in 2001.

[145] Again, this finding was short of significant at the 95 per cent confidence level in 2001.

[146] While more affluent people undoubtedly make more use of private medicine and, increasingly, cosmetic surgery, evidence of income based health inequality within the National Health Service is somewhat less clear-cut. For example, A. Dixon, J. Le Grand, J. Henderson, R. Murray and E. Poteliakhoff (2003) *Is the NHS Equitable? A Review of the Evidence,* London: London School of Economics (Health and Social Care Discussion Paper Number 11); S. Morris, M. Sutton and H. Gravelle (2005) Inequity and Inequality in the Use of Health Care in England: An Empirical Investigation, in 60 *Social Science and Medicine,* p.1250; and S. Allin and E. Mossialos (2005) *Inequity and Inequality in Health Care Use Among Older People in the United Kingdom,* paper presented at the British Household Panel Survey 2005 Conference, Colchester, 1st July 2005.

reported problems relating to unsafe or unsatisfactory rented housing or homelessness many more times as often as those earning in excess of £50,000, reflecting their lesser range of housing options and economic independence. As would be expected given their higher rates of benefit receipt, those on lower incomes and the economically inactive, particularly the unemployed, were more likely to report problems relating to welfare benefits. More than four times as many unemployed respondents as others reported such problems in 2001 and nearly six times as many in 2004.

In addition to consumer problems, and independent of income, respondents receiving welfare benefits were more likely than others to report homelessness and debt and severe money management problems, again reflecting lesser economic independence.[147] Those on benefits also appeared more likely to report problems relating to their children's education, owing possibly in part to their lesser ability to choose the schools their children attend and, once more, their lesser range of housing options – which makes them less able to move to the catchment areas of better performing schools.[148] They also reported rented housing problems more often than others.

Looking more closely at economic activity, respondents who described themselves as 'looking after the home or family,' the unemployed and respondents who were unable to work because of illness reported problems to do with neighbours more frequently than others. As was suggested above in relation to lone parents, this is perhaps a simple consequence of spending more time at home. Naturally, those respondents who were looking after the home or family also reported employment problems less frequently, along with the self-employed. They also reported problems ancillary to the breakdown of a relationship and, along with part-time employees, problems concerning children more often, reflecting their enhanced childcare role and their lack of income from employment.

The self-employed were also more likely to have reported problems relating to mental health. However, it is not immediately apparent what the association is between self-employment – which encompasses a heterogeneity of forms of work[149] –

---

[147] See, also, R. Burrows (1997), above, n.107, and Department of Trade and Industry (2004), above, n.119.
[148] S. Gibbons and S. Machin (2003) Valuing English Primary Schools, in 53 *Journal of Urban Economics,* p.197.
[149] See, for example, A. Dale (1986) Social Class and the Self-Employed, in 20 *Sociology*, pp.430-434, and B. Casey and S. Creigh (1988) Self-employment in Great Britain: Its definition in the Labour Force Survey, in tax and social security law, and in labour law, in 2 *Work, Employment and Society*, p.381.

and problems relating to mental health. Indeed, the results of the EUROSTAT ill-health module of the 1999 Labour Force survey indicated that the self-employed were less likely than employees to report conditions such as work-related stress.[150] Possibly, though, those with mental health problems and those facing discrimination and difficulties in adapting to employment are more likely to become self-employed.

Respondents who were unable to work because of illness reported domestic violence, personal injury and clinical negligence more often than others. They also reported discrimination more than four times as often as others.

Unemployed respondents also more frequently reported being victims of domestic violence. This is in line with the 2001 British Crime Survey and also ties in with findings of a recent large-scale longitudinal study of the risk of domestic violence after childbirth.[151]

Finally, employment problems were most frequently reported by the unemployed, demonstrating the immediate economic impact that can be brought about by justiciable problems of this type. Indeed, whereas 14 per cent of unemployed respondents reported employment problems in 2001, just 6 per cent of other respondents did. In 2004, there was an even greater contrast, with 18 per cent and 5 per cent reporting such problems respectively. Unemployed respondents were also more likely than others to report money/debt and rented housing problems.[152]

The 2004 survey included additional questions to enable tracking of economic activity over the survey reference period. As a result, it was possible to explore the extent to which a change for the worse preceded, accompanied or followed justiciable problems. Overall, it was found that respondents reported changes for the worse before 4 per cent of justiciable problems occurred, at the same time as 2 per cent of problems occurred and following 5 per cent of problems. However, patterns varied greatly between problem types. So, while rented housing (6 per cent), police treatment (11 per cent) and welfare benefits (12 per cent) problems were more likely to have

[150] J.R. Jones, C.S. Huxtable and J.T. Hodgson (2001) *Self-Reported Work-Related Illness in 1998/99: Results from EUROSTAT Ill-Health Module in the 1999 Labour Force Summer Quarter*, London: Health and Safety Executive.
[151] E. Bowen, J. Heron, A. Waylen and D. Wolke (2005) Domestic Violence Risk During and After Pregnancy: Findings from a British Longitudinal Study, in *BJOG: An International Journal of Obstetrics and Gynaecology*, Vol.112, No.8. The study found that the risk of domestic violence generally increased along with social adversity.
[152] Unemployment has recently been described as 'an important driver' of many aspects of social exclusion; particularly 'poverty, homelessness, physical and mental ill-health, drug abuse, social capital and transport': J. Bradshaw et al. (2004), above, n.118, p.25.

42

followed on from changes for the worse, employment problems were more likely to have preceded them (12 per cent). Homelessness and discrimination problems were very common both prior to (11 per cent and 12 per cent respectively) and in the aftermath of (15 per cent and 7 per cent respectively) changes for the worse in economic activity.

Housing and Tenure Types

The type of housing in which respondents lived and their form of tenure, both linked to their economic circumstances, had a significant influence in predicting most problem types. The most notable exception to this was domestic violence. Indeed, it is probably a further reflection of economic circumstances that saw respondents who lived in public sector rented accommodation less likely than any others to report consumer problems and more likely to report problems relating to homelessness.[153] Unsurprisingly, those who had mortgages or owned their own houses most often reported consumer problems. Economic factors were also the most likely reason behind the greater number of reported problems relating to debt[154] and welfare benefits for those respondents living in flats or the rented housing sector.[155] Of course, living in high-density housing and the rented housing sector are related, so respondents living in flats were more likely than others to report rented housing problems.

Respondents living in high-density housing, particularly in the public rented sector, were also much more likely to report problems with neighbours, at least in part as a consequence of living alongside many more neighbours who could potentially create such problems.[156] In contrast, those living in detached houses were least likely to report such problems.

---

[153] Those living in private sector rented accommodation also reported these problems relatively often.

[154] Unsurprisingly, there was indication that respondents with mortgages were more likely to report problems with investment services.

[155] In the case of both these problem types, tenure was significant in 2001, but not housing type. Housing type was significant in 2004, but not tenure.

[156] This was not quite significant in 2004 in respect of the public rented sector, although those living in public sector rented accommodation were almost twice as likely as those with any other form of tenure to report problems with neighbours.

Respondents who lived in detached houses were also less likely to report problems relating to personal injury, and there was a suggestion that they were less likely to report discrimination or problems relating to mental health.[157]

Finally, respondents with mortgages or living in the rented sector were more likely than others to report having been divorced in the surveys' reference periods.

Justiciable Problems and the Family

The type of family unit that respondents lived in had a significant influence in predicting a broad range of the problem types studied.

Lone parent respondents were more likely to report many problem types than respondents living in other types of family. This is a matter of particular concern given the steady increase over the past thirty years in the number of lone parent households. Lone parent households now account for 22 per cent of all households with dependent children.[158] Part of the reason for this greater propensity to report problems is that lone parent respondents appeared likely to report both those types of problems associated with being single and those associated with having children.[159] They were also, of course, more likely to report problems associated with family breakdown as, although the origins of lone parent families include childbirth outside of a relationship,[160] lone parenthood most often results from such a breakdown.[161]

It is not surprising that lone parent and other unmarried respondents were more likely than married respondents to report divorce. They were also more likely to report problems ancillary to relationship breakdown; although, reflecting the presence of children, lone parents in particular and other unmarried respondents with children appeared the most likely to report these kinds of problems. Lone parents were also

---

[157] See, for example, D. Meltzer, T. Fryers and R. Jenkins (2002) *Social Inequalities and the Distribution of Common Mental Disorders*, Cambridge: Institute of Public Health.

[158] Census 2001 estimate. Dataset KS20P available at www.neighbourhood.statistics.gov.uk. See, also, National Statistics (2003) *Social Trends 33,* London: The Stationery Office.

[159] The problems of being single are tied up with the economics of being single. As Bradshaw et al. have recently observed, 'Singles have twice the risk of living in poverty than couples without children and single pensioners have a higher risk than pensioners who are part of a couple': J. Bradshaw et al. (2004), above, n.118.

[160] The number of lone parent families resulting from births to 'unattached mothers' has increased over recent years: J. Haskey (1998) One Parent Families and their Dependent Children in Great Britain, in 91 *Population Trends,* p.5. However, there is also evidence that 'the proportion of lone parents who [are] single never partnered mothers appears to have stabilised at around a quarter': A. Marsh and J. Perry (2003) *Family Change 1999-2001,* London: Department for Work and Pensions, p.26.

[161] A. Marsh and J. Perry (2003), above, n.160, p.26.

much more likely to report problems relating to maintenance payments and the division of assets.

Lone parents were also most likely to report having experienced domestic violence,[162] suggesting that the violence might possibly have played a part in the breakdown of an abusive relationship. However, the change in personal circumstances that results from relationship breakdown, especially for those with whom any children from the relationship come to live, leaves lone parents particularly vulnerable to a range of further problems, many of which can constitute elements of social exclusion.

For example, a report by the National Council for One Parent Families and the homelessness charities Crisis and Health Action for Homeless People stated:

> 'Lone parenthood is associated with downward mobility in the housing market. One-parent families are more likely than others to be in public-sector housing or lower standard private housing.'[163]

Consequently, lone parent respondents were found to be more likely than others to report problems to do with rented housing,[164] especially problems to do with unsafe or unsatisfactory rented housing. Whereas in 2001 problems to do with rented housing were reported by 19 per cent of lone parents, they were reported by just 3 per cent of others. Likewise, in 2004 such problems were reported by 8 per cent of lone parents, compared to 3 per cent of others. Furthermore, in 2001 more than ten times as many lone parents as others reported problems concerning unsafe or unsatisfactory rented housing.

---

[162] Interestingly, single respondents appeared generally more likely than others to report domestic violence, both in 2001 and 2004. This is in keeping with the findings of the 2001 British Crime Survey: S. Walby and J. Allen (2004), above n.110, p.85.

[163] National Council for One Parent Families, Crisis, Health Action for Homeless People (2001) *A Secure Start for Young Families: the housing and support needs of young lone mothers*, London: NCOPF.

[164] This was significant within the regression models in 2001, but not 2004. However, as we describe below, in simple frequency terms lone parents reported many more such problems in 2004. Also, in 2001 lone parents (along with cohabitees without children) were more likely to report problems with owned housing. However, this was not found to be the case in 2004, and goes against the overall picture of married and co-habiting respondents reporting more such problems, reflecting their greater earning potential. However, the problems with owned housing reported by lone parents were different from those reported by married and co-habiting respondents, relating more often to communal repairs and conveyancing and not at all to planning matters. No lone parent reported a problem relating to repossession of the family home in 2001, and only one did so in 2004.

As with quality of housing, the general standard of living of lone parents has been reported to be much lower than that of the rest of the population.[165] Thus, lone parents (and to a lesser extent other single respondents) were more likely to report money/debt problems.[166] This drop in living standard relates in part to the obstacles faced by lone parents in gaining employment, resulting in considerably lower rates of employment (although as a consequence of the New Deal for Lone Parents the gap is narrowing).[167] Accordingly, although this was not highlighted by regression analysis, lone parent respondents least often reported employment problems in both 2001 and 2004. Also, lone parents are far more likely to receive welfare benefits than the rest of the population. It has been estimated that in 2001 half of lone parents in Britain were receiving income support and one-third received Working Families Tax Credit.[168] Thus, although this was again not highlighted by regression analysis, lone parents disproportionately reported problems concerning welfare benefits.[169]

There was, though, a difference between employment patterns in relation to female and male[170] lone parent respondents. In 2001, female lone parents were less likely to be working than their male counterparts (42 per cent, compared to 50 per cent)[171] and more likely to be receiving welfare benefits (90 per cent, compared to 67 per cent).[172] They were also considerably more likely to be in part-time employment if they were working (26 per cent, compared to 6 per cent).[173] In consequence, female lone parents reported welfare benefits problems more frequently than male lone parents, although the difference was not statistically significant. In 2004, a similar picture emerged, with female lone parents again less likely to be working (48 per cent,

---

[165] See, for example, P. Wilcox (2000) Lone Motherhood: The Impact on Living Standards of Leaving a Violent Relationship, in 34(2) *Journal of Social Policy and Administration*, p.176, and C. Chambaz (2001) Lone Parent Families in Europe: A Variety of Economic and Social Circumstances, in 35(6) *Journal of Social Policy and Administration*, p.658.

[166] See, also, Department of Trade (2004), above, n.119.

[167] The percentage of female lone parents in work increased from 44 per cent in 1997 to 50 per cent by 2001: National Council for One Parent Families (2001) *One Parent Families Today: The Facts*, London: National Council for One Parent Families. See, also, A. Marsh and J. Perry (2003), above, n.160. J. Millar and T. Ridge (2001) *Families, Poverty, Work and Care – A Review of the Literature on Lone Parents and Low Income Couple Families with Children*, London: Department for Work and Pensions (Research Report No.153).

[168] Eighty-six per cent of lone parents in the 2001 survey were receiving one or more welfare benefits. See further, National Council for One Parent Families, Crisis, Health Action for Homeless People (2001), above, n.163, and National Council for One Parent Families (2001), above, n.167.

[169] 2001: $\chi^2_1 = 7.98$, $p < 0.01$. 2004: $\chi^2_1 = 7.91$, $p < 0.01$.

[170] Men comprised 15 per cent of lone parents in both the 2001 and 2004 surveys.

[171] $\chi^2_{24} = 41.37$, $p < 0.001$.

[172] $\chi^2_3 = 11.52$, $p < 0.01$.

[173] $\chi^2_{24} = 41.37$, $p < 0.001$.

compared to 61 per cent) and more likely to be receiving welfare benefits than their male counterparts (86 per cent, compared to 57 per cent). They were also more often in part-time employment (23 per cent, compared to 7 per cent) and more often reported benefits problems, although again the difference was not significant.

As a result of the 'major emotional'[174] impact of relationship breakdown, and the fact that many lone parents are unable to work, have no partner to share responsibilities or 'engage in reflective dialogue regarding parenting issues,'[175] have limited financial resources and live in unsuitable housing, lone parents can be susceptible to experiencing psychiatric and other health problems.[176] It is not surprising, therefore, that lone parents were more likely to report justiciable problems relating to mental health than those living in other types of family.

Finally, as would be expected, lone parents, along with other respondents with resident children, were more likely than others to report problems relating to children.[177] They were also both more likely than others to report problems relating to neighbours, perhaps reflecting the greater amount of time spent in the home or friction between neighbours introduced by the presence of children.

As with economic activity, the 2004 survey included additional questions to enable tracking of family types over the survey reference period. As a result, it was possible to explore the extent to which changes for the worse preceded, accompanied or followed justiciable problems. Overall, it was found that respondents reported changes for the worse before 3 per cent of justiciable problems occurred, at the same time as 1 per cent of problems occurred, and following 4 per cent of problems. However, relatively few changes were observed away from family type problems.[178]

---

[174] G. Allan, S. Hawker, G. Crow (2001) Family Diversity and Change in Britain and Western Europe, 22(7) *Journal of Family Issues,* p.819, at p.828. See also, for example, P.R. Amato (2000) The Consequences of Divorce for Adults and Children, 62 *Journal of Marriage and the Family*, p.1269.

[175] T. Tsushima and V. Gecas (2001) Role Taking and Socialisation in Single Parent Families, in 22(3) *Journal of Family Issues*, pp.267-288.

[176] See, for example, J. Millar and T. Ridge (2001) *Families, Poverty, Work and Care − A Review of the Literature on Lone Parents and Low-income Couple Families with Children*, London: Department for Work and Pensions, Research Report No 153, and J. Popay and G. Jones (1990) Patterns of Health and Illness Amongst Lone Parents, 19(4) *Journal of Social Policy*, p.499.

[177] Lone parents were more likely than other respondents with resident children to report problems relating to children, reflecting the link between domestic violence and such problems. See, further, P. Pleasence, N.J. Balmer, A. Buck, A. O'Grady, M. Maclean and H. Genn (2003), above, n.105.

[178] Eleven per cent of respondents reported a change for the worse in their family type prior to a divorce, 7 per cent prior to problems ancillary to relationship breakdown, and 12 per cent prior to domestic violence. Unsurprisingly, 39 per cent reported a change for the worse following divorce, 14 per cent following problems ancillary to relationship breakdown, and 19 per cent following domestic violence.

Moreover, there was little pattern to changes outside of this context, with the single exception being in relation to homelessness problems, which accompanied or followed a breakdown of relationship on around 10 per cent of occasions.

Long-Standing Ill-Health And Disability

Health and disability status had a significant influence in predicting 14 of the 18 problem types studied: consumer, neighbours, money/debt, employment, personal injury, rented housing, owned housing,[179] welfare benefits, relationship breakdown, clinical negligence, domestic violence, discrimination, mental health and unfair police treatment.

It has been said that 'of all the disadvantaged groups in society, the disabled are the most socially excluded,' and that as a consequence 'life opportunities remain severely restricted for many.'[180] Disabled people and those with long-standing ill-health often experience disadvantage in the labour market,[181] and the consequent economic hardship suffered means that poverty is a 'key factor in the modern constitution of disability.'[182] Thus, it was found that respondents to both surveys who reported long-standing ill-health or disability were far more likely than others to report discrimination problems. Indeed, no fewer than half of all the discrimination problems reported through the 2001 survey concerned disability discrimination. Respondents who reported long-standing ill-health or disability were also more likely to report problems concerning employment, money/debt and welfare benefits. So, for example, in both 2001 and 2004, such respondents reported problems relating to welfare benefits at twice the rate of others.

Disabled people and those with long-standing ill-health are also prone to being 'selected out'[183] of home ownership and, despite the system of prioritisation for social housing, are 'often relegated to housing of poorer standard.'[184] Consequently,

---

[179] 2001 only.
[180] M. Howard (1999) *Enabling Government: Joined up Policies for a National Disability Strategy*, London: Fabian Society.
[181] M. Howard, A. Garnham, G. Fimister, J. Veit-Wilson (2001) *Poverty: The Facts*, London: CPAB.
[182] B. Hughes (2002) Bauman's Strangers: Impairment and the invalidation of disabled people in modern and post-modern cultures, in 17 *Disability and Society*, p.571, at p.580.
[183] D. Easterlow, S.J. Smith and S. Mallinson (2000) Housing for Health: The Role of Owner Occupation, in 15 *Housing Studies*, p.367.
[184] British Medical Association (2003) *Housing and Health: Building for the Future*, London: British Medical Association, p.22.

respondents who reported long-standing ill-health or disability were more likely to report problems relating to rented housing. They were also more likely to report problems relating to homelessness.[185]

Again, people with physical or mental incapacities are 'at greater risk of all forms of abuse and violence than are the general population,'[186] and because of their greater exposure to clinical procedures, are at greater risk of being further injured or disabled through clinical intervention. Thus, respondents who reported long-standing ill-health or disability were much more likely to report problems relating to domestic violence and clinical negligence. In fact, ill or disabled respondents reported domestic violence around twice as often and clinical negligence more than twice as often as others.

Respondents who reported long-standing illness or disability, which includes mental illness or impairment, were also much more likely to report justiciable problems related to mental health,[187] being much more exposed to the defining circumstances of such problems. In addition, being more exposed to the activity of neighbours, as a consequence of being likely to spend longer periods of time at home, they were more likely to report problems to do with neighbours.

Of course, illness and disability not only increase vulnerability to the experience of justiciable problems. Problems can also cause, or exacerbate pre-existing illness and disability.

Clearly, negligent accidents, clinical negligence and domestic violence can do so – and, as well as the immediate physical consequences of the latter, such violence can also have serious psychological effects, which can manifest themselves in many ways, including post-traumatic stress disorder and battered wife syndrome.[188] Likewise, housing in a state of disrepair[189] and overcrowded households can bring

---

[185] See, further, M. Crane and A. Warnes (2000) Evictions and Prolonged Homelessness, in *Housing Studies,* Vol.15, No.5.

[186] British Medical Association (1998) *Domestic Violence: A Health Care Issue?* London: British Medical Association, p.22. See, also, World Health Organisation (2005), above, n.119, p.15.

[187] In fact, they reported mental health related justiciable problems five times more often than others.

[188] See, for example, British Medical Association (1998), above, n.186, and L. Walker (1979) *The Battered Woman,* New York: Harper and Row.

[189] When we looked only at rented housing problems relating to unsafe or unsatisfactory housing, long-standing ill-health or disability was not a significant predictor. However, unemployment as a result of ill-health was.

about physical and psychological ill-health.[190] Also, problems relating to discrimination[191] and employment[192] can lead to psychological ill-health, as can (frequently related) problems to do with debt.[193]

As well as domestic violence, non-violent problems relating to the family, such as divorce and disputes ancillary to relationship breakdown, can also cause long-term psychological ill-health, both on the part of adult and child family members – particularly as these disputes become more acrimonious.[194] Thus, respondents reporting disputes ancillary to relationship breakdown were much more likely than others to report a long-standing illness or disability, especially if disputes related to the division of assets. However, there was no link between illness and disability and divorce on its own, consistent with the idea that people cope better with less problematic separations.

Further, a secondary analysis of data from the British Household Panel Survey has found that mortgage indebtedness adversely impacts on health and increases the likelihood that men will visit general practitioners.[195] Indeed, it was recently suggested that 'the stress caused by mortgage arrears and repossession needs to be viewed as a major health issue.'[196] Consistent with this, respondents who reported long-standing ill-health or disability were found to be more likely than others to report problems relating to owned housing, and also to be more likely to report problems relating to repossession.

---

[190] See, for example, British Medical Association (2003), above n.184; S. Hunt (1997) Housing Related Disorders, in J. Charlton and M. Murphy (eds.) *The Health of Adult Britain 1841-1994*, London: The Stationery Office; and World Health Organisation (2005), above, n.119, p.16.

[191] G.C. Gee (2002) A Multilevel Analysis of the Relationship Between Institutional and Individual Racial Discrimination and Health Status, in 92 *American Journal of Public Health,* p.615.

[192] At the very least in so far as they bring about unemployment and through that ill-health. See, S.H. Wilson and G.M. Walker (1993) Unemployment and Health, in 107 *Public Health,* p.153.

[193] See, for example, S. Edwards (2003) *In Too Deep: CAB Clients' Experience of Debt,* London: Citizens Advice Bureaux, and J. Sharpe and J. Bostock (2002) *Supporting People with Debt and Mental Health Problems: Research With Psychological Therapists in Northumberland,* Newcastle: Department of Psychological Services and Research, North Tyneside and Northumberland NHS Mental Health Trust.

[194] See, for example, P.R. Amato (2000), above, n.174, P.R. Amato and B. Keith (1991) Parental Divorce and the Well-Being of Children: A Meta-analysis, in 110 *Psychological Bulletin,* p.26, and G.R. Kitson and L.A. Morgan (1990) The Multiple Consequences of Divorce: A Decade Review, in 52 *Journal of Marriage and the Family,* p.913.

[195] S. Nettleton and R. Burrows (1998) Mortgage Debt, Insecure Home Ownership and Health: An Exploratory Analysis, in 20 *Sociology of Health and Illness,* p.731, and S. Nettleton and R. Burrows (2000) When a Capital Investment Becomes an Emotional Loss: The Health Consequences of the Experience of Mortgage Possession in England, in 15 *Housing Studies,* p.463.

[196] British Medical Association (2003), above n.184, p.59.

Again, the 2004 survey included additional questions to enable disability and health status to be tracked over the survey reference period. As a result it was possible to explore the extent to which changes for the worse followed justiciable problems. Overall, it was found that long-standing ill-health or disability followed 2 per cent of problems, with the strongest associations found with employment (4 per cent), rented housing (4 per cent), clinical negligence (4 per cent) and homelessness problems (7 per cent).

CRIME AND JUSTICIABLE PROBLEMS OF DIFFERENT TYPES

While crime victimisation was associated generally with the experience of justiciable problems, there were important differences in the form of association across the various crimes studied. Victims of theft were particularly likely to report problems relating to consumer transactions, employment, neighbours, rented housing and money or debt. Victims of vandalism tended to report a similar range of problems, although they were also more likely to report problems relating to relationship breakdown, domestic violence, children and clinical negligence. Not surprisingly, the association between victims of vandalism and those who reported problems with neighbours was particularly strong. Victims of burglary reported particularly high rates of problems relating to consumer transactions and rented housing, as well as unfair police treatment and homelessness, while victims of robbery reported higher rates of discrimination and relationship breakdown. Finally, victims of assault reported higher rates of most justiciable problem types, with particularly high levels of divorce and domestic violence, as well as problems relating to discrimination, neighbours, rented housing, money/debt, children, personal injury, mental health, immigration, unfair police treatment and homelessness.

TEMPORARY ACCOMMODATION AND PROBLEMS OF DIFFERENT TYPES

Given that, as described above, respondents to the survey of people living in temporary accommodation were much more often lone parents, substantially younger, much less economically active and on considerably lower incomes than 2001 and 2004 survey respondents, it is not surprising that they reported a very different pattern of experience of the different types of justiciable problem (Figure 2.2).

Given that complications with housing will have been the reason for many respondents to the temporary accommodation survey living in such accommodation, it is not surprising that they were far more likely than 2001 or 2004 survey respondents to report problems relating to rented housing (52 per cent, compared to 4 per cent and 3 per cent respectively).[197] However, aside from this inherent difference, the reporting rate of problems concerning rented housing would have been expected to be much higher among a sample with such a young profile, and including such a high proportion of lone parents.

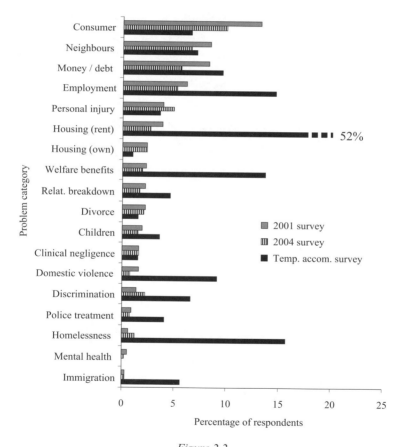

Figure 2.2
Comparison of Problem Incidence Between Surveys

---

[197] $\chi^2{}_1 = 847.83$, p < 0.001. Based on 2001 data.

The high proportion of lone parents did not translate into a significantly higher reporting rate of problems relating to children, although such problems were reported more frequently by respondents to the temporary accommodation survey. However, there were in fact similar numbers of households containing children in the three surveys. Whereas almost all children within households included in the temporary accommodation survey were in lone parent families, however, the great majority of children within households in the 2001 and 2004 surveys were in two parent families.

Again, as more than half of respondents to the temporary accommodation survey were black and minority ethnic,[198] it is not surprising that the reporting rates of problems relating to immigration and discrimination were much higher than those in the general population surveys.[199] Likewise, as almost three times as many respondents to the temporary accommodation survey as to the 2001 survey reported being in receipt of means tested welfare benefits, a much higher incidence of justiciable problems relating to welfare benefits was inevitable.[200] The reporting rate of employment problems was also higher among respondents to the temporary accommodation survey,[201] perhaps linking to the higher unemployment rates they also reported.

Although most problem types were reported more frequently by respondents to the temporary accommodation survey, consumer problems were reported considerably less frequently by them, reflecting their substantially lower incomes and consumer activity.

THE EXPERIENCE OF MULTIPLE JUSTICIABLE PROBLEMS

Respondents to the 2001 survey reported 4,214 justiciable problems; 4,050 if trivial problems are excluded.[202] This equates to an average of just over 2 problems per respondent who reported a problem. Respondents to the 2004 survey reported 2,889 problems; 2,865 if trivial problems are excluded. This equates to an average of around

---

[198] Fifty-two per cent, compared to 6 per cent of respondents in the 2001 survey (8 per cent unweighted) and 9 per cent in the 2004 survey (8 per cent unweighted).

[199] $\chi^2_1 = 106.13$, p < 0.001 (immigration); $\chi^2_1 = 32.34$, p < 0.001 (discrimination). Based on 2001 data.

[200] $\chi^2_1 = 96.53$, p < 0.001. Based on 2001 data.

[201] $\chi^2_1 = 23.37$, p < 0.001. Based on 2001 data.

[202] For the definition of 'trivial' in this context, see H. Genn (1999), above, n.3, p.13. 3,817 non-trivial problems were reported in the 18 substantive justiciable problem categories.

1³/₄ problems per respondent who reported a problem. This is a significant reduction.[203]

In both 2001 and 2004, problems were distributed unevenly among those who reported them (see Figure 2.3). Experiencing justiciable problems has an additive effect. Each time a person experiences a problem they become increasingly likely to experience additional problems. So, for example, of the 37 per cent of respondents who reported one or more justiciable problems in 2001, 46 per cent reported two or more, and of those, 47 per cent reported three or more. This pattern continued as the number of problems increased, culminating in 88 per cent of respondents who reported eight or more problems reporting nine or more.[204] A similar picture emerged in 2004.[205]

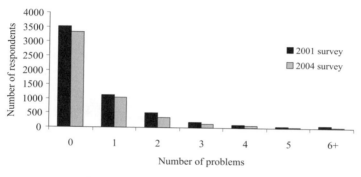

Figure 2.3
Number of Justiciable Problems Reported

As certain population groups are more vulnerable than others to a range of justiciable problems (including people with a long-standing illness or disability, lone parents and those receiving welfare benefits), and as the experience of justiciable problems can itself increase such vulnerability (through, for example, bringing about illness or disability, lone parenthood or unemployment), the proportion of respondents

---

[203] A change in the number of problems reported between the two surveys was analysed using a multilevel Poisson regression, controlling for household effects. Analysis found a significant reduction in the number of problems per respondent in 2004 equivalent to around 0.2 problems per respondent (0.8 in 2001 vs. 0.6 in 2004).

[204] This is similar to the pattern of incidence of crime. See, for example, H. Genn (1988) Multiple Victimisation, in M. Maguire (ed.) *Victims of Crime: A New Deal?* Milton Keynes: Open University Press.

[205] In 2004, of the 33 per cent of respondents who reported one or more justiciable problems, 37 per cent reported two or more, and of those, 44 per cent reported three or more. Eighty-five per cent of respondents who reported eight or more problems reported nine or more.

in vulnerable groups increased as the number of problems reported increased. As can be seen from Figure 2.4, for example, whereas 27 per cent of respondents who reported just one problem in 2004 also reported a long-standing illness or disability, the figure rose to 50 per cent among those respondents who reported six or more problems.[206] Likewise, while 30 per cent of respondents who reported one problem were in receipt of welfare benefits, the figure rose to 52 per cent among those who reported six or more problems, and for lone parents the figures were 4 per cent and 13 per cent respectively.[207] Multi-level Poisson regression confirmed that respondents in these population groups, along with those living in high-density housing, in the rented sector,[208] male respondents, and those with low or high incomes (2004 only) were significantly more likely to report multiple problems than others.[209] A peak in age was also observed in both surveys, corresponding to the age of respondents most likely to report the most problems. This peak was at around 38 years old in 2001 and around 34 in 2004.

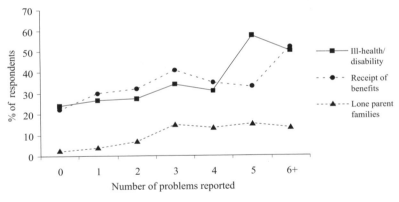

Figure 2.4
Multiple Problems and Personal Circumstances (2004)

Also, as people experience multiple problems, they become increasingly likely to experience problems that play a direct role in social exclusion. For example, whereas 2 per cent of respondents who reported one problem reported a problem

---

[206] In 2001, the figures were 27 per cent and 38 per cent respectively.
[207] In 2001, the figures were 24 per cent and 52 per cent respectively for those in receipt of welfare benefits and 4 per cent and 24 per cent respectively for lone parents.
[208] 2001 only.
[209] Further technical details are available at www.lsrc.org.uk.

relating to homelessness, 17 per cent of respondents who reported six or more problems did so.[210] Again, whereas 1 per cent of respondents who reported one problem in 2004 reported a problem relating to unsafe or unsatisfactory rented housing, 21 per cent of those who reported six or more problems did so.[211] Also, whereas 5 per cent of respondents who reported one problem in 2004 reported a divorce, 21 per cent of those who reported six or more problems did so.[212]

To a large extent, these differences in reporting rates reflect the general increased incidence of problems among those who experience many problems. However, some problem types become more prevalent as the number of problems increases.

To establish which problem types become more prevalent, the relative incidence of each problem type was calculated as the number of problems reported increased. The results indicated that the relative likelihood of respondents reporting problems ancillary to relationship breakdown, problems relating to homelessness, unfair police treatment[213] and particularly domestic violence increased significantly along with the number of problems reported. A non-linear increase was also observed for rented housing problems, which became most common where respondents reported large numbers of problems.[214] In contrast, the relative likelihood of respondents reporting problems relating to consumer transactions, neighbours and personal injury[215] decreased markedly as the number of problems reported increased. Some problem types also showed peaks in likelihood. For example, in 2004, money or debt problems were most common when accompanied by one or two additional problem types,[216] whereas divorce was most common either in isolation or accompanied by a large number of additional problem types.

TRIGGER PROBLEMS

It is no surprise that domestic violence was reported relatively frequently by respondents who had experienced multiple problems. Domestic violence is

---

[210] The figures were less than 1 per cent and 9 per cent respectively in 2001.
[211] The figures were 2 per cent and 17 per cent respectively in 2001.
[212] The figures were 3 per cent and 20 per cent respectively in 2001.
[213] Most apparent in 2001.
[214] For example, in 2004, rented housing problems accounted for 4 to 6 per cent of incidence for those reporting 1 to 4 problem types, but 10 per cent of incidence for those with 5 or more types of problem.
[215] Most apparent in 2004.
[216] Two or three additional problem types in 2001.

symptomatic of dysfunctional relationships and can lead directly to separation and divorce.[217] These problems in turn can entail disputes regarding maintenance and the division of property. Also, the need for one or both parties to move home, along with changes to income and expenditure patterns following separation, can bring about problems relating to homelessness, suitability of accommodation and financial hardship. Moreover, if there are children involved, these problems can be exacerbated by a parent with primary care responsibilities having additional difficulties in obtaining or retaining employment, and a consequent increased likelihood of dependency on maintenance, child-support and welfare benefits.[218] Domestic violence can also stem from other justiciable problems. For example, losing a job has been shown to increase the likelihood of abusing a partner.[219]

Again, it is no surprise that homelessness was reported relatively frequently by respondents who had experienced multiple problems. Homelessness is itself 'evidence of multi-dimensional problems,'[220] and as well as often being preceded or followed by social, economic and/or mental health problems,[221] some or all of which may be justiciable, it can also increase vulnerability to further problems. Living on the streets, for example, increases contact with the police, increases the likelihood of physical assault, increases the likelihood of alcohol and substance abuse, reduces employment opportunities and increases dependency on welfare benefits.

---

[217] See, for example, M. Straus, R. Gelles and S. Steinmetz (1980) *Behind Closed Doors,* New York: Anchor.

[218] L.J. Weitzman and M. Maclean (eds.) (1992) *Economic Consequences of Divorce,* Oxford: Clarendon Press; G. Davis, S. Cretney and J. Collins (1994) *Simple Quarrels: Negotiations and Adjudications in Divorce,* Oxford: Clarendon Press; J. Eekelaar, M. Maclean and S. Beinart (2000) *Family Lawyers: The Divorce Work of Solicitors,* Oxford: Hart Publications; P. Wilcox (2000) Lone Motherhood: The Impact on Living Standards of Leaving a Violent Relationship, in 34 *Journal of Social Policy and Administration,* p.176; G. Davis, G. Bevan, S. Clisby, Z. Cumming, R. Dingwall, P. Fenn, S. Finch, R. Fitzgerald, S. Goldie, D. Greatbach, D. James and J. Pearce (2000) *Monitoring Publicly Funded Family Mediation,* London: Legal Services Commission; G. Allan and G. Crow (2001) *Families, Households and Society,* Basingstoke: Palgrave; Office of the Deputy Prime Minister (2002) *The Provision of Accommodation and Support for Households Experiencing Domestic Violence in England,* London: Office of the Deputy Prime Minister.

[219] D.N. Kyriacou, D. Anglin, E. Taliaferro, S. Stone, T. Tubb, J.A. Linden, R. Muelleman, E. Barton and J.F. Kraus (1999) Risk Factors For Injury To Women From Domestic Violence, in 341(25) *New England Journal Of Medicine,* p.1892.

[220] S. Parker, L. Limbers, E. McKeon (2002) *Homelessness and Accommodation Models for People Living with Mental Health Problems,* Rozelle, New South Wales: Mental Health Coordinating Council.

[221] For a discussion of the link between mental illness and homelessness see, for example, G. Sullivan, A. Burnam and P. Koegel (2000) Pathways To Homelessness Among The Mentally Ill, in 35(10) *Social Psychiatry And Psychiatric Epidemiology,* p.444. See, also, Office of the Deputy Prime Minister (1996) *More than a Roof: A Report into Tackling Homelessness,* London: Office of the Deputy Prime Minister. See, also, J. Bradshaw et al. (2004), above, n.118, p.68 et seq., which discusses three types of driver of homelessness; structural, risk factor and trigger. Risk factors included family breakdown, debt, unemployment, low income, lack of qualifications and ill-health.

As well as domestic violence, relationship breakdown and homelessness problems, other justiciable problem types have been suggested as being comparatively more likely to either cause further problems, or follow on from earlier problems. For example, *Paths to Justice* documented how personal injury and work related ill-health may lead to unemployment or diminish employment opportunities, especially where a victim experiences a substantial degree of residual disability.[222] This in turn can lead to an increased risk of experiencing problems relating to welfare benefits and debt,[223] even if compensation is obtained in relation to the original injury or illness.[224] Serious personal injury and work related ill-health can even lead to other members of a victim's household having to give up work to become carers.[225] Evidently, also, personal injury can be caused by unsafe working conditions.

The above findings in relation to vulnerable populations also suggest a broader causal link between employment problems and money/debt and welfare benefits problems, reflecting the financial hardship that can follow from becoming unemployed. Indeed, all justiciable problems that lead to a reduction in income or diminish employment opportunities would seem likely to increase vulnerability to money/debt and welfare benefits problems. Thus, problems relating to clinical negligence, mental health and immigration might also be expected to do so.

To confirm the justiciable problem types most likely to act as triggers of other problems, a repeated measures General Linear Model was used to compare the number of justiciable problems reported as occurring before and after instances of each individual problem type. In addition, having transformed problem orders to a range from zero (first in sequence) to one (last in sequence), a median test[226] was used to establish whether problems were more likely to be found at the beginning or end of sequences of problems. Sequences of four or more problems in 2001 and three or more in 2004 were examined.[227]

---

[222] H. Genn (1999), above, n.3, p.35.

[223] D. Harris, M. Maclean, H. Genn, S. Lloyd-Bostock, P. Fenn, P. Corfield and Y. Brittan (1984) *Compensation and Support for Illness and Injury,* Oxford: Clarendon Press.

[224] Law Commission (1994) *Personal Injury Compensation: How Much is Enough?* London: Law Commission (Report No. 225).

[225] *Ibid.*

[226] A nonparametric test for multiple independent samples. It produces a chi-squared test of whether more observations were greater than or less than or equal to the median for each problem type. We combine problems in the resulting contingency table to compare specific problems to all other problems combined.

[227] The change was necessary in light of the reduced number of problems reported in 2004.

As anticipated, marginal means from the General Linear Model showed that more problems were reported to follow than to precede the three problem types relating to dysfunctional relationships: domestic violence, divorce and problems ancillary to relationship breakdown.[228] Also, divorce and relationship breakdown problems were significantly more likely to have been reported towards the beginning than towards the end of a sequence of justiciable problems.[229] In fact, around half of all divorces reported as occurring in a sequence of problems were reported as being the first problem in the sequence.[230] In contrast, just 15 per cent were reported as being the last problem.[231] Domestic violence, too, often occurred at the beginning of such sequences, with over 40 per cent of instances reported as being first in a sequence. [232] However, while more than a quarter of relationship breakdown problems were reported as being the first problem in such sequences, they were more often reported towards the middle, reflecting the greater likelihood of other family problems preceding them.[233] Thus, when the McNemar test[234] was used to establish which problem type in each pair of problem types was more likely to occur first when both were reported, there was a suggestion that divorce was more likely to occur before relationship breakdown problems, and that domestic violence was more likely to occur before divorce, although no significant differences were observed in 2004. It

---

[228] There was a clear difference in the triggering effect of the problems studied in both 2001: $F(17) = 2.41$, $p < 0.01$ and 2004: $F(17) = 3.61$, $p < 0.001$. For 2001, marginal means = 1.1 before vs. 1.5 after (domestic violence) (not significant); 0.6 before vs. 1.1 after (divorce); 0.9 before vs. 1.2 after (relationship breakdown). The difference in marginal means for domestic violence was not quite significant. For 2004, marginal means = 0.9 before vs. 1.8 after (domestic violence); 0.7 before vs. 1.3 after (divorce); 0.8 before vs. 1.1 after (relationship breakdown). For 2004, the difference in marginal means for relationship breakdown did not reach significance.

[229] In 2001, for divorce, there were 26 problems less than or equal to the median compared to 10 greater than the median ($\chi^2_1 = 5.34$, $p < 0.05$, comparing divorce to all other problems). For relationship breakdown, there were 41 less than or equal to the median compared to 19 greater than the median ($\chi^2_1 = 5.75$, $p < 0.05$, comparing relationship breakdown to all other problems). In 2004, for divorce, there were 38 problems less than or equal to the median compared to 10 greater than the median ($\chi^2_1 = 6.96$, $p < 0.01$). For relationship breakdown, there were 49 less than or equal to the median compared to 21 greater than the median ($\chi^2_1 = 4.42$, $p < 0.05$, comparing relationship breakdown to all other problems).

[230] Sixty-one per cent in 2001 (20 of 33) and 46 per cent in 2004 (12 of 26).

[231] Thus, divorce was significantly more likely to be reported in first than last position in both 2001 ((20 v. 5) $\chi^2_1 = 8.82$, $p < 0.01$) and 2004 ((12 vs. 4) $\chi^2_1 = 4.12$, $p < 0.05$).

[232] In 2001, this corresponded to 20 problems, compared to nine reported as occurring last in such sequences: $\chi^2_1 = 3.97$, $p < 0.5$. In general in 2001, however, although domestic violence was more often observed towards the beginning than the end of sequences of problems, the findings in this regard were not statistically significant. There were 29 problems less than or equal to the median compared to 17 greater than the median: $\chi^2_1 = 1.82$, $p = 0.18$. This was also the case in 2004, with marginal failure to reach statistical significance despite a large discrepancy: 23 problems less than or equal to the median compared to eight greater than the median, $\chi^2_1 = 3.46$, $p = 0.06$.

[233] Thirty-five per cent in 2001 and 25 per cent in 2004.

[234] A nonparametric test for two related dichotomous variables.

also appeared that, in 2001, domestic violence, divorce and relationship breakdown problems were all more likely to be reported as occurring before money/debt problems, reflecting the increased likelihood of experiencing financial difficulties following the breakdown of a relationship.[235] Numbers were too small in 2004 to confirm this. Domestic violence and divorce were also more likely to be reported as occurring before consumer problems, although this may reflect in large part the tendency of respondents to report only recent consumer problems.[236] In addition, it appeared in 2001 that divorce was more likely to be reported as occurring before problems relating to rented housing and children; reflecting again the financial impact of relationship breakdown, the need for sometimes speedy relocation, and the impact of relationship breakdown on children's education.[237] Again, though, numbers were too small to confirm this in 2004.

As anticipated, more problems were reported to follow than to precede personal injury problems, though the difference was not statistically significant in either 2001 or 2004.[238] Personal injury was, though, significantly more likely to have been reported as occurring first than last in a sequence of four or more problems.[239] However, because of the small number of instances of some problem types and the size of the effect observed here, it was not possible to establish any likely knock-on problem types – although again personal injury was more likely to be reported as occurring before consumer problems.

There was some indication that more problems followed than preceded problems relating to homelessness, mental health and immigration, although the findings were not significant.[240]

---

[235] $\chi^2 = 6.50$, p < 0.01 (domestic violence); $\chi^2 = 3.45$, p < 0.05 (divorce); $\chi^2 = 8.76$, p < 0.01 (relationship breakdown).

[236] An analysis of the reliability of autobiographical memory in relation to the different types of justiciable problems was set out in Pleasence et al. (2004) *Causes of Action: Civil Law and Social Justice,* first edition, Norwich: Stationery Office.

[237] p = 0.046 (rented housing); p = 0.011 (children) (exact test used, owing to small numbers: Mehta and Patel (1996) *SPSS Exact Tests 7.0 for Windows.* Chicago, IL: SPSS Inc.). See, for example, J. Sparkes and H. Glennerster (2002) Preventing Social Exclusion: Education's Contribution, in J. Hills, J. Le Grand and D. Piachaud (eds.) *Understanding Social Exclusion,* Oxford: Oxford University Press, and L. Trinder, J. Connolly, J. Kellett and C. Notley, (2005) *A Profile of Applicants and Respondents in Contact Cases in Essex,* London: Department for Constitutional Affairs.

[238] Marginal means = 0.62 before vs. 0.76 after in 2001 and 0.79 before vs. 1.00 after in 2004.

[239] 16 vs. 6, $\chi^2_1 = 4.34$, p < 0.05. This difference was non-significant in 2004.

[240] Marginal means = 1.03 before vs. 1.22 after (homelessness) in 2001, 0.98 before vs. 1.00 after in 2004; Marginal means = 0.68 before vs. 1.00 after (mental health) in 2001, 1.00 before vs. 1.78 after in 2004; Marginal means = 0.27 before vs. 0.73 after (immigration) in 2001, 0.67 before vs. 1.78 after in 2004. Also, in sequences of four or more problems, both mental health and immigration problems were

Finally, as already indicated, consumer problems were more likely to have been reported to follow on from than to precede other problems,[241] and at the end rather than the beginning of sequences of problems.[242]

THE BROADER IMPACT OF JUSTICIABLE PROBLEMS

It is clear from the above sections that justiciable problems can bring about a range of social, economic and health problems. To help further describe and quantify this broad impact, respondents to the 2004 survey were asked additional questions concerning the nature of the adverse consequences that followed from any justiciable problems identified. They were also asked about the extent to which problems interfered with day-to-day life.

Adverse consequences were reported in relation to over half of all problems reported in 2004.[243] Adverse health consequences followed from 34 per cent of problems,[244] loss of confidence from 17 per cent, loss of income or employment from 16 per cent,[245] violence or damage to property from 8 per cent,[246] loss of a home from 6 per cent and breakdown of a relationship from 4 per cent (excluding divorce and problems ancillary to relationship breakdown). Respondents also stated that they had spent all or most of their time worrying about almost 40 per cent of problems. In addition, they reported that they had often experienced great difficulty carrying on living normally while experiencing problems.

Adverse consequences and interference in day-to-day life did not, of course, follow uniformly from all problem types. As would be expected, physical ill-health was most likely to follow from accidents, clinical negligence and domestic

---

more often first than last, but numbers were very small, so again the results were not statistically significant.

[241] Marginal means = 0.75 before vs. 0.53 after in 2001 and 1.13 before vs. 0.67 after in 2004.

[242] For 2001, χ^2_1 = 14.94, p < 0.001, comparing consumer problems to other problems combined (64 problems less than or equal to the median, 98 greater). For 2004, χ^2_1 = 18.48, p < 0.001, comparing consumer to other problems combined (63 problems less than or equal to the median, 83 greater). Consumer problems were also significantly more likely to have been reported as occurring last rather than first in sequences of four or more problems (68 v. 32) in 2001: χ^2_1 = 17.3, p < 0.001 and (53 v. 25) in sequences of three or more in 2004: χ^2_1 = 12.45, p < 0.001.

[243] Fifty-two per cent (1350 of 2583).

[244] Twenty-seven per cent stress related illness and 16 per cent physical ill health. Eighteen per cent reported only stress related illness, 7 per cent only physical illness and 9 per cent both.

[245] Fifteen per cent loss of income and 6 per cent loss of employment.

[246] Four per cent personal violence and 6 per cent damage to property.

violence.[247] However, it also followed on from 9 per cent of other problems. Indeed, 18 per cent of employment problems led to physical ill-health and even consumer problems, which were the least likely to result in physical ill-health,[248] led to it in 2 per cent of cases. Stress related ill-health was most likely to result from problems ancillary to relationship breakdown and domestic violence, being reported on more than half of all such occasions.[249] It was also more likely to flow from problems relating to employment, homelessness and mental health than problems of other types. Again, though, even in the case of consumer problems,[250] stress related ill-health was reported on 10 per cent of occasions.

Of those who reported physical ill-health consequent to a justiciable problem, 80 per cent visited a general practitioner (66 per cent), hospital (42 per cent) or other health care worker (13 per cent).[251] While respondents who reported personal injury or clinical negligence problems were more likely than others to visit a hospital,[252] there was little difference in the relative likelihood of respondents visiting a general practitioner.[253] The mean number of visits to a general practitioner was six, to a hospital as an out-patient was ten, and to another health care worker was two. Of those who reported stress related ill-health, 26 per cent received treatment from a general practitioner (22 per cent), counsellor (4 per cent), community psychiatric nurse (2 per cent) or other health care worker (2 per cent).[254]

Loss of income was most likely to follow from problems concerning employment, welfare benefits, personal injury and relationship breakdown, being reported on 45 per cent, 36 per cent, 23 per cent and 20 per cent of occasions respectively. Loss of income was very unlikely to follow from problems with

---

[247] $\chi^2_{17} = 653.25$, p < 0.001. Standard Pearson Residuals = 18.8 (personal injury), 8.5 (clinical negligence) and 2.9 (domestic violence). Standardised residuals exceeding around two or three indicate a lack of fit of the null hypothesis (independence) in that cell: A. Agresti (2002) *Categorical Data Analysis*, 2nd Edition, Hoboken, NJ: Wiley, p.81.
[248] Standard Pearson Residual = -8.0.
[249] Standard Pearson Residuals = 5.4 (relationship breakdown) and 4.4 (domestic violence).
[250] Standard Pearson Residual = -7.2.
[251] Based on data collected during main interviews. 11 per cent of those who reported ill-health consequent to a justiciable problem also reported spending time in hospital as an in-patient, for an average of 9.5 days. The majority of these respondents had suffered personal injuries or clinical negligence.
[252] $\chi^2_{16} = 46.14$, p < 0.001. Standard Pearson Residuals = 2.4 (personal injury) and 0.9 (clinical negligence).
[253] $\chi^2_{16} = 13.69$, p = 0.622.
[254] Of those respondents who only reported stress-related illness, 22 per cent received clinical treatment. Of these, 19 per cent visited a general practitioner, 3 per cent a counsellor and 2 per cent a community psychiatric nurse. The average number of visits to a general practitioner was nine, to a counsellor was 6 and to a community psychiatric nurse was 49.

neighbours or consumer problems.[255] Similarly, loss of employment frequently followed employment problems. This occurred 33 per cent of the time.[256] Of course, in many cases employment problems involved people being sacked or made redundant (25 per cent[257]). However, aside from issues such as these, 8 per cent of respondents reported that their employment problems were resolved by leaving their job. Also, while loss of employment was less common as a consequence of personal injury or relationship breakdown problems, it was still reported on 6 per cent of occasions. As with loss of income, loss of employment rarely followed on from problems with neighbours or consumer transactions.[258]

Where respondents reported losing a job as a consequence of a problem, 70 per cent went on to experience a period of unemployment and, of these, 59 per cent then went on to claim unemployment related benefits.[259] Thirty-seven per cent had not found a new job at the time of interview[260] and, of the remainder, over one-third did not find another job for three months or more. Moreover, 48 per cent of those who did start a new job were paid less than they were previously, although 36 per cent were paid more.[261]

Physical assault was a common feature of relationship breakdown. In all, 9 per cent of divorces and 19 per cent of problems ancillary to relationship breakdown were reported to have resulted in assault. Outside of the family, violence was also likely in connection with problems with neighbours. Ten per cent of neighbour problems involved assault and a further 19 per cent involved property damage. In addition, discrimination problems were more likely than others to involve assault.[262] In only five of the 18 problem categories, were there no reports of assault: welfare benefits, personal injury, clinical negligence, mental health and immigration. Problems relating to consumer transactions, money/debt, housing and employment also saw violence in 1 per cent or fewer instances.

---

[255] $\chi^2_{17} = 331.22$, $p < 0.001$; Standard Pearson Residuals = 12.2 (employment), 5.1 (welfare benefits), 2.1 (personal injury), 2.0 (relationship breakdown), -6.0 (neighbours) and -5.8 (consumer). The average loss was put at £2,290.

[256] $\chi^2_{17} = 450.27$, $p < 0.001$; Standard Pearson Residual = 18.1 (employment).

[257] Also, a further 10 per cent of problems concerned threats of sack or redundancy.

[258] Standard Pearson Residual = -3.9 (neighbours) and -4.8 (consumer).

[259] Based on data collected during main interviews. Sixty-six of 94 respondents reported unemployment. Thirty-two of 66 reported claiming benefits as a result. Respondents who claimed benefits did so for an average of 19 weeks.

[260] Based on 90 responses.

[261] Twenty-seven of 57 respondents were paid less, 20 were paid more.

[262] $\chi^2_{17} = 296.83$, $p < 0.001$. Standard Pearson Residuals = 12.2 (domestic violence), 7.1 (relationship breakdown), 5.3 (neighbours) and 1.9 (discrimination).

Of those respondents who reported being assaulted or property damage as a result of experiencing a justiciable problem, 51 per cent contacted the police. Of these, around two-thirds requested that police attend the scene immediately.

Unsurprisingly, loss of a home was most likely to follow from family and rented housing problems, although this was not the case with owned housing problems.[263] It was least likely to follow from consumer problems.[264] Although there was not a significantly greater likelihood of problems with neighbours leading to people leaving their home, 7 per cent of respondents who reported these problems stated that the problem was resolved by moving.

Most of those who lost a home moved to a new home straight away. However, 46 per cent spent a period in temporary accommodation, two people moved to a refuge or shelter and one spent time sleeping rough.[265]

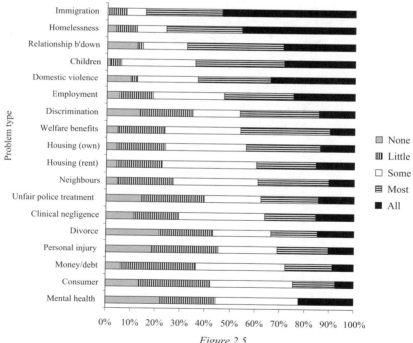

Figure 2.5
Time Spent Worrying About Problem

---

[263] $\chi^2_{17} = 366.97$, p < 0.001. Standard Pearson Residuals = 10.7 (divorce), 5.1 (relationship breakdown), 3.0 (domestic violence) and 2.7 (rented housing).
[264] Standard Pearson Residual = -5.6.
[265] Based on data collected during main interviews.

Loss of confidence was most likely to follow from employment and discrimination problems. This outcome was reported on more than one-third of all occasions.[266] It was also a common feature of relationship breakdown, noted in just under one-third of divorces. Again, loss of confidence was least likely to follow consumer problems,[267] although it was still reported on 9 per cent of occasions.

As has already been indicated, the breakdown of a relationship was most likely to follow from domestic violence.[268] While it was far less likely to follow other problems, it was not uncommon elsewhere. For example, it was said to have been a consequence of 9 per cent of discrimination problems and 8 per of employment problems.[269] Again, it was least likely to follow consumer problems.[270]

As regards the amount of time respondents worried about problems and the extent to which they were able to live normally while experiencing them, those who had experienced problems concerning immigration, homelessness, domestic violence, children and problems ancillary to relationship breakdown were in the gravest position. As can be seen from Figure 2.5 above, more than 60 per cent of respondents who reported each of these problem types said they had spent all or most of their time worrying about them. This compares to just 24 per cent who said the same in respect of consumer problems and 33 per cent in respect of divorce. While just 22 per cent of people who experienced problems concerning mental health spent all or most of their time worrying about them, this was at odds with reports about the extent to which they were able to live normally while experiencing such problems. Using the latter measure, mental health related problems appeared to be the sixth most serious type.

As well as different adverse consequences being reported in relation to different problem types, some problems were more likely than others to result in multiple adverse consequences. So, as is illustrated by Figure 2.6, victims of domestic violence reported the most number of adverse consequences, followed by those who had experienced problems related to employment, relationship breakdown and discrimination. The one respondent who reported experiencing every form of adverse consequence attributed this to a divorce.

---

[266] χ^2_{17} = 193.25, p < 0.001. Standard Pearson Residuals = 6.3 (employment) and 6.9 (discrimination).
[267] Standard Pearson Residual = -4.8.
[268] χ^2_{17} = 183.81, p < 0.001. Standard Pearson Residual = 6.6.
[269] Standard Pearson Residual = 1.8 (employment) and 1.4 (discrimination).
[270] Standard Pearson Residual = -3.3.

Those who suffered consumer problems and problems concerning owned housing and unfair police treatment reported the least number of adverse consequences.

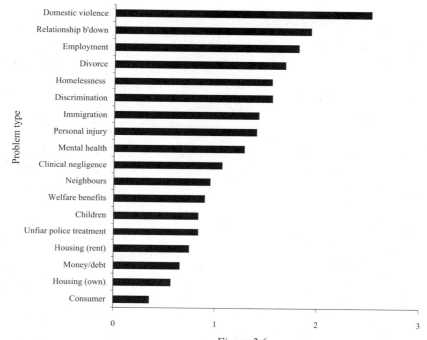

Figure 2.6
Mean Number of Adverse Consequences

PROBLEM CLUSTERS

Problem types do not have to cause or follow on from one another in order for there to be a connection between them. Connections can also stem from coinciding characteristics of vulnerability to problem types, or coinciding defining circumstances of problem types. Thus, a connection between owned housing and consumer problems reported in *Paths to Justice* can now be attributed to both problem types being most likely to be experienced by those on higher incomes who own their own homes and have a greater number of academic qualifications. In some instances, connections may stem from patterns of causation and vulnerability and coincidence of defining circumstances (e.g. problems relating to children and the care and control or financial support of children).

Hierarchical cluster analysis was used to establish general and underlying connections between different problem types.[271] Average between groups linkage was employed as the clustering method. Then, by reference to the position of problems in sequences of problems within individual clusters, the typical ordering of problems associated with each of the main clusters was established.

The results of the hierarchical cluster analysis are summarised in two dendrograms set out in Figures 2.7 and 2.8. Dendrograms are commonly used to summarise cluster analysis results. They illustrate the complete clustering procedure and the divisions made at each stage of analysis.

As anticipated – given that family type problems appear to follow on from one another, are each most frequently reported by people aged between 25 and 44, and have substantially overlapping defining circumstances – a distinct cluster of family problems is evident, comprising domestic violence, divorce and relationship breakdown problems. In 2001, the cluster also included problems regarding children. This same cluster was also revealed by a secondary hierarchical cluster analysis of *Paths to Justice* data (Figure 2.10). In fact, almost half of all family problems were reported as having occurred in combination with one or more other family problems.

As has been reported elsewhere,[272] and as is suggested by Figure 2.9, domestic violence, which in both 2001 and 2004 occurred in combination with one or more other family problems in over 40 per cent of all instances,[273] often appeared to lie behind the experience of other family problems. Thus, in 2001, where domestic violence was reported in combination with a divorce, it generally occurred first, and its existence increased substantially the likelihood of problems ancillary to the divorce being reported.[274]

---

[271] See P. Pleasence, N. J. Balmer, A. Buck, A. O'Grady and H. Genn (2004) Multiple Justiciable Problems: Common Clusters and their Social and Demographic Indicators, in *Journal of Empirical Legal Studies,* Vol.1, No.2. The hierarchical cluster analysis was based on similarity matrices of problem types included within the 2001 and 2004 surveys. As data were binary, similarities between problem types were used, rather than dissimilarity or distance measures. For a discussion of dissimilarity/distance measures and all other matters relating to cluster analysis, see B.S. Everitt, S. Landau and M. Leese (2001) *Cluster Analysis,* London: Arnold. Jaccard coefficients were used as similarity measures. Jaccard coefficients are calculated for two given problems (*i and j*) as, $s_{ij} = a/(a + b + c)$, where a corresponds to the experience of both problem types and b and c are off diagonals (zero-one and one-zero). Co-absences (zero-zero) were ignored as individuals who had experienced both problems clearly had something in common, while this was not necessarily the case for those who had experienced neither problem (i.e. clusters were based on the experience rather than the absence of problems).

[272] P. Pleasence, N.J. Balmer, A. Buck, A. O'Grady, M. Maclean and H. Genn (2003), above, n.67.

[273] Over 50 per cent in 2001.

[274] $\chi^2_1 = 7.56$, $p < 0.01$.

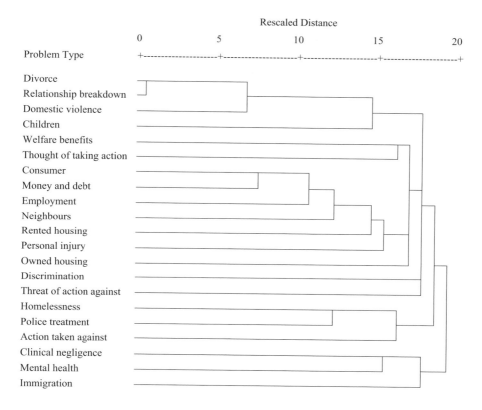

Figure 2.7

Dendrogram Using Average Linkage (Between Groups) (2001)

Outside of divorce, violence was equally likely to occur before or after problems ancillary to relationship breakdown. If violence occurred before problems ancillary to relationship breakdown, this was not as long before as in the case of divorce, suggesting that domestic violence is tolerated for longer within marriage. However, violence still appeared to be strongly linked with problems ancillary to relationship breakdown, being reported in one-third of all instances.

68

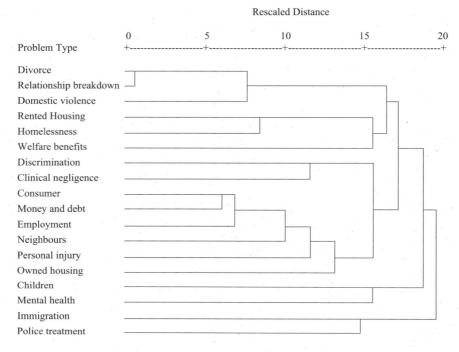

Rescaled Distance

Figure 2.8

Dendrogram Using Average Linkage (Between Groups) (2004)

The existence of domestic violence also substantially increased the likelihood of problems relating to children occurring. So, in 2001 whereas 14 per cent of respondents who reported domestic violence also reported children related problems (mostly concerning education),[275] just 2 per cent of other respondents did so.[276] Moreover, 29 per cent of respondents who reported domestic violence and problems ancillary to the breakdown of a relationship reported problems related to children, compared to 2 per cent who reported neither.[277] Numbers were too small in 2004 to draw comparisons. Problems related to children were generally experienced at the end of sequences of problems within the 'family' cluster.

---

[275] If education problems are looked at alone, the increased likelihood is only marginally less substantial: $\chi^2_1 = 50.23$, p < 0.001.

[276] $\chi^2_1 = 64.19$, p < 0.001.

[277] $\chi^2_1 = 135.53$, p < 0.001.

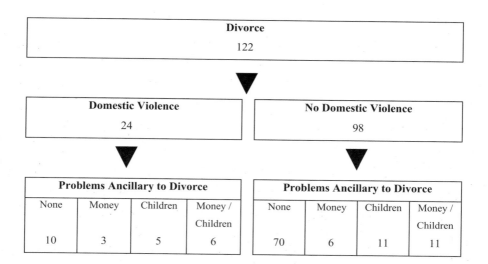

Figure 2.9

Family Problems Relating to Divorce (2001)

Hierarchical cluster analysis of 2001 data also indicated a problem cluster involving homelessness, unfair treatment by the police, and action being taken against the respondent. Factor analysis also revealed this cluster,[278] although it suggested an additional component in problems relating to rented housing. In fact, over half of all homelessness problems reported in 2001 were reported in combination with a rented housing problem, and the expanded cluster principally embodied a cycle of rented housing and homelessness problems. Hierarchical cluster analysis of 2004 data also connected homelessness and problems concerning rented housing and, further, indicated that both are linked to benefits problems. This ties up with the fact that those who reported homelessness problems or lived in the rented housing sector were much more likely than others to be in receipt of benefits. The 2004 analysis did not include the residual problem category of action being taken against the respondent, so it is not possible to compare it with the 2001 analysis in this respect. Neither did it link homelessness problems with unfair treatment by the police, although those who reported homelessness problems were more likely than others to report problems with the police. In 2004, unfair police treatment was instead linked with immigration

---

[278] Details of this factor analysis were set out in P. Pleasence et al. (2004), above, n.236, p.165.

problems, possibly as a consequence of the increasing use of the criminal law in relation to immigration issues.

The inclusion of unfair treatment by the police in a 'homelessness' cluster makes sense in light of both police and homelessness problems being most often experienced by young people in receipt of welfare benefits. It also reflects the increased vulnerability to police problems that accompanies extended periods of time being spent on the streets and the social problems associated with the homeless population (e.g. alcohol and drug abuse). Possibly this latter connection explains why police related problems seemed to occur at any stage in sequences of problems within the cluster. Rented housing problems, in contrast, were reported at the beginning and end of sequences of problems within the cluster, although more typically at the beginning rather than the end in 2004. This may be explained by the disproportionate reporting of problems relating to unsafe and unsatisfactory rented housing accommodation by respondents reporting homelessness. These types of problems very much characterise routes into and out of homelessness.

A third cluster identified by hierarchical cluster analysis involved a broad range of problem types including those relating to consumer transactions, money/debt, employment, neighbours, personal injury, rented housing, owned housing, welfare benefits and discrimination. Within this cluster there were also further more defined clusters, most particularly a core cluster incorporating problems relating to consumer transactions, money/debt, neighbours and employment, and at another level, personal injury, owned housing and, in 2001, rented housing problems. The central four-problem element of this core cluster was structurally identical in both 2001 and 2004. Moreover, although rented housing problems were more closely associated with the homelessness cluster in 2004, 55 per cent of respondents reporting rented housing problems also reported one or more problems relating to consumer transactions, money/debt, employment, neighbours, personal injury or owned housing.

Unlike the family cluster, the structure of which also clearly emerged from a secondary analysis of *Paths to Justice* data, the structure of this broad cluster appears at first to have differed somewhat from the equivalent cluster drawn from *Paths to Justice* data. For example, the dendrogram set out in Figure 2.10 suggests more of a connection between owned housing and consumer problems, and less of a connection between consumer and money/debt problems. This may, though, be due to the different composition of the owned housing and money categories within the *Paths to*

Justice dataset. For example, in the *Paths to Justice* study, owned housing problems included problems relating to neighbours, and money problems included problems relating to welfare benefits. Thus, there can actually be seen to be a startling degree of consistency between the three sets of survey findings.

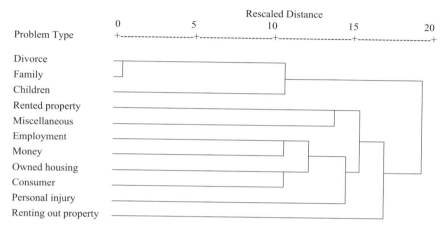

Figure 2.10

Dendrogram Derived from Secondary Analysis of Paths to Justice Data

The connections between employment and personal injury problems have been described above, as have those between employment, personal injury and money/debt problems. Where these problems occurred in combination, personal injury generally came first, and money/debt problems last.

In addition, money/debt problems can lead to downward mobility in the housing market, along with general difficulties relating to mortgage and rental payments, thus increasing vulnerability to rented housing problems. As a result, as was demonstrated above, respondents in the rented housing sector were more likely to report money/debt problems than others.

Of the seven core problems in this 'economic' cluster, money/debt problems most often overlapped with consumer problems, perhaps reflecting the overreaching economic activity of some of those who face money/debt problems. Over one-third of 2001 survey respondents, and around one-quarter of 2004 survey respondents, who reported money/debt problems also reported a consumer problem.[279] However, because of the common experience of consumer problems, over one-fifth of 2001 respondents and around one-sixth of 2004 respondents who reported each of the other cluster problems also reported consumer problems; as did significant numbers of respondents reporting non-cluster problems, with the exception of problems relating to homelessness in 2001,[280] and mental health and homelessness in 2004.[281]

Reporting of problems with neighbours did not overlap *substantially* with reporting of any of the other individual economic cluster problems. However, problems with neighbours are associated with high-density housing – which is more common in the rented housing sector (leading to respondents in the sector being more vulnerable to such problems) – and with extended periods being spent at home, a possible consequence of both employment and personal injury problems. Interestingly, though, factor analysis of 2001 survey data suggested that, where problems concerning consumer transactions and neighbours occur in combination, it is unlikely that employment and personal injury problems will also occur, and vice versa.[282]

While other problem clusters emerged from hierarchical cluster analysis – such as one, in 2001, involving clinical negligence, mental health and immigration problems and one, in 2004, involving discrimination and clinical negligence – these were not consistent between the two surveys.

PROBLEM CLUSTERS AND PATTERNS OF VULNERABILITY

As with individual problems, experience of multiple problems falling within identified problem clusters does not affect people uniformly across the population. Multi-level Poisson regression was used to test the influence of a range of social and demographic predictors on the number of problems reported within each of the above clusters.[283]

---

[279] Thirty-four per cent (158 of 465) in 2001, 23 per cent (63 of 279) in 2004.
[280] Eight per cent (3 of 36).
[281] Three per cent (2 of 61) for homelessness and none of eleven for mental health.
[282] Details of this factor analysis were set out in P. Pleasence et al (2004), above, n.236, p.165.
[283] The independent variables used in the analysis were the same as those set out in note 64 above. By using Poisson regression, the number of cluster problems was modelled, rather than simply the presence or absence of problems. Further details of the analysis are set out at www.lsrc.org.uk.

As with each of the four types of family problem, and reflecting the impact of such problems, lone parents, those who reported long-standing ill-health or disability and those living in the rented housing sector were more likely than others to report problems within the family cluster. In contrast, married respondents were less likely than others to do so. Asian respondents were also less likely than others to report family cluster problems. As with the individual problem types within the family cluster, the peak age of respondents reporting multiple family cluster problems was around 40. In all, 80 respondents reported multiple family cluster problems in 2001 and 46 in 2004.

Reflecting the economic disadvantage of those people experiencing problems within the homelessness cluster, economically inactive respondents, those in receipt of welfare benefits and those with low incomes were more likely than others to report homelessness cluster problems. The same was also true of those living in the rented housing sector, both public and private. In addition, respondents who reported long-standing ill-health or disability were more likely than others to report homelessness cluster problems; perhaps in part reflecting the 'relegation' of those with a long-term ill-health or disability to poor quality housing. Consistent with the findings relating to homelessness, the youngest respondents appeared most likely to report problems within this cluster. In all, 69 respondents reported multiple homelessness cluster problems in 2001 and 46 in 2004.

Finally, reflecting the incidence and range of problems encompassed by the economic problem cluster, the social and demographic associations with this cluster were not dissimilar to those found for the experience of justiciable problems in general. This was so for both the four-problem and seven-problem core clusters. Thus, reflecting the broad links between the experience of justiciable problems and social exclusion, those on benefits, those living in high density housing, those who reported long-standing ill-health or disability and those with the lowest incomes[284] were more likely than others to report problems within the economic problem clusters. Conversely, respondents who were married and had children were less likely than others to do so. However, the inclusion within the clusters of problem types also associated with affluence – such as consumer problems – led to those with mortgages and those with the highest incomes also being more likely than others to report cluster

---

[284] This finding in relation to income was observed in 2004 only.

problems.[285] Reporting of economic cluster problems peaked for respondents in their mid-thirties. In all, 671 respondents reported multiple seven-problem economic cluster problems in 2001 and 417 in 2004, while 510 respondents reported multiple four-problem cluster problems in 2001 and 275 in 2004.

SUMMARY

Thirty-six per cent of respondents to the 2001 survey and 33 per cent of respondents to the 2004 survey reported having experienced one or more justiciable problems during the preceding three-and-a-half years. This is a significant decrease, in part explained by differences in the social and demographic profile of the 2001 and 2004 samples. Evidently, though, such problems remain ubiquitous.

While all sections of the population experience problems, experience is far from being randomly distributed. Experience reflects not only chance, but also underlying differences in life circumstances that entail differences in vulnerability to problems. In general terms, those 2001 and 2004 survey respondents who reported long-standing ill-health or disability, lone parents, those living in the rented housing sector and in high-density housing, those who were unemployed and on very low incomes, and those aged between 25 and 44 were more likely than others to report problems. Thus, although there was also a tendency for those on very high incomes to report problems at higher than average rates, it seems that 'socially excluded' groups are particularly vulnerable to experiencing justiciable problems. This was starkly illustrated by the fact that more than four-fifths of respondents to the temporary accommodation survey reported one or more problems during the same time period.

From the 2004 survey data regarding respondents' experiences of crime, a picture also emerged of substantial commonality between patterns of crime and civil justice problems. So, almost half of those respondents who reported having been victims of crime also reported having experienced a justiciable problem. As crime victimisation and offending are closely associated, the same was also true of a similar proportion of self-reported offenders.

---

[285] The picture emerging from the analysis was subtly different between 2001 and 2004, mortgage status being significant in relation to both the four-problem and seven-problem core clusters in 2001, but not 2004 and income being significant in relation to both the four-problem and seven-problem core economic clusters in 2004, but not 2001.

Of course, the reported incidence of individual problem types, and the population groups most vulnerable to them varied greatly. Common problems, such as those that arose from consumer transactions, arose from 'defining circumstances' routinely experienced across the adult population. In contrast, rare problems, such as those that arose from a change of country of abode, residence status or citizenship, arose from defining circumstances far from the routine. Those who most often experienced the 'defining' circumstances of individual problem types were, all else being equal, also most vulnerable to experiencing the problems themselves. However, all else was not always equal. Physical make-up, experience, resources and disposition were also observed to influence patterns of vulnerability.

Age was found to be an important influence in predicting all problem types except those relating to neighbours, personal injury, clinical negligence and mental health. In addition, gender, while not found to be a significant influence in predicting problems in general, was an important influence in predicting such things as domestic violence and unfair treatment by the police. Similarly, ethnicity, though not an important predictor in general, was found to be particularly influential in predicting problems concerning discrimination and immigration.

Furthermore, aspects of respondents' economic and housing circumstances had a significant influence in predicting most problem types. However, unlike age, gender and ethnicity, economic circumstances can change as a result of the experience of justiciable problems. The findings in this regard therefore reflect not only patterns of vulnerability to justiciable problems, but also their economic impact. So, for example, employment problems were most likely to be reported by the unemployed.

Tracked demographic data from the 2004 survey shed new light on the direction of causation between problems and changes in economic activity. Analysis indicated that, whereas changes for the worse in economic activity tended to precede problems concerning rented housing, welfare benefits and unfair treatment by the police, they tended to follow on from employment problems.

In large part indicating the impact of relationship breakdown, the type of family in which respondents lived had a significant influence on predicting a range of problem types. Thus, lone parents were more likely than other respondents to have reported problems concerning, for example, rented housing, money/debt and mental health. The particular vulnerability of lone parents reflects susceptibility both to problems affecting single people and problems affecting parents.

Lastly, respondents who reported long-standing ill-health or disability were more likely than others to report most problem types. Such respondents were particularly vulnerable to a range of justiciable problems associated with social exclusion, including problems with discrimination, employment, money/debt, welfare benefits and rented housing. As well as ill-health and disability increasing vulnerability to justiciable problems, these factors can also be brought about or worsened by justiciable problems. This is obviously so in relation to negligent accidents, clinical negligence and domestic violence. However, there is also evidence that housing in a state of disrepair and overcrowded households can bring about physical and psychological ill-health, as can problems relating to discrimination, employment, debt and relationship breakdown. Analysis of tracked demographic data from the 2004 survey indicated that problems relating to employment, rented housing, clinical negligence and homelessness were most likely to bring about long-standing ill-health or disability.

As respondents to the survey of people living in temporary accommodation were much more often lone parents, younger, much less economically active and on considerably lower incomes than their general population survey counterparts, unsurprisingly they reported a very different pattern of experience of problems. This included increased rates of problems relating to rented housing, employment, welfare benefits, discrimination and immigration.

Reinforcing the disadvantage of those who are vulnerable to justiciable problems, the experience of such problems has an additive effect. So, each time a person experiences a problem, they become increasingly likely to experience additional problems. As certain population groups (including people with a long-standing illness or disability) are more vulnerable than others to a range of justiciable problems, and as the experience of justiciable problems can itself increase such vulnerability (through, for example, bringing about ill-health or disability) the proportion of respondents in vulnerable groups increased as the number of problems reported increased. Also, as respondents experienced multiple problems, they became increasingly likely to have experienced problems that play a direct role in social exclusion. Of course, to a large extent this is simply a consequence of their experiencing increasing numbers of problems. However, some problem types, such as those relating to homelessness and domestic violence, became more prevalent as the number of problems increased. In contrast, some problem types, such as those relating to consumer transactions and personal injuries, became less prevalent as the number of problems increased.

Although the experience of problems has an additive effect, not all problem types were associated with the same risk of additional problems. Domestic violence, divorce, relationship breakdown, and personal injury problems all appeared more likely than other problem types to trigger additional problems. This is unsurprising. Domestic violence has been shown to be symptomatic of dysfunctional relationships and can lead directly to separation and divorce, which, in turn, can lead to disputes regarding maintenance and the division of property. The changes in living arrangements and economic circumstances following separation can also bring about problems relating to, for example, rented housing and financial hardship. Furthermore, *Paths to Justice* documented how personal injury and work related ill-health can diminish employment opportunities and lead to unemployment, which, in turn, can lead to problems relating to welfare benefits and debt, even if compensation is obtained in relation to the original injury or illness.

In addition to being able to examine the relationship between social and demographic factors and the experience of different problem types, data from the 2004 survey allowed an estimate to be generated of the broader impact of problems. It transpired that over one-third of problems resulted in a deterioration of health, and a substantial proportion in a loss of confidence, income, employment, a home or family. Evidently, problems also sometimes involved or led to violence. Of those respondents who reported becoming ill as a result of a problem, the majority went on to utilise health services, most often a general practitioner. Of those who reported losing their job, many went on to claim unemployment benefits. Of those who reported violence, the majority went on to involve the police. The cost to the public of justiciable problems is evidently substantial.

Problem types do not have to cause or follow on from one another in order for there to be a connection between them. Connections can also stem from coinciding characteristics of vulnerability to problem types, or coinciding defining circumstances of problem types. Hierarchical cluster and factor analysis identified three principal problem clusters. The most distinct, a 'family' cluster, was comprised of problems relating to domestic violence, divorce, relationship breakdown and children. This same cluster was also revealed by a secondary hierarchical cluster analysis of the *Paths to Justice* data. A 'homelessness' cluster comprised problems relating to rented housing, homelessness, welfare benefits and unfair treatment by the police. Lastly, an 'economic' cluster comprised problems relating to consumer transactions, money/debt, neighbours and employment problems, and at another level, problems relating to rented housing, owned housing and personal injury.

As with individual problems, experience of multiple problems falling within identified problem clusters is not randomly distributed. Respondents who reported long-standing illness or disability were more likely to report multiple problems within all three clusters. Lone parents and those living in rented housing were also more likely than others to report multiple problems within the family cluster. Respondents receiving welfare benefits, those on low incomes and those living in rented housing were more likely than others to report multiple problems within the homelessness cluster; as were also the youngest respondents. Finally, those receiving welfare benefits, living in high-density housing, on low or high incomes and those with mortgages were more likely than others to report multiple problems within the economic cluster.

3

Inaction and Action:
Responses to Justiciable Problems

This chapter sets out the ways in which people deal with justiciable problems. Using information obtained from screen interviews, it highlights the sense of powerlessness and helplessness often experienced by people who face such problems. It also examines the different rates of action and use of advice services associated with different problem types and population groups. As part of this examination, it reveals how individual and household problem resolution strategies can become entrenched, and how awareness of local advice services is linked to whether or not people take any action to resolve problems. The chapter then details the many sources from which people attempt to obtain advice and, using information obtained from main interviews, reveals the manner in which people seek advice, the difficulties they experience in doing so and the nature of help received by those who are successful in doing so. Through this, it illustrates how people's choices of advisers, although often logical and apposite, can be uncertain and unpromising. It also illustrates the phenomenon of referral fatigue, whereby the more times people are referred on elsewhere by an adviser, the less likely they become to act on a referral. Finally, the chapter describes how advice is paid for

INACTION AND ACTION

Not everyone who experiences a justiciable problem will take action to resolve it. As Felstiner, Abel and Sarat depicted in their influential model of disputing behaviour, before action can be taken, a problem must be recognised as such.[286] People faced with the constituent elements of a justiciable problem will not always regard them as problematic. As suggested in the preceding chapter, sensitivity as well as vulnerability to problems varies between differently constituted population groups. People's perceptions of specific sets of circumstances are influenced by, for example, their familiarity with them, understanding of them, and general expectations. These, in turn, are influenced by, for example, their age, education, economic situation and physical, social and cultural environment. So, for instance, as expectations of standards of behaviour vary between people of different ages, young people are less likely to regard 'neighbour nuisance' as problematic.[287] Also, as physical strength and the experience of physical violence vary between people of different gender, men are less likely to regard an assault by a partner as upsetting or frightening, and consequently as problematic.[288]

As the Hughes Commission noted, even if the constituent elements of a justiciable problem are regarded as problematic, action to resolve it will still be unlikely if it is believed that nothing can be done to effect a satisfactory resolution.[289] Of course, as was observed in *Paths to Justice*, people who take no action to resolve a problem because they think nothing can be done make this judgment without the benefit of advice and, therefore, without the benefit of an opportunity to identify solutions they are not personally aware of.[290] As few people are familiar with the complexities of the framework of civil law that bears on everyday life, the existence

---

[286] W. Felstiner, R. Abel and A. Sarat (1981) The Emergence and Transformation of Disputes: Naming, Blaming, Claiming ..., 15 *Law and Society Review*, p.631. The five-part aetiology of how 'injurious experiences' (here taken as equivalent to 'justiciable problems') may become lawsuits involves the recognition of circumstances as "injurious" (naming); the identification of them as a grievance for which another is responsible (blaming); the confrontation of the wrongdoer with a complaint (claiming); and finally, if the response of the wrongdoer is unsatisfactory, the decision to pursue a remedy through the courts. Felstiner, Abel and Sarat described the five stages as 'subjective, unstable, reactive, complicated and incomplete,' and the model is very much a 'starting point' (H. Genn (1999), above, n.3) for an understanding of the decision making process.

[287] 'Acceptable behaviour to a young person can be difficult for an elderly neighbour to tolerate': Social Exclusion Unit (2000) *National Strategy for Neighbourhood Renewal: Report of Policy Action Team 8: Anti-Social Behaviour*, London: The Stationery Office, paragraph 1.1. Also, in this instance young people will themselves often constitute 'the problem.' See, further, T. Newburn (2002), above, n.117, and M. Rutter, H. Giller and A. Hagell (1998) *Antisocial Behaviour by Young People*, Cambridge: Cambridge University Press.

[288] See, for example, C. Mirrlees-Black (1999), above, n.113, and C. Kershaw, T. Budd, G. Kinshott, J. Mattinson, P. Mayhew and A. Myhill (2000) *The 2000 British Crime Survey*, London: Home Office (Home Office Statistical Bulletin 18/00), pp.36-7.

[289] Hughes Commission (1980) *Report of the Royal Commission on Legal Services in Scotland*, Edinburgh: HMSO (Cmd. 7846).

[290] H. Genn (1999), above, n.3, p.69.

of unidentified solutions is no doubt commonplace. Thus, the Hughes Commission advocated that education and the provision of general information regarding rights and obligations and the means available to effect them is essential to the promotion of just solutions to justiciable problems.

Furthermore, if people believe that something can be done to resolve a problem, action may still not be taken because of concerns about the physical, psychological, economic or social consequences of doing so.[291] Such inaction perhaps constitutes a simple personal preference, reflecting the inherent cost of taking action, or, alternatively, reflecting structural failings in the civil justice infrastructure.

The 2001 and 2004 surveys both indicated that a substantial proportion of those who experience justiciable problems take no action to resolve them, though the proportion was significantly lower in 2004 (10 per cent, compared to 19 per cent). The 2004 proportion was also significantly lower than the 16 per cent figure reported in relation to screen interview data in *Paths to Justice.*[292] The reason for this decrease in the proportion of people reporting they took no action to resolve problems is not altogether clear. It may in part be a consequence of decreasing problem incidence set against a backdrop of maintained or increased levels of advice provision.[293] It may also be in part a consequence of the increasing availability of easily accessed telephone advice services.[294] Certainly, the results set out below demonstrate that the use of the telephone in obtaining advice is now extremely common. It may also be that people are becoming generally more inclined to take action to deal with

---

[291] H. Genn (1999), above, n.3, p.70.

[292] H. Genn (1999), above, n.3, p.38. This figure is substantially higher than the frequently quoted 5 per cent figure reported in relation to *Paths to Justice* main interview data (p.68).

[293] The Law Society and Citizens Advice both, for example, indicate recent supply side increases. The number of solicitors on the solicitors' roll increased from 109,553 in 2001 to 121,165 in 2004; although the number of organisations in which they worked was virtually unchanged (B. Cole (2002) *Law Society Annual Statistical Report,* London: Law Society; B. Cole (2005) *Law Society Annual Statistical Report,* London: Law Society). Also, the number of Citizens Advice service outlets increased from around 2,000 to almost 3,400 between 2001/2 and 2004/5; the number of Bureaux now being 475 (Citizens Advice (2002) *Annual Report,* London: Citizens Advice; Citizens Advice (2005) *Annual Report,* London: Citizens Advice).

[294] For example, National Debtline assisted around 2,000 clients per month in 2002, its first year of operation, rising to around 5,000 per month in 2005. It aims to assist 12,500 clients per month by 2008: Money Advice Trust (2005) *Annual Report and Accounts,* London: Money Advice Trust. Similarly, Community Legal Service Direct received around 11,000 calls per month in August 2004, its first full month of operation, rising to more than 50,000 calls per month by the end of 2005: Legal Services Commission (2005) *Annual Report 2004/5,* London: The Stationery Office; Department for Constitutional Affairs (2005) *A Fairer Deal For Legal Aid,* Norwich: HMSO. In addition, The National Domestic Violence helpline assisted with 74,000 calls in 2003/4, its first year of operation. Details are available at www.womensaid.org.uk. Finally, Consumer Direct aims to complete its national roll-out by 2006. Details are available at www.consumerdirect.gov.uk.

problems. Nevertheless, it remains the case that a great many people facing problems take no action to resolve them.

In 2001 the most common reason for inaction was that respondents 'did not think anything could be done' (31 per cent of problems where no action was taken; 6 per cent of problems overall), supporting findings elsewhere and confirming a 'profound need for knowledge ... about obligations, rights, remedies, and procedures' for resolving justiciable problems.[295] So as to differentiate between when respondents thought nothing could be done because they were unaware of available options and when they thought that any action would ultimately be ineffective, 2004 respondents were presented with a broader range of potential reasons for inaction. Accordingly, while again one-third of respondents who took no action to resolve a problem believed nothing could be done, it became clear that this was most often because they thought that, whatever action was taken, it would make no difference (22 per cent). Uncertainty as to rights (7 per cent) and uncertainty as to what to do or where to get help (8 per cent) were less frequently mentioned. It is possible, however, that those who reported *only* that they thought action would be ineffective (20 per cent) were not fully aware of their options. Findings elsewhere indicate that uncertainty regarding rights and uncertainty regarding sources of advice are closely linked. The 2005 Individuals' Awareness, Knowledge and Exercise of Employment Rights Survey, for example, indicated that those who are least aware of their rights at work are also least likely to know where to turn to get advice about employment problems.[296] However, it was not possible to confirm this using 2004 data as the numbers were too small.

Despite relatively few respondents reporting that issues of awareness lay behind inaction, awareness of nearby advisers appeared to link strongly with whether or not action was taken to resolve problems. By merging information on the whereabouts of advisers detailed on the Legal Services Commission's management systems with 2004 survey data, it was possible to establish that inaction was far more common among respondents who were unaware of advisers in their locality than among respondents who were aware of local advisers. Fourteen per cent of the former took no action to resolve problems, compared to around 8 per cent of others. Interestingly, though, even among respondents who were clearly unaware of local

[295] H. Genn (1999), above, n.3, p.255.
[296] J. Casebourne et al. *Findings from the Individuals' Awareness, Knowledge and Exercise of Employment Rights Second Benchmark Survey*. London: Department of Trade and Industry, Employment Relations Research Series Number 51, forthcoming.

advisers, fewer than 12 per cent of those who took no action to resolve problems indicated that they had not known what to do or where to go. The sense that advice would make little difference remained much more common; accounting for one-third of reasons given for inaction.

The link between awareness and strategy is important. Around 33 per cent of respondents who lived within two miles of a solicitors' firm,[297] 27 per cent of those who lived within two miles of a Citizens Advice Bureau and 8 per cent of those who lived within two miles of a Law Centre were unaware of the fact that they did so. In all, 39 per cent of respondents were not aware of any solicitor, Citizens Advice Bureau or Law Centre within two miles of their home, and 64 per cent of these respondents were wrong in relation to at least one adviser type.

Around one-third of respondents took no action to resolve problems because, for various reasons, they felt there was no need to do so. Hence, on 18 per cent of occasions in 2004, action was said to have been unnecessary as the problem was either over and done with or was expected to resolve itself. Neither of these options was presented to respondents in 2001, although in that year, 9 per cent of respondents described action as unnecessary as a result of activity on the part of others. Also, in both 2001 and 2004, it was reported on 10 per cent of occasions that action was unnecessary as there was no 'dispute' and nobody was regarded as having been in the wrong. Furthermore, a number of problems where no action was taken were described as of insufficient importance to warrant action (12 per cent in 2001; 7 per cent in 2004).

Concerns about the potential cost of action were reported as a reason for inaction on only relatively few occasions (4 per cent in 2001; 2 per cent in 2004); as were concerns about the time it might take to reach a resolution (6 per cent in both 2001 and 2004). In fact, not wanting to (further) damage a relationship (8 per cent in 2001; 3 per cent in 2004), being 'scared to do anything' (6 per cent in 2001; 3 per cent in 2004) and the likely stress of acting (9 per cent in 2004)[298] were more often cited as reasons for inaction than concerns about cost.

Also, on 3 per cent of occasions when 2004 respondents took no action to deal with problems, the reason given was because it was too early to take action.

---

[297] Only solicitors' firms holding a Specialist Quality Mark were included.
[298] This option was not presented to respondents in 2001.

84

Often respondents who took no action to resolve problems discussed their situation with friends and relatives and, when they did, friends and relatives were much more likely to encourage them to act than not to act (32 per cent compared to 4 per cent in 2001; 12 per cent compared to 4 per cent in 2004).[299] Respondents' reasons for inaction in the face of a contrary recommendation by friends or relatives were similar to reasons in general, but with the virtual absence of lack of importance or dispute. This suggests that problems were more likely to be discussed if there was a greater interest in action being taken.

In *Paths to Justice* it was commented that the reasons for failure to take action provided by 'lumpers'[300] conveyed, on the whole, 'a rather negative and powerless quality.'[301] This was most acute in respect of those problems in relation to which respondents reported combinations of reasons for not acting. For example, a profound sense of powerlessness and helplessness was indicated by respondents who reported that they did not act because they were both scared to do so and believed that, in any event, nothing could be done (1 per cent in 2001; 2 per cent in 2004) – particularly as their problems appeared serious and chronic (relating to their employment, relationships, or living environment).

Consistent with findings elsewhere, reasons for inaction varied significantly by problem type. Respondents most often thought nothing could be done to resolve employment, discrimination, money/debt and mental health problems.[302] They least often thought nothing could be done to resolve consumer and personal injury problems.[303] Drawing upon the more detailed data obtained in 2004, it appeared that those who believed nothing could be done to resolve employment problems were generally either unaware of their rights or, along with those who had faced discrimination or domestic violence, did not think that action would make any

[299] In 2001, just over half of those respondents who did not act to resolve a problem discussed their situation with friends or relatives. Twenty-three per cent of them did so with a partner (44 per cent of those who discussed their situation with anyone). These figures are derived from information obtained from main interviews. No equivalent information was collected in 2004.
[300] W. Felstiner, R. Abel and A. Sarat (1981), above, n.286.
[301] H. Genn (1999), above, n.3, p.70.
[302] In 2001, respondents who did not act to resolve problems reported believing nothing could be done for 38 per cent of employment problems, 53 per cent of discrimination problems and 34 per cent of money/debt problems. In 2004, the figures were 69 per cent, 47 per cent and 53 per cent respectively. In 2001, the figure for mental health problems was 64 per cent. There were insufficient mental health related problems reported in 2004 for the purposes of this analysis.
[303] In 2004, respondents who did not act to resolve problems reported believing nothing could be done in respect of 15 per cent of consumer problems and 25 per cent of personal injury problems. In 2001, the figures were 22 per cent and 31 per cent respectively.

difference to their case. None of the respondents reported that they did not know what to do. In contrast, respondents who thought nothing could be done to resolve money/debt problems frequently reported not knowing what they could do. They also often reported being unaware of their rights. Perhaps reflecting the proliferation of advertising of no-win no-fee personal injury claim services, those not acting to resolve personal injury claims most often knew what could be done to resolve them. However, these respondents, along with those who had faced a divorce, were most likely to consider there was no need to act; frequently because problems were regarded as involving no dispute.[304] Respondents who took no action to resolve problems with housing and neighbours were least likely to consider there was no need to act.[305]

Respondents who took no action in relation to problems concerning neighbours and, in 2001 but not 2004, unfair treatment by the police most often expressed concerns about the damage that action might have caused on-going relationships; relationships that were doubtless often unsatisfactory to start with.[306]

Those who took no action to resolve problems with neighbours, along with those who took no action in relation to employment or domestic violence problems, also more frequently reported that they had been scared to act.[307] Unsurprisingly, those who took no action to resolve consumer problems least frequently did so.

---

[304] Fifty-nine per cent of respondents in 2001 and 54 per cent of 2004 respondents who did not act to resolve personal injury problems stated there had been no need to act. Sixty-one per cent of these 2001 respondents and 52 per cent of the 2004 respondents stated that this was because there was no dispute involved. Similarly, 68 per cent of 2001 and 43 per cent of 2004 respondents who did not act in relation to a divorce stated there had been no need to act. Sixty-nine per cent of these 2001 respondents and 40 per cent of the 2004 respondents stated that this was because there was no dispute involved.

[305] Twenty-two per cent of respondents in 2001 and no 2004 respondents who did not act to resolve owned housing problems stated there had been no need to act. In 2001, 12 per cent of those who took no action to resolve rented housing problems and 17 per cent of those who took no action to resolve problems with neighbours stated there had been no need to act. However, little difference was observed between these and other problem types in 2004.

[306] Twenty-eight per cent of 2001 respondents who took no action in relation to unfair police treatment were worried about damaging an on-going relationship. However, this was not the case in respect of any 2004 respondents. Eighteen per cent of 2001 and 10 per cent of 2004 respondents who took no action in relation to problems with neighbours were worried about damaging an on-going relationship.

[307] Fourteen per cent of respondents in 2001 and 10 per cent of 2004 respondents who did nothing to resolve problems with neighbours reported being scared to act. The same was true of 8 per cent of 2001 respondents and 13 per cent of 2004 respondents who did nothing to resolve employment problems. In 2001, 24 per cent domestic violence victims who did nothing to resolve the problem reported being scared to do so. The number of domestic violence victims in 2004 did not allow for comparison. Fear of acting to resolve domestic violence problems is recognised as an issue across the world. See, for example, World Health Organisation (2005), above, n.119, pp.18-20. That report also noted that victims are unlikely to act to resolve problems if violence is considered 'normal' within a culture (p.19). For details of government initiatives to help victims of domestic violence, see Home Office (2005), above, n.110.

Concerns about the resources that can be involved in resolving problems were most often reported by those who took no action to resolve problems regarding money/debt, clinical negligence and, in 2001, mental health and consumer transactions.[308] They were least often reported by those who took no action in relation to personal injury and employment problems.[309] In 2001, concerns about the cost of action were most likely to be reported by those who did nothing to resolve problems ancillary to relationship breakdown, and least likely to be reported by respondents who took no action to resolve employment problems.[310] In 2004, there were too few cost concerns to be able to draw comparisons. As will become clear below, cost concerns in relation to problems ancillary to relationship breakdown are consistent with a general perception that such problems should be dealt with through a solicitor. Respondents who considered getting advice from a solicitor, but did not go on to do so, were more likely to cite cost concerns than those who considered getting advice from other types of adviser.[311]

PATTERNS OF INACTION

As with the reasons given for taking no action to resolve problems, the proportion of occasions on which no action was taken varied by problem type. In addition, it varied between differently constituted population groups. Multi-level binary logistic regression was used to test the influence of problem type and a range of social and demographic predictors on the likelihood of respondents having acted to resolve problems.[312]

Problem type was the most influential predictor. Those faced with problems relating to clinical negligence, discrimination, unfair police treatment, personal injury, neighbours, mental health, employment and domestic violence were less likely than

---

[308] In 2001, the percentages were 12 per cent (money/debt), 13 per cent (clinical negligence), 21 per cent (mental health) and 16 per cent (consumer). In 2004, they were 20 per cent (money/debt) and 18 per cent (clinical negligence). There were insufficient mental health problems reported in 2004 to draw comparisons. In 2004, no respondents who did nothing to resolve consumer problems reported insufficient resources as the reason why.

[309] In 2001, the percentages were 1 per cent (personal injury) and 1 per cent (employment). In 2004, they were 4 per cent (personal injury) and 0 per cent (employment).

[310] Eighteen per cent and 0 per cent respectively.

[311] 2001: $\chi^2_1 = 142.3$, p < 0.001; Standardised Pearson Residuals = 9.8; 2004: $\chi^2_1 = 7.78$, p < 0.05; Standardised Pearson Residuals = 2.5.

[312] The analysis was reworked from the first edition of this book to enable improved analytical techniques to be used. See, further, n.64 above. Further technical details and output tables are available for download from www.lsrc.org.uk.

others to take action to resolve them; although in the last three cases the results were significant only in 2001.[313] This list is striking in the degree to which it consists of problems associated with either substantial imbalance of knowledge, standing and institutional support, or inter-personal conflict. Thus, people facing such problems might be expected to be particularly uneasy in taking action to resolve them. This is reflected in the high levels of concern over the consequences of acting to resolve problems concerning neighbours, unfair police treatment, employment and domestic violence and the uncertainly and pessimism over how problems concerning employment, discrimination, domestic violence and mental health might be resolved. This is compounded by people with mental health problems being less likely to have someone to talk to about their problems and often describing 'the fear of making contact with other people.'[314]

Those faced with relationship breakdown and problems concerning children were more likely than others to act, as were those faced with problems relating to money/debt, welfare benefits and consumer transactions.[315] In 2001, those faced with homelessness problems were also more likely to act, but the reverse was the case in 2004. However, numbers were small on both occasions.

Beyond problem type, it appeared that older respondents were more likely than others to act to resolve problems, as were people living in households in which others had also acted to resolve problems. Experience would therefore seem to play an important part in individuals' selections of problem resolution strategies. This was emphasised by the fact that respondents who did nothing to resolve one problem were much less likely than others to act to resolve concurrent or subsequent problems. So in 2004, for example, whereas almost one-quarter of respondents who did nothing to resolve an earlier problem went on to do nothing to resolve a later one, less than one-

---

[313] The 2004 findings were, though, consistent throughout. See, also, P. Pleasence, N.J. Balmer, H. Genn, A. Buck and A. O'Grady (2003) The Experience of Clinical Negligence Within the General Population, in 9(6) *Clinical Risk*, p.211. This finding is similar to that of *Paths to Justice*: H. Genn (1999), above, n.3, p.69.
[314] J. Ritchie, C. Morrisey and K. Ward (1988) *Keeping in Touch with the Talking: The Community Care Needs of People with Mental Illness*, London: SCPR, cited in J. Bradshaw et al. (2004), above, n.118, p.56
[315] In *Paths to Justice Scotland*, respondents faced with consumer and welfare benefits problems were reported to be less likely to act: H. Genn and A. Paterson (2001), above, n.20, p.87. However, their analysis seems to be based on a contrast with those who obtained advice, and is inconsistent with information they provide elsewhere in the text that suggests a high rate of taking some form of action (p.51).

tenth of others did so.[316] Moreover, three-quarters of those who did nothing to resolve one of a number of concurrent problems also did nothing to resolve others.[317]

Likewise, those with academic qualifications were more likely than those without to act to resolve problems; though further analysis did not indicate that the number of academic qualifications was a determinant of whether or not respondents took action.

There was no indication, as suggested in both *Paths to Justice* and *Paths to Justice Scotland*, that those on higher incomes were more likely than others to act.[318] Indeed, both 2001 and 2004 survey respondents receiving means-tested welfare benefits were more likely to act than those not receiving such benefits. However, as will be shown below, income did appear to have a bearing on choice of problem resolution strategy.

Gender and ethnicity also appeared to affect the likelihood of respondents having taken action to resolve problems. Male respondents were less likely than female respondents to have taken action. So, in 2001, whereas 21 per cent of men facing problems took no action to resolve them, the same was true of only 17 per cent of women. In 2004, the figures were 11 and 9 per cent respectively. However, a mixed picture emerged in relation to ethnicity. In 2001, black and minority ethnic respondents were less likely than white respondents to have taken action to resolve problems. Accordingly, whereas 23 per cent of black and minority ethnic respondents facing problems took no action, the same was true of slightly less than 19 per cent of white respondents. However, in 2004, there was no observable difference between white and black and minority ethnic respondents in this regard, with both groups taking no action on around 10 per cent of occasions.[319]

There was some indication that black and minority ethnic respondents who did not act were more likely than their white counterparts to think that nothing could be done to help them (44 per cent compared to 30 per cent in 2001; 53 per cent compared

---

[316] $\chi^2_4 = 35.69$, $p < 0.001$. Standard Pearson Residual = 4.6. While the results in 2001 were consistent with this finding, they were not significant.
[317] $\chi^2_4 = 50.27$, $p < 0.001$. Standard Pearson Residual = 6.4.
[318] H. Genn (1999), above, n.3, p.38; H. Genn and A. Paterson (2001), above, n.20, p.87.
[319] In 2001, among black and minority ethnic respondents, Asian respondents were the least likely to take action, taking no action on 27 per cent of occasions, compared to just 14 per cent of occasions for 'other' minority ethnic respondents. However, in 2004 Asian respondents were the most likely to take action. This may reflect, as indicated in the previous chapter, the different composition of Asian respondents in the 2004 sample. Thus, it may simply indicate the limitations of analysis using the relatively small sample of black and minority respondents within the surveys.

to 31 per cent in 2004.[320] There was also indication in 2001 that black and minority ethnic respondents were more likely than white respondents to have reported having been scared to act, but there were insufficient numbers in 2004 to confirm this.[321]

There were no noticeable differences in the likelihood of action having been taken to deal with problems between respondents in different forms of housing or in different family types. Also, neither economic activity nor long-term illness or disability appeared to influence whether action was taken.

PATTERNS OF ACTION

When action was taken to resolve justiciable problems, just under two-thirds of respondents (63 per cent in 2001, 65 per cent in 2004)[322] reported that they sought formal advice, of either a 'rights-based' or 'personal' nature,[323] to assist them in the resolution process. The remainder handled their problems alone, without ever seeking such advice (37 per cent in 2001; 35 per cent in 2004).[324] In handling problems alone, respondents most often simply talked or wrote to 'the other side' involved in a dispute, and attempted to negotiate a solution.[325] Of course, the fact that they did not seek formal advice did not mean they sought no information or support at all in taking action. On 8 and 14 per cent of occasions, in 2001 and 2004 respectively, respondents obtained information from a self-help guide (4 per cent in 2001; 8 per cent in 2004) and/or an internet site (4 per cent in 2001; 9 per cent in 2004), and on around one-third of occasions they discussed their situation with friends or relatives prior to or while acting.[326] The increase in people obtaining information from self-help guides

---

[320] 2001: $\chi^2_1 = 4.8$, $p < 0.05$. 2004: $\chi^2_1 = 6.04$, $p = 0.024$.

[321] $\chi^2_1 = 6.14$, $p = 0.013$.

[322] Overall, this equated to 51 per cent in 2001 and 59 per cent in 2004.

[323] Formal advice can take many forms, and may involve little or no reference to rights or formal dispute resolution processes. This terminology, recently set out by Kenrick, draws a useful distinction between advice that is focused on 'legal and human rights, entitlements and responsibilities' (rights-based advice) and advice that encompasses 'what has traditionally been termed 'personal support' within the youth sector.' See, further, J. Kenrick (2002) *Rights to Access: Meeting Young People's Needs for Advice,* London: Youth Access, p.2. However, while a detailed description of the advice and assistance provided by 'formal advisers' is set out in a later section, typological complexities and the associated difficulties that faced respondents who were asked to describe the advice they received meant that it was not possible to always reliably ascertain its form.

[324] Overall, this equated to 30 per cent in 2001 and 31 per cent in 2004.

[325] They did so on 95 per cent of occasions in 2001 and 91 per cent in 2004.

[326] This figure is derived from information obtained from 2001 main interviews. Thirty-six per cent of friends and relatives recommended that action should be taken. Just 1 per cent of friends and relatives recommended against action being taken. In 2004, there were again more friends and relatives who encouraged action than discouraged it.

90

and the internet between 2001 and 2004 reflects a general increase in the number of leaflets available and use of the internet.

A small proportion of respondents who handled their problem alone went beyond the normal practice of negotiating directly with 'the other side' and became involved in court or tribunal proceedings,[327] though they did so far less often than those who had sought advice in dealing with problems.[328] The extent to which this difference is a consequence of the types of problems they faced, the preferred methods of advice providers, or the relative seriousness of problems is discussed below.

Also, on a very few occasions those who handled problems alone utilised an Ombudsman or a mediation service.[329] Once more, though, this was less often than for those who sought advice.[330]

Again, multi-level binary logistic regression was used to test the influence of problem type and a range of social and demographic predictors on the likelihood of respondents who took action to deal with problems having sought advice in doing so.

Problem type was again found to be the most influential predictor. However, different problem types were associated with seeking advice, as compared to simply taking action. So, for example, whereas those faced with consumer and money/debt problems were more likely than others to take action to resolve them, they were much less likely than others to seek advice once they took action. Indeed, in both 2001 and 2004, less than half of those who took action to resolve these types of problems sought advice. Conversely, whereas those who faced personal injury problems were less likely than others to take action in the first instance, they were much more likely than others to seek advice once they did.[331]

---

[327] Two per cent in 2001; 4 per cent in 2004. The questions were substantially revised in 2004 to improve clarity.

[328] Eleven per cent in 2001; 17 per cent in 2004. The questions were substantially revised in 2004 to improve clarity. The difference in the figures stemming from the two surveys should not, therefore, be taken to indicate any increase in the use of formal process. For a discussion of changes in the volume and form of litigation in recent years, see J. Peysner and M. Seneviratne (2005) *The Management of Civil Cases: The courts and the Post-Woolf Landscape,* London: Department for Constitutional Affairs.

[329] Two and 1 per cent respectively in 2001; 1 per cent and 0.2 per cent in 2004. However, in 2004 a further 1 per cent of respondents who handled problems alone reported that they had a mediation session planned for the future.

[330] Three and 7 per cent respectively in 2001; 4 and 4 per cent respectively in 2004.

[331] Eighty-four per cent in 2001; 85 per cent in 2004. In 2001, the same was true of victims of domestic violence. They sought advice on 88 per cent of occasions on which they took any action. However, while in 2004, victims of domestic violence who took action to resolve problems again sought advice on over 70 per cent of occasions, they rarely did nothing to resolve the problem (5 per cent).

Also, those who took action in relation to problems concerning homelessness, immigration, employment, divorce or ancillary to relationship breakdown were more likely than others to seek advice.[332] In addition, there was evidence that respondents who took action to resolve rented housing problems were more likely to seek advice if the problem concerned unsafe or unsuitable accommodation (shown in the previous chapter to be a defining element of the homelessness problem cluster).[333]

Similar to the finding in relation to action to resolve problems in general, respondents in their mid-forties were most likely to obtain advice. However, younger and older respondents were both less likely to do so, perhaps reflecting differing knowledge of, or attitudes towards, available advice services.[334]

In 2001, white and black and minority ethnic respondents who acted to resolve problems sought advice at almost identical rates, and there was no significant difference in rates in 2004.[335] However, this masked significant differences between black and other respondents. Both the 2001 and 2004 models indicated that black respondents were less likely than others to obtain advice. These findings are, though, slightly at odds with those of a recent Citizens Advice survey, which found both a broad difference between white and black and minority ethnic respondents in advice seeking rates and a greater advice-seeking rate on the part of Asian respondents.[336] Furthermore, the Citizens Advice results were based on a larger 'booster' sample of black and minority ethnic respondents than those included within the 2001 and 2004 surveys. As indicated in the previous chapter, the 2001 and 2004 survey findings relating to specific ethnic category respondents may not be as representative.

While not entirely consistent, the 2001, 2004 and Citizens Advice survey findings do echo those in the health field, where white people appear more likely than

---

[332] In 2001, those who took action to resolve problems sought advice for about 95 per cent of homelessness problems, 87 per cent of immigration problems, 73 per cent of employment problems, 81 per cent of problems ancillary to relationship breakdown and 96 per cent of divorces. The figures were 85 per cent, 73 per cent, 80 per cent, 81 per cent and 90 per cent respectively in 2004. See, further, P. Pleasence, N.J. Balmer, A. Buck, A. O'Grady and H. Genn (2003) Family Problems: Who Does What and When: Further Findings from the LSRC Survey of Justiciable Problems, 33 *Family Law*, p.822.

[333] This evidence stems from simple chi-square tests: 2001: $\chi^2_1 = 8.25$, p < 0.01; 2004: $\chi^2_1 = 12.34$, p < 0.001.

[334] This is consistent with the findings of a range of earlier studies. See, further, J. Kenrick (2002), above, n.323, pp.9-11 and pp.17-18. Kenrick notes, in particular, that younger people are more likely to seek informal advice than access mainstream advice services.

[335] Sixty-three per cent and 62 per cent respectively in 2001: $\chi^2_1 = 0.002$, p > 0.95. Sixty per cent and 57 per cent respectively in 2004: $\chi^2_1 = 1.58$, p > 0.21.

[336] MORI (2004), above, n.80, p.15.

black and minority ethnic people to utilise medical services.[337] In England, this has been found to be especially so where black and minority ethnic people are unable to speak English.[338] It also appears that culturally rigid health care services act as a barrier to health care.[339] Some studies of advice services, too, have highlighted the need for translation services and cultural empathy to lower barriers to comprehensive service provision, and there is evidence that some black and minority ethnic people consider that 'seeing an adviser from another cultural identity would cause difficulties.'[340]

Also, as with taking no action to deal with problems, respondents were more likely to handle problems alone if they had previously done so.[341] So in 2004, for example, whereas 42 per cent of those who had previously handled a problem alone did so in relation to the problem in question, the same was true of just 29 per cent of others. Moreover, 48 per cent of those who handled one of a number of concurrent problems alone also handled others alone.[342] Interestingly, the fact that a respondent had previously obtained advice did not appear to affect problem resolution strategies; although where a respondent obtained advice for one of a number of concurrent problems, they were much more likely to obtain advice for others.[343]

While whether respondents possessed academic qualifications was not significant within the statistical models, a more detailed examination of the level of qualifications held revealed that respondents became more likely to handle problems alone as their qualifications increased. Thus, in 2001, 48 per cent of respondents with

---

[337] See, for example, C.M. Ashton, P. Haidet, D.A. Paterniti, T.C. Collins, H.S. Gordon, K. O'Malley, L.A. Petersen, B.F. Sharf, M.E. Suarez-Almazor, N.P. Wray and R.L. Street (2003) Racial and Ethnic Disparities in the Use of Health Services – Bias, Preference, or Poor Communication? in 18(2) *Journal Of General Internal Medicine*, p.146; and K.A. Sproston, L.B. Pitson, and E. Walker (2001) The Use of Primary Care Services by the Chinese Population Living in England: Examining Inequalities, in 6(3-4) *Ethnicity & Health*, p.189.
[338] K.A. Sproston, L.B. Pitson, and E. Walker (2001), above, n.337.
[339] Q. Ngo-Metzger, M.P. Massagli, B.R. Clarridge, M. Manocchia, R.B. Davis, L.I. Iezzoni and R.S. Phillips (2003) Linguistic And Cultural Barriers To Care, in 18(1) *Journal Of General Internal Medicine*, p.44.
[340] S. Hughes (2002) *Addressing the Advice Needs of Black and Minority Ethnic Communities*, Brighton: Brighton and Hove Community Legal Service Partnership, pp.2-3. See, also, J. Hobson and P. Jones (2003) *Methods of Delivery: Telephone Advice Pilot: Evaluation Report*, London: Legal Services Commission, paragraph 1.21, and A. Griffith (2005) *Regional Planning and Its Limitations*, London: Advice Services Alliance, p.17 and pp.37-38.
[341] 2001: $\chi^2_2 = 57.62$, p < 0.001. Standard Pearson Residual = 5.4. 2004: $\chi^2_4 = 27.97$, p < 0.001. Standard Pearson Residual = 3.8.
[342] $\chi^2_4 = 10.36$, p < 0.05. Standard Pearson Residual = 1.5.
[343] $\chi^2_4 = 9.97$, p < 0.05. Standard Pearson Residual = 2.1 (2004). However, those who had tried and failed to obtain advice in the past were more likely to again try and fail to obtain advice: $\chi^2_4 = 10.76$, p < 0.05 (2004). The same was also true in respect of concurrent problems: $\chi^2_4 = 40.20$, p < 0.001 (2004).

higher degrees who took action to resolve problems did not seek advice in doing so. In contrast, the same was true of only 37 per cent of those with no qualifications. In 2004, the figures were 46 per cent and 31 per cent respectively.

There were no significant differences in the likelihood of advice being sought by those who took action to deal with problems between respondents on different incomes, in different forms of housing, in different family types or between female and male respondents. Overall, though, female respondents who acted to resolve problems sought advice more often than their male counterparts (65 per cent compared to 60 per cent in 2001; 66 per cent compared to 65 per cent in 2004).[344] Also, if those who sought advice were compared to those who either handled their problems alone or took no action to deal with them, then differences between the strategies adopted by women and men again became apparent, although the difference was not significant in 2004.[345] These findings therefore reflect those in the health field, where women appear more likely than men to utilise medical services – at least from adolescence onwards.[346]

ADVICE AND SERIOUSNESS

In addition to the above, there was evidence that the likelihood of respondents having sought advice increased along with the seriousness of the problems they faced. In 2001, for example, respondents were asked how important it had been to sort out problems. They were more likely to describe problems about which they had sought advice as 'very important to sort out' (86 per cent, compared to 75 per cent).[347] In 2004, respondents were provided with a broader range of possible answers. Similarly, though, they were more likely to describe problems for which advice was sought as 'extremely' important to resolve (51 per cent, compared to 38 per cent), and less likely to describe them as only 'moderately,' 'mildly' or 'not at all' important to resolve (19 per cent, compared to 29 per cent).[348] In 2004, respondents were also asked how difficult it was to live normally while problems were ongoing and how

---

[344] 2001: $\chi^2_1 = 10.88$, $p < 0.01$. 2004: $\chi^2_1 = 0.43$, $p < 0.51$.

[345] 2001: $\chi^2_1 = 17.17$, $p < 0.001$. 2004: $\chi^2_1 = 1.58$, $p < 0.21$.

[346] K.D. Bertakis, R. Azari, L.J. Helms, E.J. Callahan and J.A. Robbins (2000) Gender Differences In The Utilization Of Health Care Services, in 49(2) *Journal Of Family Practice*, p.147; A.V. Marcell, J.D. Klein, I. Fischer, M.J. Allan and P.K. Kokotailo (2002) Male Adolescent Use Of Health Care Services: Where Are The Boys? in 30(1) *Journal Of Adolescent Health*, p.35.

[347] $\chi^2_1 = 25.03$, $p < 0.001$.

[348] $\chi^2_{10} = 79.40$, $p < 0.001$. The question utilised an 11 point scale (0-10) with indicative phrasing.

94

much of their time they had spent worrying about them. Those who had sought advice were more likely to have found it 'extremely' difficult to live with problems (16 per cent, compared to 8 per cent) and less likely to have found it only 'moderately,' 'mildly' or 'not at all' difficult to live with them (48 per cent, compared to 71 per cent).[349] Likewise, those who had sought advice were markedly more likely to have spent 'all' or 'most' of their time worrying about problems (47 per cent, compared to 27 per cent) and much less likely to have spent 'little' or 'none' of their time doing so (23 per cent, compared to 39 per cent).[350]

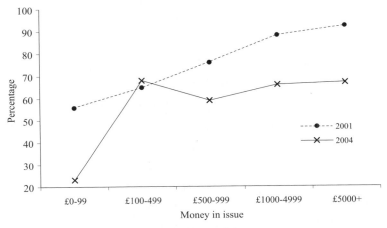

Figure 3.1
Percentage of Problems Where Advice Sought
by Sum of Money Involved

As is illustrated in Figure 3.1, when respondents' objectives in acting concerned money, the likelihood of them having sought advice increased in relation to the amount.[351] Whereas in 2001 advice was obtained in relation to just 56 per cent of problems involving sums less than £100, it was obtained in relation to 92 per cent of problems involving sums of £5,000 or more. In 2004, the figures were 23 per cent and 67 per cent respectively.

---

[349] $\chi^2_{10} = 126.34$, p < 0.001. The question utilised an 11 point scale (0-10) with indicative phrasing.
[350] $\chi^2_5 = 114.38$, p < 0.001.
[351] We used ordinal logistic regression with the amount of money involved as our response variable and 'sought advice' as against 'did not seek advice' as a single dichotomous predictor: $Wald_1 = 32.6$, p < 0.001 (2001); $Wald_1 = 3.44$, p = 0.064 (2004).

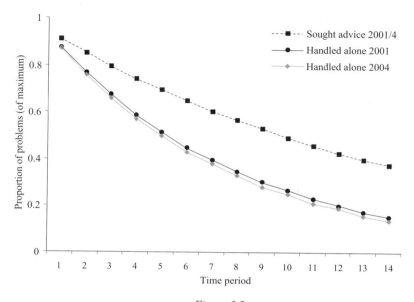

Figure 3.2
Proportion of Problems Recalled from Each of Fourteen
Time Periods Making Up the Reference Period (Fitted)

As has been explained elsewhere, the relative likelihood of respondents recalling particular problem types that occurred early on in the survey reference period provides a further indication of their seriousness. In short, problems that are forgotten quickly are likely to be less serious than those that take longer to forget.[352] To establish whether problems that respondents attempted to resolve on their own were forgotten more quickly than problems about which respondents sought advice, simple exponential decay functions, using non-linear regression, were fitted to the number of problems starting in each of fourteen time periods that together made up the survey reference periods as a proportion of the highest number of problems starting in any time period. This was done for problems that respondents attempted to resolve on their own and then for problems about which advice had been sought. In both cases, and for both 2001 and 2004 data, the functions fitted the data well.

As can be seen from Figure 3.2, problems that respondents had sought advice about appeared to be forgotten less quickly than those that respondents attempted to

---

[352] P. Pleasence et al. (2004), above, n.236, Appendix C.

resolve on their own. The decay coefficients were 0.07 and 0.13 respectively in 2001 and 0.07 and 0.14 in 2004. Even with the relatively small number of time periods, the confidence intervals for these coefficients did not overlap, indicating significant differences. Also, when problem types were ranked according to similarly derived decay coefficients, there was a significant correlation between that ranking and the ranking of problem types according to the likelihood of advice being sought.[353] Once again, it appears that the likelihood of respondents having sought advice increased along with the seriousness of the problems they faced.

PHYSICAL BARRIERS TO ADVICE

Supporting previous findings from both the United Kingdom and elsewhere, information obtained from both the 2001 and 2004 surveys indicated that respondents who sought formal rights-based or personal advice in dealing with justiciable problems did so from a wide range of types of adviser.[354] These included solicitors' firms, Citizens Advice Bureaux and other advice agencies, local authorities, the police, health workers, trade unions and professional bodies, employers, insurance companies, politicians, social workers, Jobcentres, financial institutions, court staff, churches, government departments, claims agencies, housing associations, the media, banks, schools and trade associations. However, 15 per cent of those who sought advice in 2001 and 16 per cent in 2004 were not successful in obtaining it.[355]

Unsuccessful attempts to obtain advice were most likely to be reported in connection with problems relating to housing; particularly problems concerning neighbours and rented housing.[356] In 2001, 24 per cent of those who sought advice

---

[353] Again, including only problems where some action was taken. Spearman correlation coefficient = 0.720, p < 0.01 (2001); Spearman correlation coefficient = 0.671, p < 0.01 (2004).

[354] See, for example, H. Genn (1999), above, n.3, H. Genn and A. Paterson (2001), above, n.20, and G. Maxwell, C. Smith, P. Shepherd and A. Morris (1999), above, n.20. Also, for example, in the context of welfare benefits, Bryson noted in the early 1990s that people seek advice from many types of professional they come into contact with. He wrote that 'these informal advisors include staff in various branches of the health, social and probation services as well as others such as personnel officers and religious leaders': A. Bryson (1994) *Information and Advice about Benefits*, London: Policy Studies Institute, p.5.

[355] Eight per cent overall in 2001 and 7 per cent in 2004.

[356] 2001: χ^2_{17} = 84.01, Monte Carlo p < 0.001; Standardised Pearson Residuals (SPR) = 4.0 and 1.5 respectively. 2004: χ^2_{17} = 63.37, Monte Carlo p < 0.001; SPR = 2.8 and 1.2 respectively. In 2001, there were also significantly more unsuccessful attempts to obtain advice in relation to homelessness (SPR = 4.9). This was not so in 2004 (SPR = 0.2). However, the problem identification questions in 2004 enquired into homelessness within the context of other problems as well as on its own. In 2004, those facing problems relating to unfair police treatment were also more likely to fail in their attempts to

about problems with neighbours failed to obtain any, compared to 13 per cent of those who sought advice about other problems.[357] In 2004, the figures were 18 per cent and 11 per cent respectively. Conversely, unsuccessful attempts were least likely to be reported in connection with family problems – particularly divorce – and personal injury.[358] As will become clear from the next section, these different rates of success in obtaining advice can in large part be explained by the fact that different types of advice service are commonly used in relation to different problem types. For example, respondents were more likely to try to obtain advice from local councils in connection with problems relating to neighbours (36 per cent in 2004) and rented housing (31 per cent in 2004) than in connection with other problems (11 per cent in 2004),[359] and unsuccessful attempts to obtain advice were frequently reported in relation to local councils. Indeed, in 2004, 28 per cent of attempts to obtain advice from local councils were unsuccessful, compared to just 17 per cent for other advisers.[360] On the other hand, respondents were more likely to try to obtain advice from solicitors in connection with problems related to family (50 per cent in 2004) and personal injury (31 per cent in 2004) than in connection with other problems (10 per cent in 2004),[361] and unsuccessful attempts to obtain advice were least frequently reported in relation to solicitors. In fact, just 5 per cent of attempts to obtain advice from solicitors were unsuccessful.[362]

The most frequent reason given for an attempt to obtain advice having been unsuccessful was that an adviser had been unable to provide any help. There was some indication that generalist advice agencies, such as Citizens Advice Bureaux,[363] were less likely than specialist advisers, such as solicitors, to be unable to help. Of

---

obtain advice (SPR = 3.9). Indeed, over 40 per cent of them failed to do so. In 2001, the figure was 25 per cent.

[357] The figure was 20 per cent for rented housing problems.

[358] 2001: Standardised Pearson Residuals = -2.7 and -2.7 respectively; 4 and 5 per cent respectively. 2004: Standardised Pearson Residuals = -3.4 and -2.2 respectively; 0 and 5 per cent respectively. In 2004, those facing problems relating to children were also less likely to fail in their attempts to obtain advice (SPR = -2.2). They did so on just 2 per cent of occasions.

[359] In 2004, data was obtained for almost all problems identified through the screen interviews, while 2001 data was obtained only in relation to problems discussed in main interviews. For this reason, only 2004 findings are presented. $\chi^2_{17} = 387.37$, $p < 0.001$; Standard Pearson Residuals = 9.6 (neighbours) and 4.8 (rented housing).

[360] Figures based on 2004 data. See, further, n.356 above.

[361] $\chi^2_{17} = 563.75$, $p < 0.001$; Standard Pearson Residuals = 15.8 (divorce), 9.2 (relationship breakdown), 1.5 (domestic violence), -0.4 (children) and 5.7 (personal injury). Within family problems, divorce was most strongly associated with solicitors (79 per cent) and problems concerning children were least associated with solicitors (15 per cent). See, further, n.356 above.

[362] Figures based on 2004 data. See, further, n.356 above.

[363] Though not generalist non-advice organisations.

course, a respondent stating that they were unsuccessful in obtaining advice because an adviser was unable to 'help' raises some problems of interpretation. An adviser being unable to help potentially covers a broad range of possibilities; for example, the adviser was not in a position to give advice about the respondent's problem; they did not know the answer to the respondent's questions; or they did not think there was anything that could be done to resolve the respondent's problem.[364] Also, on some occasions it was suggested that advisers had not grasped the nature of the problem, although this may have been because the adviser was not skilled to deal with such problems. One respondent commented:

"They could not understand what I was saying." (2004)

There may therefore have been more than a simple difference between forms of advice lying behind these differences.

Another common reason given for an attempt to obtain advice being unsuccessful was difficulty getting through on the telephone. This problem was, though, reported far less often in 2004, perhaps reflecting the likely increase in supply relative to problem incidence consequent on the overall drop in incidence.[365]

Although the picture in 2004 was not clear, data from 2001 suggested that this reason was significantly more likely to have been offered by those who had sought to obtain advice from Citizens Advice Bureaux. This supports other recent findings, including those of a recent survey commissioned by Citizens Advice itself.[366] In 2001,

---

[364] This could include advice being offered that was not what respondents "wanted to hear" (2004 respondent). This highlights a limitation of general population surveys in relation to the assessment of the quality of professional services. Information asymmetry entails that consumers are often poorly placed to assess the accuracy or appropriateness of advice: Social Market Foundation (1994) *Organising Cost-Effective Access to Justice,* Social Market Foundation Memorandum Number 7; and G. Bevan (1996) Has There Been Supplier-Induced Demand for Legal Aid? In 15 *Civil Justice Quarterly,* p.98.

[365] In 2004, 87 per cent of respondents who tried unsuccessfully to obtain advice *did* successfully contact the person/organisation from which they were attempting to obtain advice. It was not possible to derive an equivalent figure for 2001

[366] MORI (2004), above, n.80, p.30. MORI found that of those people who considered going to a Citizens Advice Bureau, the two most common reasons for not having done so were waiting times (14 per cent) and problems getting through on the telephone (13 per cent). For black and minority ethnic respondents to the MORI survey, the figure for waiting times rose to 25 per cent. Also, see, for example, H. Genn (1999), above, n.3, p.76, H. Genn and A. Paterson (2001), above, n.20, p.94, and, from earlier, T. Goriely (1997) *Resolving Civil Disputes: Choosing Between Out of Court Schemes and Litigation,* London: Lord Chancellor's Department, and G. Petterson, P. Sissons and M. Wann (1995) *Users' Views of CAB Services,* London: NACAB. A 1998 National Association of Citizens Advice Bureaux report indicated that 80 per cent of telephone calls were met with an engaged tone, although

more than half the unsuccessful attempts to obtain advice from Citizens Advice Bureaux were reported as foundering due to problems getting through to an adviser.[367] The frustration felt by respondents in not being able to get through on the telephone was clearly evident:

"I rang them and no one answered. It was a waste of time." (2001)

"[The CAB is] inaccessible, not near to where we live and when you phone you could not get through." (2001)

Difficulties experienced in telephoning advisers were sometimes compounded by the hours of operation of many advice services. Service providers that are more focused on face-to-face advice, such as solicitors and Citizens Advice Bureaux, tend to focus delivery of their services on normal working hours – especially if they are delivered by the same individuals.[368] This poses a double problem for those who cannot get through to such services on the telephone, and cannot attend in person because, for example, they have to work during normal working hours. As one respondent said:

"Being in full-time work and having children ... [There is a] lack of time to actually get [to] or telephone them." (2001)

Respondents who sought advice from service providers that are more focused on telephone advice, such as insurance companies, reported relatively few problems contacting advice services, both by telephone and in general. Dedicated telephone advice services are commonly provided on a 24-hour basis, making it easier for

---

telephone systems have improved since then: National Association of Citizens Advice Bureaux (1998) *The CAB Service and Community Legal Services: A Paper for the Lord Chancellor*, London: NACAB.
[367] $\chi^2_{17} = 563.75$, p < 0.001; Standardised Pearson Residual = 5.7.
[368] An analysis of 2003 data on 146 Citizens Advice Bureaux in North London, the West Midlands and Yorkshire and Humberside indicated that only one-third (53) offered some sort of out-of-hours service. Furthermore, out-of-hours services were generally restricted to a few hours on one day per week, with advice offered by appointment only. The Citizens Advice Bureau in Scarborough, however, had a 24-hour telephone advice line, and some bureaux had internet advice facilities. Camden Citizens Advice Bureau operated an outreach service, where people who contact the bureau by telephone can arrange a face-to-face meeting in their own home. The survey was carried out using data obtained from the Community Legal Services Directory: Legal Services Commission (2003) *Community Legal Services Directory*, 5th edition, London: Legal Services Commission. Information supplied by Citizens Advice in October 2005 indicated that at that time only 13 per cent of bureaux routinely opened in evenings and 4 per cent at the weekend. Also, while there were ten 24-hour recorded helplines, there were no 24-hour staffed helplines and no national helpline.

people to contact them at a time that is convenient for them. Accordingly, respondents to the recent Citizens Advice survey who did not consider using a Citizens Advice Bureau indicated that they would be more likely to consider doing so if a 24-hour telephone helpline was available, or if opening hours were more flexible.[369]

In 2001, respondents reported that 47 per cent of unsuccessful attempts to obtain advice were via the telephone. Moreover, the telephone was used at some stage in 73 per cent of cases in which there was an unsuccessful attempt to obtain advice. In 2004, the figures were 41 and 59 per cent respectively. This, along with the fact, detailed below, that the telephone is used in the majority of cases where advice is successfully obtained highlights both the significance of the telephone in the provision of easily accessible advice and assistance and the danger of failing to meet demand through telephone services.

As well as unsuccessful attempts to contact advisers by telephone, respondents also sometimes reported attempts failing because they had to 'wait too long' to see an adviser, or they received no reply to a letter requesting advice.

Only rarely did respondents complain that they had been unable to obtain advice because an adviser had been too far away.[370] Nevertheless, it has recently been reported that 'there is a general lack of supply of advice services' in rural areas.[371] Although there is a comparatively high level of car ownership among residents of rural areas, making it 'relatively straightforward' for them to visit geographically distant service locations, accessing services can be extremely difficult for those people without cars.[372] As one early 1990s study of access to advice services in rural areas found, 'elderly women living on their own faced serious, almost overwhelming, problems.'[373] The continuing development of telephone and internet advice services appears to be mitigating the problem of providing advice services in rural areas, but it most likely will remain into the future, and those affected will continue to be particularly disadvantaged within our society.

---

[369] MORI (2004), above, n.80.

[370] Three per cent of occasions and 2 per cent of all reasons provided in 2001. No occasions in 2004.

[371] Consumers' Association (2000) *The Community Legal Service: Access for All?* London: Consumers' Association, p.37.

[372] M. Blacksell, K. Economides and C. Watkins (1991) *Justice Outside the City: Access to Legal Services in Rural Britain,* Harlow: Longman.

[373] *Ibid.* For details of the cross-government strategy for developing partnerships to meet the needs of older people, see H.M. Government (2005) *Opportunity Age – Meeting the Challenges of Ageing in the 21st Century,* London: The Stationery Office, Chapter 5.

THE IMPACT OF BARRIERS TO ADVICE

Comparing the numbers of occasions on which respondents successfully obtained advice with the number of occasions on which they sought advice, but obtained none, we found that respondents who attempted to obtain advice, whether rights-based or personal, from solicitors and health professionals – and to a lesser extent Citizens Advice Bureaux and trade unions – were more likely than those who attempted to obtain advice from elsewhere to report actually obtaining it.[374]

Respondents in 2004 were unsuccessful in attempts to obtain advice from solicitors on only 5 per cent of occasions, and from health professionals on only 8 per cent of occasions, compared to 19 per cent of occasions overall. In relation to solicitors, this probably reflects in part the broad geographical distribution of solicitors' firms, as well as their general appropriateness for advising on matters of civil justice. In relation to health professionals, this probably reflects more the context in which advice is most likely to be provided – namely scheduled appointments with patients – and, as will become clear below, the nature of the narrow range of problems about which health professionals are consulted. Those who sought advice from trade unions, Citizens Advice Bureaux, other dedicated independent advice agencies and insurance companies were successful at a rate broadly in line with the overall rate: 85 per cent, 84 per cent, 81 per cent and 80 per cent respectively.

Those who sought advice from local councils, employers, the police and 'other' advisers were, though, significantly less likely than others to have been successful in obtaining it, doing so on just 67 per cent, 72 per cent, 75 per cent and 76 per cent of occasions respectively.[375] In large part, this is likely to have been a consequence of these advisers lacking the knowledge and skills necessary to provide appropriate advice. This became particularly apparent when the 'local council' category was broken down further. Within councils, advice was more often successfully obtained from specific advice services and trading standard officials (80 per cent) than general enquiries staff (66 per cent).

---

[374] $\chi^2{}_9 = 124.50$, $p < 0.001$; Standardised Pearson Residuals = -7.0 (solicitor) and -3.3 (health professionals). Only 2004 data were used for this analysis, as these data provided a greater degree of detail and were more comprehensive than the 2001 data. See, further, the below section on sources of advice.
[375] Standardised Pearson Residuals = 4.1 (local council), 3.0 (employer), 2.1 (police) and 2.6 (other).

102

If advisers from whom respondents considered getting advice but failed to do so are also included in the analysis, solicitors and health workers continue to stand out as sources of advice from which advice was most likely to be subsequently obtained (89 per cent of occasions in both instances). Employers and local councils also continue to stand out as advisers from which advice was least likely to be obtained (63 per cent and 66 per cent respectively). However, Citizens Advice Bureaux and other independent advice agencies join them in this regard (67 per cent and 65 per cent respectively). This ties up with the 2001 survey finding that those who considered obtaining advice from Citizens Advice Bureaux were less likely than those who considered obtaining advice elsewhere to actually obtain it.[376] This appears to reflect the relatively small number of Citizens Advice Bureaux[377] and a general perception, evidenced in the Citizens Advice survey, that they can be quite difficult to access.[378] Thus, in both 2001 and 2004, those who considered but did not use Citizens Advice Bureaux more often than others mentioned concerns about how to approach them and the time involved and stress of doing so. They were also more likely to have believed that doing so would make no difference to their situation, though numbers were small.

In both 2001 and 2004, more than two-thirds of those respondents who were unsuccessful in their attempts to obtain advice tried, in any event, to resolve problems alone. However, important differences in behaviour were observed in relation to different problem types. Respondents were less likely to give up trying to resolve problems concerning money/debt and rented housing, and more likely to give up trying to resolve problems concerning neighbours, unwilling to further jeopardise their situation without support.[379]

In the 2004 survey main interviews, those respondents who were unsuccessful in their attempts to obtain advice were asked why they had not gone on to make further attempts to do so. Twenty-two per cent of them indicated there had been no need, as the problem was either resolved or in the process of being resolved.

[376] $\chi^2_8 = 69.62$, p < 0.001; Standardised Pearson Residual = 5.1.
[377] There are just 475 Citizens Advice Bureaux across England and Wales, compared to 9,211 solicitors' firms. Citizens Advice do, though, provide information through around 3,400 outlets, and the continuing development of these types of service will no doubt increase the effectiveness of Citizens Advice in reaching those populations that wish to make use of their services. See, further, above, n.293.
[378] MORI (2004), above, n.80.
[379] 2001: $\chi^2_{17} = 135.78$, p < 0.001; Standardised Pearson Residuals (SPR) = -2.7 (rented housing) and -2.9 (money/debt). 2004: $\chi^2_{15} = 43.64$, p < 0.001; SPR = -1.4 (rented housing) and -1.6 (money/debt). In 2001, respondents were also less likely to give up with problems concerning homelessness, welfare benefits, children and ancillary to relationship breakdown. In 2004, they were also less likely to give up with consumer problems. This analysis is based on screen interview data.

However, a further 27 per cent of respondents indicated that they simply didn't know where to go next to get advice – suggesting that in total around 13 per cent of respondents who did not get advice about problems did not know where to go for advice.[380] In addition, 7 per cent of respondents who failed in their efforts to obtain advice stopped trying to do so because it would have been too stressful, and 5 per cent because they were scared to keep going. As with doing nothing to resolve problems, this last reason was provided in relation to problems concerning employment, neighbours and domestic violence. A couple of respondents raised concerns about costs; on both occasions in relation to personal injury.

SOURCES OF ADVICE

While in 2001 detailed information on successful sources of rights-based and personal advice was collected only through main interviews, in 2004 much of this information was collected through screen interviews. Thus, a fuller and more representative picture came to light.

Overall, advice was obtained in relation to 43 per cent of problems in 2001 and 52 per cent of problems in 2004. This equated to 1,389 problems in total in 2004, about which advice was obtained from 2,143 advisers, an average of around 1.5 advisers per problem. Sixty-three per cent of respondents obtained advice from only one adviser, 25 per cent from two advisers, 8 per cent from three advisers, and the remaining 4 per cent from four advisers or more.

As can be seen from Figure 3.3, in 2004, 20 per cent of advisers were solicitors and 11 per cent were Citizens Advice Bureaux or other independent dedicated advice agencies (including, for example, independent advice agencies, consumer advice services and Law Centres). Additional dedicated advice services were also included within the 'local council' category (one in seven of these advisers, equivalent to 2 per cent of all advisers), which was the next largest category after solicitors. As indicated above, the remainder were of a broad range of types. For the purposes of analysis, the five most common – the police, health professionals, trade unions and professional bodies, employers and insurance companies – are separated out below. These together accounted for 28 per cent of advisers.

---

[380] This figure is based on those respondents who did nothing to resolve problems, handled them alone or tried but failed to get advice.

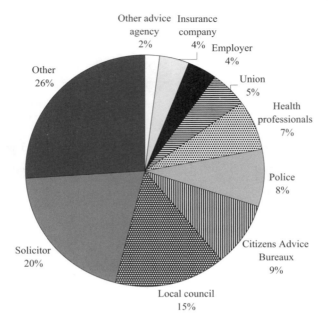

Figure 3.3
Advisers From Whom Advice Successfully Obtained

Of the 'other' types of advisers, the most common were MPs and local councillors (2 per cent), commercial non-advice organisations (excluding financial institutions) (2 per cent), social workers (2 per cent), government departments (1 per cent), Jobcentres (1 per cent) and financial institutions (1 per cent).[381] There was no evidence in either 2001 or 2004 that social landlords were major providers of advice, although a recent report by Matrix Research and Consultancy has suggested that registered social landlords perceive themselves as providing substantial volumes of advice on civil justice matters.[382] Of course, it may be that social landlords provide a great deal of information and advice to people about housing and welfare related issues, but not generally in the context of problems that are regarded as being difficult

---

[381] If local councillors and social workers, who are usually employed by local councils, had also been included in the 'local council' category, then it would have been roughly equivalent in size to the solicitor category.

[382] Matrix Research and Consultancy (2005) *Estimating the Size and Nature of the Civil Legal Advice Sector in England and Wales,* London: Matrix, p.53.

to solve.[383] Remarkably, the Matrix report also concluded that 'local authority departments are unlikely to account for a large percentage of ... advice provision.'[384] In this case, though, it may be that such departments – which accounted for 7 per cent of all advisers used by 2004 survey respondents – do not regard the assistance they provide as advice, but rather as service delivery. This highlights the potential conflict of interest, detailed below, that arises when people seek help about problems from the 'other side.' Local council departments may often regard the 'advice' they provide as being part of a negotiation or dispute resolution process.

Thirty per cent of 2004 respondents who obtained advice from one or more advisers obtained advice from a solicitor *at some point*, 21 per cent from a local council, 16 per cent from a Citizens Advice Bureau or other advice agency, 13 per cent from the police, 11 per cent from a health professional, 7 per cent from a trade union or professional body, 7 per cent from an employer, 6 per cent from an insurance company, and 40 per cent from another adviser. This compares to 33 per cent of 2001 respondents who obtained advice having done so from a solicitor at some point, 22 per cent from a CAB or other advice agency, and 10 per cent from a trade union or professional body.[385] It would seem, therefore, that the increase in the percentage of problems about which advice is obtained has not led to a proportionate increase in the use of mainstream advisers, but rather to an increase in the use of local council services and departments, health professionals and the broad range of 'other' advisers detailed by respondents. So, while solicitors provided advice in relation to a slightly greater proportion of problems in 2004 (16 per cent, compared to 14 per cent),[386] they did so in relation to 3 per cent fewer problems about which advice was obtained and on 2 per cent fewer occasions overall.

Very different patterns of advisers were associated with different points in sequences of advisers, reflecting in part a progression from generalist to specialist

---

[383] Indeed, it may be that problems are not regarded as difficult to solve precisely because timely information and advice are provided by social landlords at the point when problems are about to or are starting to arise.

[384] Matrix Research and Consultancy (2005), above, n.382, p.49. The Matrix Research and Consultancy findings also contrast with the results of the *Paths to Justice* surveys and other Scottish surveys: H. Genn (1999), above, n.3; Genn and A. Paterson (2001), above, n.20, C. Palmer and C. Managhan (2001), above, n.50; and J. Law et al. (2004), above, n50.

[385] Comparisons between other adviser types are not possible owing to the limited information collected in the 2001 screen interviews.

[386] Advice agencies provided advice in relation to a similar proportion of problems (8 per cent, compared to 9 per cent).

rights-based advisers, but also apparent confusion on the part of some respondents as they tried to navigate an advice maze.[387]

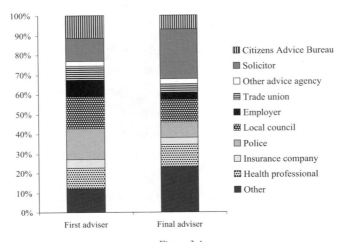

Figure 3.4
First and Final Advisers in Sequences of Two or More (2001)

Using main interview data relating to those respondents who obtained advice from two or more advisers to help deal with a justiciable problem, ordinal regression was used with a logit link function to determine the relative likelihood of different types of adviser being used earlier or later in a sequence of advisers.[388] Citizens Advice Bureaux tended to be used earlier in sequences than solicitors. Thus as is shown by Figures 3.4 and 3.5, Bureaux became less commonly used as respondents progressed through sequences of advisers, whereas solicitors became more commonly used. In fact, in 2001 81 per cent of those Citizens Advice Bureaux mentioned were first advisers, compared to 60 per cent of solicitors. The figures were 75 and 65 per cent respectively in 2004. Furthermore, whereas 67 per cent of 2001 respondents who obtained advice from a solicitor in the first instance obtained advice from nowhere else, the same was true of only 28 per cent of respondents who obtained advice from a Citizens Advice Bureau in the first instance. The figures were 55 and 46 per cent respectively in 2004.

---

[387] 2001: χ^2_{40} = 121.59, p < 0.001; 2004: χ^2_{90} = 29.83 p < 0.001. There did not, though, appear to be equivalent movement from advisers associated with personal advice to advisers associated with rights-based advice.

[388] χ^2_{24} = 63.76, p < 0.001. See, for example, P. McCullagh (1980) Ordinal Regression Models, in 42(2) *Journal of the Royal Statistical Society, Series B (Methodological)*, p.109. Further details and output tables can be downloaded from www.lsrc.org.uk.

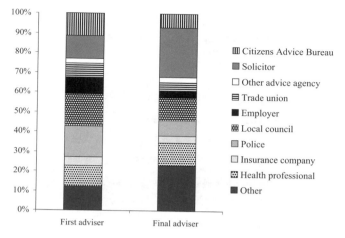

Figure 3.5
First and Final Advisers in Sequences of Two or More (2004)

Employers were also more likely to be used earlier in sequences than solicitors, and there were indications in 2004 that the same was true of local councils and the police. In contrast, other dedicated advice agencies were more likely to be used later in sequences. While this is in keeping with the notion of orderly procession towards specialist rights-based advisers, health professionals and 'other' advisers were also more likely to be used later in sequences.[389] Furthermore, 74 per cent of respondents in 2001 and 61 per cent of respondents in 2004 who obtained advice from 'other' advisers in the first instance obtained advice from nowhere else, despite the fact that the great majority of such sources were generalist or supporting in character, and some seemed unlikely sources of good advice (e.g. the Head Boy of a local school).

Interestingly, second advisers more often happened to be friends or relatives of respondents than first advisers,[390] suggesting a degree of confusion and despair about

---

[389] The finding in respect of health professionals perhaps reflects an increased need for 'personal' advice on the part of those people whose problems lead to them obtaining advice from multiple advisers. More specifically, it may also reflect the health impact of justiciable problems described in Chapter 2, or the health impact of dealing with problems described in Chapter 4. The finding in respect of 'other' advisers was significant in 2001 only.

[390] In 2001, 11 per cent of second advisers were friends or relatives, compared to 8 per cent of first advisers. This difference was just short of being statistically significant: $\chi^2_2 = 2.95$, p = 0.086. Overall, 9 per cent of advisers were friends or relatives. In 2004, the figures were 8 per cent and 7 per cent respectively: $\chi^2_2 = 0.33$, p = 0.567. A further 1 and 2 per cent respectively were organisations in which friends or relatives worked.

108

where to obtain advice on the part of some respondents who were unable to obtain all the advice they needed from a first adviser.

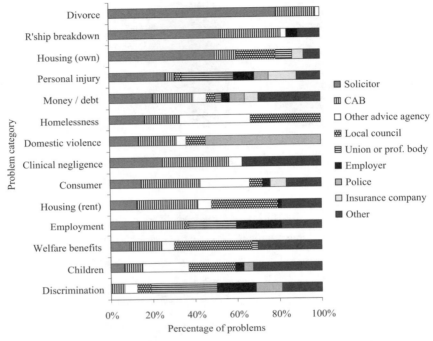

Figure 3.6
First Adviser by Problem Type (2001)

Some confusion is also indicated by respondents' choices of first advisers, which, confirming earlier findings, varied greatly between problem types.[391] Some first sources of advice appeared unlikely and unpromising. This may, to some extent, have been owing to a degree of creativity in choices, perhaps necessitated by the unavailability of local advice services. However, again, it seems likely that on many occasions it was, rather, uncertainty that lay behind choices. For example, the extraordinary range of first advisers associated with problems concerning children indicates real uncertainty as to the most effective way of responding to these problems. A substantial percentage of both 2001 and 2004 respondents who had faced such problems first obtained advice from an 'other' adviser, and although many of

[391] 2001: $\chi^2_{152} = 806.12$, p < 0.001; 2004: $\chi^2_{144} = 975.3$, p < 0.001.

these advisers were social workers or people within the educational system – who might be expected to be able to provide, at least to some extent, both personal and rights-based advice – there were also instances of advice being provided by housing associations, Jobcentres and others with little obvious expertise or capacity to help. Also, many respondents who reported a personal injury problem first obtained advice from a health professional, which, while convenient and perhaps valuable in personal terms, would not necessarily have yielded any constructive rights-based advice.

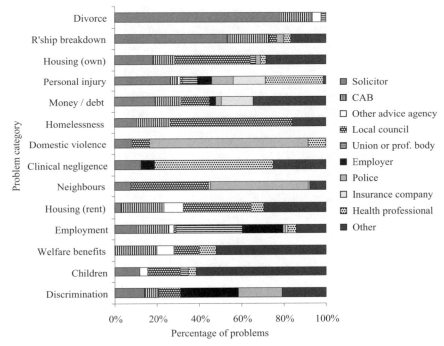

Figure 3.7
First Adviser by Problem Type (2004)

Furthermore, it appears that a number of respondents may in the first instance have obtained advice from the 'other side' to disputes. For example, many respondents who obtained advice on employment problems first obtained advice from their employers. While some advisers described as employers may have been advice services operated on behalf of employers, it seems unlikely that this would account for all these instances. Similarly, advice concerning public rented housing problems was frequently obtained from local council housing departments. Also, doctors were frequent advisers on clinical negligence problems, although it is likely that at least some of these doctors were providing only 'personal' advice and/or reports in support of claims. Furthermore, many 'other' advisers appeared to be commercial organisations with which respondents were in dispute, such as garages, retailers, tour operators and utility companies.

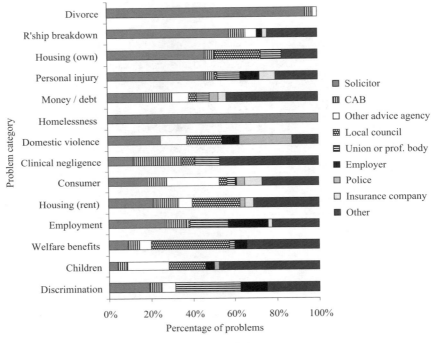

Figure 3.8
Final Adviser by Problem Type (2001)

Although it is possible that sometimes an opposing party in a dispute might provide a person with dispassionate and valuable advice or an internal complaints process, it seems unlikely that advice from an opposing party could ever be as dispassionate and valuable as advice from an independent adviser.

Related to this, it is worth noting that Palmer and Monaghan's qualitative interviews with Scots who had experienced civil legal problems identified the seeking of advice from opposing parties as 'the strongest barrier' to accessing legal information and advice. This was because the source of a problem was often 'regarded as having responsibility for resolving the problem.' Thus, for example, 'if a respondent had a dispute with a Benefits Office or a local authority department, they did not normally look beyond that organisation for help in resolving the issue.'[392]

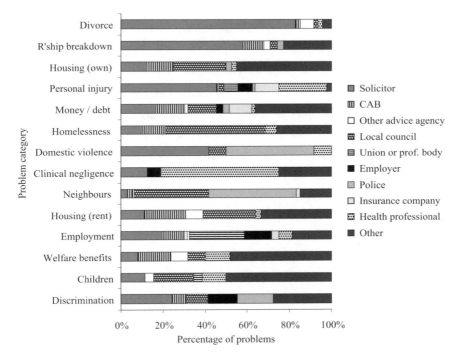

Figure 3.9
Final Adviser by Problem Type (2004)

However, aside from the above, the 'fit' of first advisers to problem type was for the most part seemingly sensible and appropriate (Figures 3.6 and 3.7). So, for example, respondents who had been involved in a divorce generally first obtained advice from solicitors (79 per cent in 2001, 75 per cent in 2004) and advice agencies. Those who had faced problems relating to homelessness generally first obtained advice from solicitors, advice agencies and local councils, which have a responsibility for local housing matters. Those who had experienced domestic violence first obtained advice from solicitors, advice agencies, local councils, which often provide

---

[392] See, further, C. Palmer and C. Monaghan (2001), above, n.50, p.25.

112

shelters, and, particularly, the police. Likewise, those who had experienced problems with their neighbours usually first sought help from local councils and the police.

Also, demonstrating the common use of appropriate experienced advisers, those who had experienced consumer problems, for example, often obtained advice from consumer advice agencies or trading standards services. Those who had experienced employment problems often obtained advice from a trade union or professional body.

As can be seen from Figures 3.8 and 3.9, respondents' final[393] advisers differed between problem types to almost as great an extent as first advisers.[394] As indicated above, though, final advisers were much more likely to be solicitors. However, they were also more likely to be 'other' advisers, suggesting that the uncertainty apparent in relation to some first advisers could remain throughout the advice seeking process.

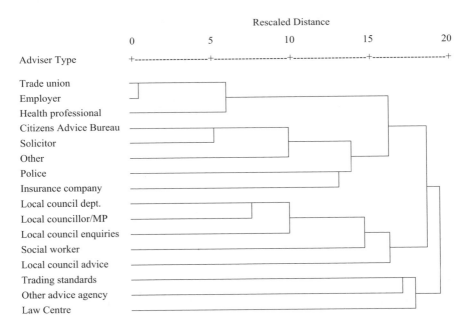

Figure 3.10

Dendrogram Using Average Linkage (Between Groups) (2004)

---

[393] The final adviser would be the first adviser if advice were obtained from only one adviser.

[394] $\chi^2_{152} = 650.28$, $p < 0.001$.

Hierarchical cluster analysis was used to establish which adviser types were most likely to be used in combination. Average between groups linkage was employed as the clustering method. As can be seen from Figure 3.10, trade unions and employers tended to be used in combination, reflecting their common association with employment problems. Advice tended to be sought from trade unions last.[395] Elements of local councils also tended to be used in combination, suggesting that councils may have a tendency to direct people internally for advice rather than externally Within this adviser cluster, dedicated advice services and specific council departments, which would represent more specialist elements, tended to be used later in sequences. Finally, Citizens Advice Bureaux and solicitors tended to be used in combination, reflecting frequent referrals from the former to the latter as well as, perhaps, public perception of both adviser types being focused on 'legal' problems.[396]

MANNER OF ACCESS

Information on the manner in which respondents contacted and communicated with each of their advisers was collected through 2004 survey main interviews. This information, as was suggested above, indicates clearly that the telephone now plays a central role in advice provision. So, while 71 per cent of those respondents who obtained advice met face-to-face with their first adviser at some point (on an average of five occasions), initial contact was more likely to be made via the telephone (53 per cent). Indeed, two in five of those who met face-to-face with their first adviser made initial contact via the telephone. Overall, just 40 per cent of respondents who obtained advice made first contact in person.

In addition to initial contact in person and via the telephone, a small number of respondents made first contact using other methods of communication. So, for example, 3 per cent sent a letter and 2 per cent used e-mail.

Of those people who first contacted their first adviser via the telephone, just over 40 per cent used this as their sole means of communication. A small majority went on to meet advisers face-to-face (54 per cent). However, for the other methods of initial contact, only a minority of respondents went on to attend face-to-face meetings.

---

[395] This was the case on just over 70 per cent of occasions, based on 2004 main interview data.
[396] MORI (2004), above, n.80.

The manner of initial contact turned out to be important, not only in influencing the manner of general communication with an adviser, but also in influencing the manner of communication with subsequent advisers. Binary logistic regression indicated that the manner of contact with a second, third etc. adviser was 340 per cent more likely to be the same as the manner of contact with the previous adviser than another.[397] Thus, the same manner of contact was used in around seven in ten pairs of sequential advisers.

Overall, no face-to-face advice was provided in relation to 27 per cent of problems where advice was obtained. On 11 per cent of occasions advice was provided exclusively by telephone.

Of course, the manner of contact and communication with advisers and also the degree of communication with advisers was influenced by adviser type. So, particularly in the case of first advisers, Citizens Advice Bureaux and employers were most likely to be first visited in person (62 per cent and 81 per cent respectively), while the opposite was true of insurance companies (0 per cent). Insurance companies were invariably first contacted via telephone.[398] Solicitors and the police were most likely to be contacted by phone, but then provide advice face-to-face.[399] Both ultimately provided face-to-face advice on around three-quarters of occasions. Patterns for second and subsequent advisers were similar, but less pronounced. This is at least in part a consequence of the influence of previous manners of contact.

In terms of the degree of communication, the number of meetings and telephone calls held with solicitors tended to be highest (six on average), while it was generally low for Citizens Advice Bureaux and other advice agencies (two and three on average respectively).

Differences were also observed between problem types in the manner advisers were contacted, although these to some extent reflected differences in the associated adviser types. Given the strong association between the use of solicitors in connection with problems relating to divorce, relationship breakdown, owned housing and personal injury, it is no surprise that these problem types were commonly associated with face-to-face advice. Such advice was provided in 75, 61, 48 and 48 per cent of

---

[397] Expβ= 4.42, Wald=22.4, p<0.001.

[398] Respondents were also most likely to meet with employers face-to-face at some point during the advice process.

[399] Thus, on 50 per cent and 57 per cent of occasions respectively, initial phone contact was followed up with face-to-face advice.

incidences respectively. In contrast, face-to-face advice was provided in respect of just 23 per cent of money/debt problems.

The greatest number of meetings and telephone calls was associated with immigration problems (ten on average). Clinical negligence, personal injury and problems ancillary to relationship breakdown also involved more meetings and calls than other problem types. Problems concerning unfair police treatment, rented housing, money/debt and welfare benefits involved the fewest meetings and calls.

THE SUBSTANCE OF ADVICE AND ASSISTANCE

The substance of advice and assistance offered to both 2001 and 2004 respondents varied greatly by adviser type. In terms of the subject matter of advice, solicitors – the most overt rights-based advisers – most often explored respondents' legal positions, although a relatively wide range of other advisers – advice agencies, trade unions and the police in particular – also did so. This demonstrates that legal advice is not, as was theoretically the case in Germany until late last year, provided only by legal professionals.[400] Health professionals, employers and 'other' advisers least often explored respondents' legal positions. For example, health professionals did so on just 6 per cent of occasions. Here, 'personal' advice was much more common. A similar pattern emerged in relation to respondents' financial positions, although in this case the police were least likely to offer advice. However, a majority of advisers of all types discussed procedural issues.

Reflecting the subject matter of advice they tended to provide, solicitors, advice agencies, trade unions and the police most often suggested that respondents threaten or commence legal action. Indeed, solicitors suggested threatening or commencing legal action to half of those to whom they provided advice. To some extent this may have been a symptom of the predominantly legal focus of solicitors. For example, in 2001, solicitors commenced legal proceedings on 24 per cent of occasions on which they were final advisers (compared to 11 per cent for other

---

[400] See, for example, M. Kilian (2003) Alternatives to Public Provision: The Role of Legal Expenses Insurance in Broadening Access to Justice: The German Experience, in 30(1) *Journal of Law and Society*, p.31.

advisers).[401] This accounted for 43 per cent of all occasions on which legal proceedings were commenced.[402]

In 2004, this legal focus was even more evident, with legal action being commenced on 40 per cent of occasions where solicitors were final advisers (compared to 6 per cent elsewhere). However, differences in the rates of invocation of legal processes may also have stemmed from the nature of the problems that different types of adviser tended to deal with. So, while solicitors suggested threatening or commencing legal action to over half their clients, and commenced proceedings for many of them, over one-third of their clients were facing one of the four problem types relating to relationships or children and more than one-sixth of their clients were preparing to get, or were already getting, divorced.[403] As divorce inherently involves formal court process, it could not be said that formal action was suggested in relation to it on account of solicitors being involved. As with conveyancing,[404] therefore, it was often because formal legal process was required that respondents sought advice or assistance from solicitors, rather than vice versa. Overall, in both 2001 and 2004, family problems accounted for over 40 per cent of all instances of formal legal action.[405]

Those occasions on which the police suggested that formal legal action should be threatened or commenced generally involved domestic violence or problems with neighbours. It may be, however, that respondents were unclear as to the distinction between civil and criminal legal action, and thus reported suggestions or instances of criminal legal action as instances of civil legal action.

On occasion, solicitors, advice agencies, trade unions and employers suggested that respondents try mediation or conciliation to resolve their problems, although the suggestion was quite rare. For solicitors and advice agencies, mediation or conciliation tended to be suggested in relation to family problems. For trade unions and employers, the suggestion tended to be in relation to employment problems. In 2001, mediation or conciliation was reported as having been used in the context of 12

---

[401] $\chi^2_1 = 28.89$, $p < 0.001$.

[402] Fifty-four per cent of all occasions on which proceedings were commenced after advice had been obtained.

[403] Family problems accounted for 34 and 36 per cent of problems taken to solicitors in 2001 and 2004 respectively.

[404] Only very rarely are conveyances undertaken without the assistance of solicitors or licensed conveyancers.

[405] Money/debt problems accounted for 14 and 12 per cent of instances in 2001 and 2004 respectively, employment problems 8 and 14 per cent and consumer problems 10 and 5 per cent.

per cent of family problems, and 4 per cent of employment problems. The figures for 2004 were 10 per cent and 6 per cent respectively.[406] These differences are not statistically significant.[407] Overall, mediation or conciliation was used in 4 per cent of cases in 2001 and 2 per cent in 2004. This difference is significant, although the question was modified substantially in 2004, which may have had an impact on the results.[408] Aside from family problems, where mediation has been enthusiastically promoted by the government and Legal Services Commission in recent years,[409] these findings still indicate 'the very slight impact that [mediation and other alternatives to traditional methods of dispute resolution] have had on the thinking of advisers and, therefore, on the strategies adopted by the public for dealing with disputes.'[410]

In 2004, 11 per cent of advisers told respondents that there was nothing that could be done to resolve their problem. This was least often suggested by solicitors and health professionals and most often suggested by insurance companies, employers, advice agencies (other than Citizens Advice Bureaux) and 'other' advisers.

Most types of adviser routinely suggested that respondents should try to resolve their problem by talking directly to the 'other side.' In all, in both 2001 and 2004, 40 per cent of all advisers suggested this, and slightly more in the case of Citizens Advice Bureaux, reflecting their common philosophy of 'empowering' clients to deal with their own problems. The police and health professionals suggested this less often. In the former case, this was most probably because of concerns about respondents' personal safety in relation to domestic violence.

Some advisers, particularly Citizens Advice Bureaux and other advice agencies, the police, insurance companies, trade unions and health professionals also routinely referred respondents on to other advisers,[411] although this was less often the

---

[406] Drawing on main interview data, it appears that in both 2001 and 2004 only around one-third of those to whom this was suggested actually went on to try mediation or conciliation.

[407] Family: $\chi^2_1 = 1.31$, p = 0.252; employment: $\chi^2_1 = 1.11$, p = 0.293.

[408] $\chi^2_1 = 7.68$, p < 0.01. The 2001 survey included a single question that asked about court processes, mediation, conciliation and use of an ombudsman. The 2004 survey included three questions on mediation alone.

[409] See, for example, the statement of Lord Irvine, then Lord Chancellor, on 23rd March 2001, available at www.gnn.gov.uk. Also see, for example, G. Davis, G. Bevan, S. Clisby, Z. Cumming, R. Dingwall, P. Fenn, S. Finch, R. Fitzgerald, S. Goldie, D. Greatbatch, A. James and J. Pearce (2000) *Monitoring Publicly Funded Family Mediation: Report to the Legal Services Commission*, London: Legal Services Commission.

[410] H. Genn (1999), above, n.3, p.96.

[411] Trade unions were relatively less frequent referrers in 2001 and insurance companies relatively less frequent referrers in 2004.

case in 2004 than 2001. Referrals were most often to solicitors, but were commonly also to specialist advice agencies and local councils.[412] Indeed, overall, more than one-quarter of referrals were to solicitors.

Despite frequently benefiting from referrals, fewer than 10 per cent of solicitors themselves referred respondents on to other advisers, and much of the time this was to another solicitor or lawyer. The low referral rate associated with solicitors is in part a consequence of their relative level of specialism. However, it is also consistent with a narrow focus on clients' legal positions. It is also clear, though, that lawyers spend a significant proportion of their time dealing with extra-legal matters. For example, Eekelaar, Maclean and Beinart have observed that family lawyers spend a great deal of time fulfilling the traditional roles of social worker and confidante.[413]

'Other' advisers, also, only infrequently referred respondents on. Given the broad range of such advisers, and the fact that many seemed unlikely sources of good advice, this is a cause for concern. It is also a cause for concern that respondents referred on by 'other' advisers were the least likely to actually go on and obtain advice from another adviser.

In general, it appeared that those adviser types that most frequently referred respondents on were the same as those whose referrals were most likely to be acted upon.[414] So, for example, those referred on to other advisers by Citizens Advice Bureaux, the police, local councils and trade unions went on to actually obtain advice from another adviser more often than in general. Indeed, in both 2001 and 2004, more than two-thirds of those referred on by Citizens Advice Bureaux successfully obtained advice elsewhere, compared to only around one-third of those referred on by 'other' advisers.

However, the different success rates in referring people on to other advisers associated with different adviser types did not only reflect levels of experience in doing so. They also most likely reflected respondents' expectations of their advisers. While Citizens Advice Bureaux and the police, for example, may often be thought of as sources of *initial* help and advice – the place you go to when a problem arises or when you need a pointer as to what to do – solicitors, in particular, are more likely to

---

[412] Most frequently to specific council departments.
[413] J. Eekelaar, M. Maclean and S. Beinart (2000), above, n.218. See, also, G. Davis, S. Cretney and J. Collins (1994), above, n.218; and G. Bevan, G. Davis and J. Pearce (1999) Piloting a Quasi-Market for Family Mediation Amongst Clients Eligible for Legal Aid, in 18 *Civil Justice Quarterly*, p.239.
[414] 2001: Pearson correlation = 0.815, p < 0.01. 2004: Pearson correlation = 0.471, p = 0.17.

be regarded as offering tailored and specialist advice. Consequently, respondents who were referred on by solicitors may have been more likely to feel they had been inappropriately 'unloaded' elsewhere. Importantly, also, the different success rates will have reflected the fact that those adviser types least likely to have referred respondents on became more prominent later on in sequences of advisers and, as Figure 3.11 illustrates, a phenomenon of *referral fatigue* meant that the likelihood of respondents obtaining advice from an adviser to whom they had been referred declined as respondents visited more advisers.

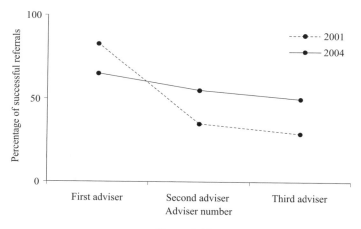

Figure 3.11
The Phenomenon of Referral Fatigue

The phenomenon of referral fatigue suggests a degree of exhaustion among members of the public as a result of being pushed from adviser to adviser. This is consistent with the vivid descriptions reported in *Paths to Justice* of respondents having sometimes to make Herculean efforts to be seen by an adviser.[415] It is perhaps not surprising that some respondents felt unable to maintain the necessary level of persistence or to invest the necessary amount of time to follow up repeated referrals in order to obtain the help they were looking for. In any event, the phenomenon of referral fatigue again demonstrates the importance of public education to create awareness among people of sources of help and assistance. Crucially, also, it demonstrates the importance of equipping those many individuals outside of the

---

[415] H. Genn (1999), above, n.3.

recognised advice sector from whom people may initially seek advice (such as health professionals, social workers and politicians) with the means to effectively direct them on to appropriate advisers if necessary, through professional education and awareness raising and through making appropriate advisers more accessible to those who are referred on to them.[416]

As well as providing general information and suggesting a course of action for respondents to take, many advisers also provided active assistance to them. Consistent with the concept of 'empowerment,' but also perhaps reflecting their limited resources, Citizens Advice Bureaux were less likely than solicitors and other advice agencies to provide active assistance to respondents, although some active assistance was provided on around half of occasions in both 2001 and 2004. As would be expected, the same was also true of employers and health professionals

In contrast, solicitors provided active assistance on around 85 per cent of occasions. In particular, they took over direct negotiation or dealings with the 'other side' to a dispute and prepared, or helped in the preparation of, paperwork on the majority of occasions – especially if they were a respondent's final adviser. Trade unions and professional bodies also took over direct negotiation or dealings with the 'other side' (generally an employer) on the majority of occasions. Unsurprisingly, given the proportion of occasions on which they recommended legal action should be threatened or taken, and the fact that they are legal professionals, solicitors attended hearings more frequently than other types of advisers. 'Other' advisers and trade unions also, though, attended hearings relatively frequently.

SATISFACTION WITH ADVISERS

Respondents who obtained advice were asked whether they would recommend those advisers they had consulted. They indicated that they would definitely or probably recommend over three-quarters of them (78 per cent in 2001, 82 per cent in 2004). However, there were differences in respondents' views of different adviser types. So, whereas in both 2001 and 2004, around 90 per cent of those who obtained advice

---

[416] The problem of how to develop appropriate and effective referral strategies between different suppliers of legal information and advice is not new and was one of the central concerns in the development of the Community Legal Service and is clearly an area that would benefit from closer analysis: See discussion in H. Genn and A. Paterson, above, n.20, p.17, and associated references, especially C. Millar (1999) *Referrals between Advice Agencies and Solicitors*, Edinburgh: Scottish Office Central Research Unit. See, also, for example, A. Bryson (1994), above, n.354.

from Citizens Advice Bureaux said they would definitely or probably recommend them, the same was true of less than 65 per cent of employers. Around 25 per cent of respondents who obtained advice from employers said that they would definitely or probably not recommend them.

Other adviser types that were particularly favoured by users were solicitors, trade unions, the police and health professionals. The fact that health professionals were also reported to have offered only limited assistance to respondents, though, indicates that attitudes to advisers are based on a wider range of adviser characteristics than simply technical knowledge, skill or assistance.[417] Thus, employers, who would often have been the other party to a dispute and frequently had a conflict of interest with those asking for advice, would therefore have had a particularly hard task in gaining more universal recommendation.

Other adviser types that were relatively poorly regarded were local councils, insurance companies and dedicated advisers other than Citizens Advice Bureaux. However, while respondents said that they would probably or definitely recommend trade unions and the police more often than dedicated advisers, this was notwithstanding the fact that respondents found them to be less 'helpful,'[418] again indicating that attitudes were based on many adviser characteristics.

Despite the concerns raised about 'other' advisers, they were reasonably well looked upon, though again this was not necessarily a reflection of knowledge, skill or assistance. It could well have been a consequence of the active support that 'other' advisers frequently provided to respondents, which may not always have been

---

[417] For further details on client satisfaction as an outcome measure for advice, see, for example, A. Sherr, R. Moorhead, and A. Paterson (1994) *Lawyers – The Quality Agenda, Volume 1: Assessing and Developing Competence and Quality in Legal Aid; The Report of the Birmingham Franchising Pilot*, London: HMSO; H. Sommerlad (1999) English Perspectives on Quality: The Client-Led Model of Quality – A Third Way, 33(2) *University of British Columbia Law Review*, p.491; R. Moorhead, A. Sherr, L. Webley, S. Rogers, L. Sherr, A. Paterson and S. Domberger (2001) *Quality and Cost: Final Report on the Contracting of Civil, Non-Family Advice and Assistance Pilot*, London: The Stationery Office. In general, satisfaction with services seems to be linked to a number of factors not immediately connected with technical knowledge, skill or utility. A report by the Cabinet Office Performance and Innovation Unit, for example, notes that expectation is an important factor, as are the aesthetic qualities of the service: N. Donovan, J. Brown and L. Bellulo (2001) *Satisfaction with Public Services: A Discussion Paper*, London: Cabinet Office. In similar vein, a recent report on client satisfaction of nursing stated that 'patients may not differentiate between nursing care and the hotel functions provided in a hospital': A.M. Dozier, H.J. Kitzman, G.L. Ingersoll, S. Holmberg and A.W. Schultz (2001) Development of an Instrument to Measure Patient Perception of the Quality of Nursing Care, in 24 *Research in Nursing and Health*, p.506.

[418] This finding is based on information about the helpfulness of advisers obtained through the 2001 survey.

effective. Offering help as regards the means to an end does not always equate to being helpful as regards the end itself.

Reasons for dissatisfaction with advisers centred upon the perceived ability or inclination of advisers to provide help, although criticism was occasionally related to cost (6 per cent in 2001, 5 per cent in 2004). Criticisms over cost were, though, generally levelled at solicitors.

The position of advisers in sequences of advisers made no difference to respondents' views on whether they would be recommended to others.

THE COST OF ADVICE

In both 2001 and 2004, respondents who had obtained advice were asked during main interviews about who had paid for it. In both years, more than three-quarters stated that they had not paid for it. On around two-thirds of these occasions, respondents described all the advice they had obtained as having been provided 'free' by advisers. On the other one-third of occasions, they described it as having involved costs met by third parties. Of those respondents who paid to receive advice, just under three-quarters paid the full cost.

To build up a clearer picture of the involvement of third parties, as well as differences in patterns of payment, 2004 respondents were asked to provide details of the source of payment for all advisers whom they had consulted. On only 11 per cent of occasions did respondents pay the full cost of advice from an adviser, and in only a further 4 per cent of cases did they pay part of the cost.

Where respondents paid nothing or only some of the cost of advice, it was generally the adviser who was described as having covered the remaining costs (65 per cent). Legal aid was the next most frequently mentioned source of subsidy (8 per cent), followed by trade unions (7 per cent) and insurance companies (6 per cent). Conditional fee arrangements were used to cover the cost of 4 per cent of advisers and employers covered a further 3 per cent of advice costs. The remainder of advisers had their costs paid by a broad range of third parties, including friends, relatives, local councils and the National Health Service.

Of course, the source of payment for advice varied greatly between different adviser and problem types. As can be seen from Figure 3.12, most adviser types were routinely described as having covered the cost of the advice they provided themselves. Evidently, general funding of advice services by commercial, charitable and government sources, as opposed to funding of advice in relation to particular problems, was rarely recognised. Interestingly, though, payments respondents made towards advice provided by insurers and unions, through premiums and subscriptions, were also rarely cited.

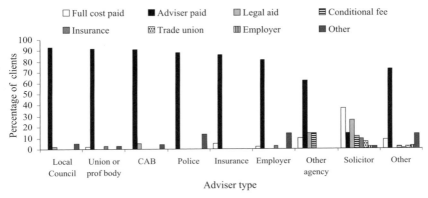

Figure 3.12
Source of Funding by Adviser Type (2004)

Solicitors were the only advisers who were described as covering their own costs on only a minority of occasions (14 per cent), probably comprising community 'open evenings,' free initial consultations and conditional fee or legal aid funded advice that was not recognised as such.[419] Solicitors were also the most likely provider of advice for which respondents had to meet costs in full (37 per cent). They were also the most likely to offer conditional fees (11 per cent).

Advice on divorce and problems ancillary to relationship breakdown, frequently provided by solicitors, was more likely than advice on other problems to be paid for by respondents themselves (57 and 30 per cent respectively).[420] It was also, along with advice on domestic violence, frequently covered by legal aid. Indeed, more than one-third of instances of advice on domestic violence were paid for in full or in

---

[419] See, for example, P. Pleasence (1998) *Personal Injury Litigation in Practice*, London: LABRU.
[420] Forty-three per cent and 28 per cent respectively, if only those cases in which respondents paid all costs were included.

part by legal aid. Similarly, advice on problems relating to owned housing, also often provided by solicitors, was more likely than advice on other problems to be paid for by respondents (21 per cent).[421]

Advice about personal injuries, again commonly associated with solicitors, was frequently paid for through conditional fees (11 per cent of instances).[422] The use of conditional fees may, though, be under-reported through the 2004 survey. Occasions on which the cost of advice on personal injuries was covered by 'other' advisers (21 per cent of instances) or insurers (16 per cent of instances) could sometimes have been instances of conditional fees that were not recognised as such. Advice on personal injuries was also frequently paid for by trade unions (10 per cent of instances), which, unsurprisingly, were also most likely to cover the costs of advice about employment problems (19 per cent of instances). Only a small number of advisers on personal injuries were reported to have been paid by legal aid, reflecting the removal of such advice from the scope of legal aid through the Access to Justice Act 1999. Similarly, though, very few respondents reported paying the full cost of their advice.

Advice was least often paid for by respondents personally if it concerned discrimination, employment, rented housing, neighbours, homelessness, welfare benefits, money/debt, domestic violence, children or personal injury. In most cases, the cost of such advice was described as being covered by advisers themselves.

Those 2004 respondents who did not pay for advice were asked whether they would have continued to seek help from their advisers if they had had to contribute towards the cost. Just over half said they would have continued to do so. More, though, said they would have done so in relation to solicitors and specialist advice agencies.[423] Reflecting levels of satisfaction with advisers, respondents least often

---

[421] Nineteen per cent, if only those cases in which respondents paid all costs were included. Respondents also frequently reported paying personally for advice on immigration and mental health related problems, although the numbers were very small.

[422] Nineteen per cent of problems. Further, 29 per cent of instances of advice on personal injuries provided by solicitors involved conditional fees. Conditional fees were introduced by the Conditional Fee Agreements Regulations 1995. For a discussion on their introduction and a commentary on conditional fee practice, see S. Yarrow and P. Abrams (1999) *Nothing to Lose? Clients' Experiences of Using Conditional Fees,* London: University of Westminster, R. Moorhead (2000) Conditional Fee Agreements, Legal Aid and Access to Justice, in 33 *University of British Columbia Law Review,* p.471, and S. Yarrow (2000) *Just Rewards? The Outcome of Conditional Fee Cases,* London: University of Westminster. See also, for example, P. Fenn, A. Gray, N. Rickman and H. Carrier (2002) *The Impact of Conditional Fees on the Selection, Handling and Outcome of Personal Injury Cases,* London: Lord Chancellor's Department.

[423] $\chi^2_9 = 41.42$, $p < 0.001$; Standard Pearson Residuals = 2.6 (solicitors) and 1.2 (other advice agencies).

said they would have paid for advice from employers and local councils.[424] In terms of problem types, respondents were most likely to say they would have paid for advice in relation to problems concerning children and least likely to say they would have paid for advice about housing problems, which were strongly associated with local councils.[425]

On average, respondents who said they would have been prepared to pay for advice had it not been delivered to them free of charge stated that they would have been prepared to spend £560 on average (median = £100).[426] Amounts varied, though, by adviser and problem type. In general, respondents indicated they would have been prepared to pay the most money for advice about family (£645), employment (£627) and personal injury advice (£556). They would have been prepared to pay the least for advice about problems concerning mental health (£20), homelessness (£26), rented housing (£62) and welfare benefits (£89).[427] Clearly, therefore, people's ability to pay, as well as the severity of problems, figured greatly in their calculations. As for advisers, unsurprisingly, given the findings in relation to problem types, respondents would have been prepared to pay most for advice from solicitors (£675), trade unions (£407) and employers (£345). They would also have been prepared to pay relatively large sums for police assistance (£772). In contrast, respondents said they would have been prepared to pay relatively little for advice from Citizens Advice Bureaux (£114) and local councils (£100).[428]

Those respondents who would not have been prepared to pay for advice if it had not been delivered to them free of charge were most likely to indicate that it would not have been appropriate, or that the responsibility lay elsewhere (36 per cent). Quite a few, though, stated simply that they could not have afforded it (29 per cent). This was particularly so in relation to solicitors and family problems. Some respondents also indicated that they did not need further advice (10 per cent) or that further advice would have been of no use to them (6 per cent). Just 6 per cent said

---

[424] Standard Pearson Residuals = -2.0 (employers) and -1.4 (local councils).
[425] χ^2_{16} = 29.45, p < 0.05. Standard Pearson Residuals = 1.4 (children), -1.9 (owned housing) and -1.8 (rented housing).
[426] The range was from £5 to £20,000.
[427] The respective median figures were £500 (family), £194 (employment), £200 (personal injury), £20 (mental health), £20 (homelessness), £66 (rented housing) and £107 (welfare benefits).
[428] The respective median figures were £278 (solicitors), £167 (trade unions), £152 (employers), £152 (police), £20 (Citizens Advice Bureaux), £50 (local councils).

they would not have been prepared to pay because the problem was not important enough.

In part reflecting the fact that both legal aid funded advice and privately funded advice were principally associated with solicitors and family problems, there was evidence that both were more likely than otherwise funded advice to be obtained in relation to more serious problems. Solicitors were more likely than other adviser types to deal with problems involving larger sums of money,[429] and, also, they were more likely to deal with problems that could be recalled after longer periods of time.[430] Family problems were also more likely to be recalled after longer periods of time.[431] Legal aid funded advice and privately funded advice were more likely than otherwise funded advice to be obtained in relation to problems involving larger sums of money[432] and problems that could be recalled after longer periods of time.[433]

---

[429] 2001: χ^2_{16} = 36.30, p < 0.01. Standardised Pearson Residuals = -3.3 (less than £1,000), 2.0 (£1,000-9,999), 2.5 (£10,000 plus). 2004: χ^2_{16} = 28.54, p < 0.05. Standardised Pearson Residuals = -2.5 (less than £1,000), 0.4 (£1,000-9,999), 2.5 (£10,000 plus). Based on final adviser.

[430] Simple exponential decay functions were fitted, using non-linear regression, to the number of problems starting in each of fourteen time periods that together made up the survey reference periods as a proportion of the highest number of problems starting in any time period. Technical details are set out at www.lsrc.org.uk. In 2001, there was little evidence of memory decay in relation to problems dealt with by solicitors. The decay coefficient was 0.04, with the lower 95 per cent confidence band equal to 0 (upper = 0.077), and the R^2 value was 0.272. For Citizens Advice Bureaux, the decay coefficient was also 0.04, with the 95 per cent confidence interval straddling 0 (-0.005 to 0.088), and the R^2 value was 0.230. In contrast, however, the decay co-efficient for 'other' advisers was 0.11, the lower 95 per cent confidence band was 0.04 (upper = 0.182), and the R^2 value was 0.582. Likewise, in 2004 there was little evidence of memory decay in relation to problems dealt with by solicitors. The decay coefficient was 0.034, with the lower 95 per cent confidence band equal to 0.001 (upper = 0.067), and the R^2 value was 0.295. For Citizens Advice Bureaux, the decay coefficient was 0.065, with the 95 per cent confidence from 0.015 to 0.116, and the R^2 value was 0.361. The decay co-efficient for 'other' advisers was 0.073, the lower 95 per cent confidence band was 0.029 (upper = 0.117), and the R^2 value was 0.516.

[431] See P. Pleasence et al. (2004), above, n.236, Appendix C.

[432] 2001: χ^2_2 = 8.33, p < 0.05. Standardised Pearson Residuals = -1.8 (less than £1,000), 0.7 (£1,000-9,999), 1.9 (£10,000 plus) (legal aid). χ^2_6 = 30.17, p < 0.001, Standardised Pearson Residuals (Private funding (all) = -2.0 (less than £1,000), 1.2 (£1,000-9,999), 1.6 (£10,000 plus). Standardised Pearson Residuals (private funding (part)) = -2.0 (less than £1,000), 0.4 (£1,000-9,999), 2.8 (£10,000 plus). 2004: χ^2_2 = 4.83, p = 0.089. Standardised Pearson Residuals = -1.6 (less than £1,000), 0.7 (£1,000-9,999), 1.2 (£10,000 plus) (legal aid); χ^2_4 = 33.30, p < 0.001, Standardised Pearson Residuals (Private funding (all) = -1.6 (less than £1,000), -1.6 (£1,000-9,999), 4.4 (£10,000 plus). Standardised Pearson Residuals (private funding (part)) = -1.7 (less than £1,000), 0.4 (£1,000-9,999), 1.6 (£10,000 plus).

[433] There was little evidence of memory decay for problems in relation to which legal aid or privately funded advice was obtained. In 2001, the decay coefficients were 0.03 and 0.01 respectively, and in each case the 95 per cent confidence interval straddled 0 (-0.041 to 0.106; -0.082 to 0.0562). Also, the R^2 values were just 0.076 and 0.011. In contrast, there was considerable evidence of decay for problems in relation to which respondents paid nothing towards their advice, and slight decay in respect of problems in relation to which otherwise funded advice had been obtained. The decay coefficients were 0.09 and 0.07 respectively, and in the former case, the lower 95 per cent confidence band was 0.0563 (above the higher 95 per cent confidence band of private funding) and the R^2 value was 0.820. In the case of otherwise funded advice, the lower 95 per cent confidence band was only marginally above 0 (0.005), and the R^2 value was 0.333. In 2004, the decay coefficients for problems about which

Also, those respondents whose advice was funded by legal aid or a trade union indicated that they found it more difficult to carry on living normally while experiencing their problems than other respondents.[434] Those whose advice was funded by a trade union also indicated that their problems were more important to resolve.[435]

INACTION, ACTION, ADVICE AND TEMPORARY ACCOMMODATION

Respondents to the 2001 survey of people living in temporary accommodation reported taking no action to deal with problems on 28 per cent of all occasions. This is far more often than respondents to the 2001 and 2004 general population surveys reported taking no action. However, respondents to the temporary accommodation survey were much more likely to have sought advice if action was taken, with 95 per cent of them (68 per cent overall) having done so; although only around three-quarters of them were successful in doing so (74 per cent, 53 per cent overall). Because of the very different pattern of problems reported by those in temporary accommodation and their very different social and demographic profile, it is not surprising that the strategies they adopted were also different; though some of the characteristics of temporary accommodation survey respondents, such as being generally younger and more often black and minority ethnic, are associated with inaction, rather than action.

As with general population respondents, strategies varied considerably by problem type.[436] Owing to the size of the sample of people living in temporary accommodation, though, it was not possible to usefully examine strategies at the level of individual problem types. Nevertheless, a simple test of correlation was able to determine that the problem types associated with higher and lower rates of inaction

---

respondents had obtained legal aid or privately funded advice were 0.005 and -0.018 respectively, and in each case the 95 per cent confidence interval straddled 0 (-0.076 to 0.086; -0.085 to 0.050). Also, the R^2 values were just 0.002 and 0.024 respectively. For problems in relation to which respondents paid nothing towards their advice, the decay coefficient was 0.060 and the lower 95 per cent confidence band was 0.029 (the higher band was 0.091) and the R^2 value was 0.59. For advice that was paid for otherwise, the decay coefficient was 0.039, the lower 95 per cent confidence band was below zero 0 (-0.041(upper band = 0.119)), and the R^2 value was 0.075.

[434] $F_1 = 6.49$, $p < 0.05$ (trade union), $F_1 = 7.87$, $p < 0.01$ (legal aid). Based on 2004 data.

[435] $F_1 = 8.58$, $p < 0.01$. This was, though, also true of those respondents who reported that the cost of advice they received was covered by advisers themselves: $F_1 = 24.82$, $p < 0.001$.

[436] $\chi^2_{48} = 12.05$, $p < 0.001$.

128

were similar for temporary accommodation and general population survey respondents.[437]

As with general population respondents, the most common reason for respondents not acting to resolve problems was that they did not think that anything could be done. However, they were significantly more likely than general population respondents to provide this reason (49 per cent),[438] and this was not just a consequence of the very different pattern of problems they experienced. When problem type was controlled for, the significance of the difference actually increased.[439] They were also significantly more likely to report that they took no action because they were scared to act (13 per cent),[440] although in this instance the difference was not significant once problem type was controlled for. Conversely, temporary accommodation respondents reported less often that they regarded problems as insufficiently important to warrant action (6 per cent), although again the difference was less marked once problem type was controlled for. The finding was, though, consistent with the notion that the problems faced by respondents to the temporary accommodation survey tended to be of a more serious nature than those faced by respondents to the general population surveys.

The problem types that were associated with higher and lower rates of advice seeking on the part of respondents who took action were also similar for respondents to the temporary accommodation and general population survey.[441] Thus, all of those temporary accommodation respondents who took action to deal with a divorce obtained advice, whereas just 30 per cent of those who took action to deal with a consumer problem obtained advice.

Reflecting the disproportionately great number of rented housing and welfare benefits problems that temporary accommodation respondents faced, they much more frequently obtained advice from local councils (30 per cent).[442] However, even when problem type was controlled for, this difference remained.[443] This may be because they had greater dealings with local councils in general, in the context of both council services and advice.

---

[437] Spearman correlation coefficient = 0.626, p < 0.01. Based on 2001 survey data.
[438] $\chi^2_8 = 28.80$, p < 0.001. Standardised Pearson Residual = 3.2. Based on 2001 survey data.
[439] $\chi^2_8 = 52.86$, p < 0.001. Standardised Pearson Residual = 5.3.
[440] Standardised Pearson Residual = 2.4.
[441] Spearman correlation coefficient = 0.523, p < 0.05. Based on 2001 survey data.
[442] $\chi^2_8 = 88.60$, p < 0.001. Standardised Pearson Residual = 7.6. Based on 2001 survey data.
[443] $\chi^2_8 = 83.77$, p < 0.001. Standardised Pearson Residual = 7.0.

Reflecting the fact that temporary accommodation respondents were much more often economically inactive, they rarely reported obtaining advice from employers, trade unions or professional bodies.[444] In the case of trade unions, though, the difference was not significant once problem type was controlled for.[445]

Lastly, in part reflecting the disproportionately smaller number of family problems that they faced, temporary accommodation respondents were less likely to have obtained advice from a solicitor (18 per cent).[446] However, they were also less likely to have obtained advice from a solicitor when problem type was controlled for.[447]

SUMMARY

No action was taken to resolve around one-fifth of problems reported through the 2001 survey and the same was true in around one-tenth of problems reported through the 2004 survey. This represents a significant decrease, likely to be in part a consequence of reduced problem incidence set against a backdrop of maintained or increased supply of advice services. It remains the case, though, that a substantial number of people take no action to resolve problems.

The reasons provided for inaction in 2001 and 2004 were broadly similar. Often respondents did not act to resolve problems because they were regarded as insufficiently important to warrant action, because there had been no dispute involved and nobody was regarded as being in the wrong, or because action became unnecessary as a result of activity on the part of others. However, despite the fact that the judgement was made without the benefit of advice, inaction most often resulted from a belief that nothing could be done. More detailed information on reasons for inaction obtained in 2004 indicated that this belief generally reflected a profound pessimism as to whether any form of action would bring about change. Uncertainty as

---

[444] $\chi^2_8 = 88.60$, $p < 0.001$. Standardised Pearson Residuals = -2.6 (employer) and -2.3 (trade union). Based on 2001 data.

[445] $\chi^2_8 = 83.77$, $p < 0.001$. Standardised Pearson Residuals = -2.3 (employer) and -0.5 (trade union). Based on 2001 data.

[446] $\chi^2_8 = 88.60$, $p < 0.001$. Standardised Pearson Residual = -1.8. The same was also true of advice agencies other than Citizens Advice Bureaux (Standardised Pearson Residuals = -1.8), though this was probably due to a significant difference in the number of consumer problems. Thus, the difference in use of such advice agencies was not apparent once problem type was controlled for. Based on 2001 data.

[447] $\chi^2_8 = 83.77$, $p < 0.001$. Standardised Pearson Residual = -3.8. Based on 2001 data.

to rights or regarding what to do or where to turn to for help was less evident. Nevertheless, a separate analysis of respondents' awareness of local advice services indicated that levels of such awareness were an important factor in determining whether respondents acted to resolve problems. Those who were unaware of local services acted much less often than others. This is important, as a great number of people are unaware of locally available services.

Also, and a matter of some concern, respondents sometimes reported having taken no action because they were too scared to act. This was a more common reason for inaction than worries about cost.

Reasons for inaction varied significantly by problem type. So, for example, respondents who did not act were most likely to believe nothing could be done to resolve problems concerning discrimination, employment, money/debt and mental health, and most likely to report they had been scared to act to resolve problems relating to employment, neighbours and domestic violence. Concerns about cost were most likely to be reported by those who did nothing to resolve problems ancillary to relationship breakdown. The proportion of occasions on which no action was taken also varied by problem type, with those who faced problems relating to clinical negligence, discrimination, unfair police treatment, personal injury, neighbours, mental health, employment and domestic violence less likely than others to take action to resolve them. In addition, gender, ethnicity and experience all influenced the likelihood of action having been taken. In the last case, this meant that older respondents, those with academic qualifications, those who had acted to resolve problems before, and those who lived in households in which other people had acted to resolve problems were all more likely than others to act to resolve problems.

When action was taken to resolve justiciable problems, just under two-thirds of respondents reported that they sought formal rights-based or personal advice to assist them. The remainder handled their problems alone; although sometimes this involved obtaining information from printed literature or the internet, or support from friends and family, or, on very rare occasions, commencing proceedings in a court or tribunal, use of an Ombudsman or mediation. As fewer people took no action to resolve problems reported in 2004, the proportion of problems about which advice was obtained was greater than in 2001.

Again, problem type had most influence on whether respondents obtained advice. However, different problem types were associated with seeking advice, as compared to simply taking action. Problem severity, ethnicity and experience also influenced the likelihood of advice having been obtained.

Those who sought advice did so from a wide range of types of adviser. However, over one-sixth of those who sought advice were unsuccessful in obtaining it. In part because different types of adviser were used in relation to different problem types, different rates of success were also associated with different problem types.

The most frequent reason given for an attempt to obtain advice having been unsuccessful was that an adviser had been unable to provide any help, followed by difficulty getting through on the telephone, waiting too long to see an adviser and receiving no reply to a letter. Only rarely did respondents complain that they had been unable to obtain advice because an adviser had been too far away. However, the reasons given for attempts to obtain advice having been unsuccessful varied by adviser type. For example, unsuccessful attempts to obtain advice from Citizens Advice Bureaux were more likely to be due to problems getting through to an adviser than unsuccessful attempts to obtain advice from elsewhere.

There was evidence that advice services operating on a commercial basis presented fewer physical obstacles to those seeking to use them. The ease of use of insurance companies' legal helplines and the geographical distribution of solicitors firms were both factors in this. However, following initial contact with an adviser, the picture changed somewhat. Non-commercial generalist advisers were more likely to be able to provide help than, for example, insurance company helplines.

More than two-thirds of respondents who unsuccessfully attempted to obtain advice also tried to resolve problems alone. The remainder gave up trying.

Of those respondents who successfully obtained advice, almost two-thirds did so from just one adviser, around one-quarter from two advisers, and the remainder from three or more advisers. The most common types of advisers were solicitors, local councils, Citizens Advice Bureaux, the police, health professionals, trade unions, employers, insurance companies and other dedicated advice services.

Where respondents obtained advice from sequences of advisers, different patterns of types of adviser were associated with earlier and later points in these sequences, reflecting in part a progression from generalist to specialist advisers, but also some confusion on the part of many respondents as they tried to navigate an advice maze. Confusion was, for example, indicated by the great range of advisers used by respondents facing some types of problem and, also, by the fact that more than three-fifths of respondents who obtained advice from 'other' advisers in the first instance obtained advice from nowhere else, despite the fact that the great majority of such sources were generalist in character, and many – such as the Head Boy of a local school – seemed unlikely sources of good advice. In addition, confusion, and even some desperation, was indicated by respondents turning to advisers who were friends or relatives more often as a second than a first source of advice and, also, by a number of respondents appearing to have obtained advice, in the first instance, from the 'other side' to disputes.

Despite the above, the fit of advisers to problem type was generally seemingly appropriate. Indeed, in relation to some problem types respondents seemed quite clear about where they should go for advice.

Highlighting the significance of the telephone in the provision of easily accessible advice and assistance, the majority of advisers detailed through the 2004 survey were first contacted via the telephone, although almost three-quarters were seen in person at some point. On just over one-tenth of occasions, advice was provided exclusively by telephone. E-mail was rarely used as a means of communication.

Interestingly, the manner of initial contact with an adviser was important not just in indicating the likely manner of subsequent communication with that adviser, but also in indicating the manner of communication with subsequent advisers.

The substance of advice and assistance offered to respondents by different types of adviser varied greatly. Unsurprisingly, in terms of the subject matter of advice, solicitors most often explored respondents' legal positions, although this was also common for advice agencies, trade unions and the police. Reflecting the subject matter of advice they tended to provide, solicitors (especially), advice agencies, trade unions and the police most often suggested that respondents threaten or commence legal action. With regard to solicitors, this may to some extent have been a symptom of their predominantly legal focus. It may also, though, have stemmed from the nature of problems that solicitors dealt with. Over one-third of their clients were facing family type problems, which together accounted for over two-fifths of all instances of formal legal action.

Overall, away from family problems, mediation and conciliation were suggested and used only rarely.

Most types of adviser routinely suggested that respondents should try to resolve their problem by talking directly to the 'other side,' and some, like Citizens Advice Bureaux, routinely referred respondents on to other advisers. Despite frequently benefiting from referrals, solicitors themselves rarely referred respondents on to other advisers, presumably owing to their relatively high level of specialism. However, their low referral rate may also again indicate a relatively narrow focus on clients' legal positions. 'Other' advisers, also, only infrequently referred respondents on to different sources of advice. Worryingly, those referred on by such advisers were the most likely to fail to actually go on and obtain advice from the source they had been referred to.

In analysing referral patterns, the phenomenon of referral fatigue became apparent. This involves the likelihood of people obtaining advice from an adviser to whom they have been referred declining as they visit more advisers. The phenomenon of referral fatigue demonstrates the importance of equipping those from whom people initially seek advice with the means to quickly and effectively refer them on when necessary.

Specialist advice providers were more likely than generalist advice providers to provide active assistance to respondents and, unsurprisingly, solicitors attended court more frequently than other types of advisers. However, 'other' advisers also attended court relatively frequently. In fact, whether or not they had the training or experience to act as effective advisers, 'other' advisers were generally very active in assisting respondents.

More than three-quarters of advisers appear to have been regarded by respondents as satisfactory. However, there were differences in respondents' views of different adviser types. Solicitors and Citizens Advice Bureaux were among the most favoured, and employers the least favoured. This last finding most likely in part reflects the potential conflict of interest employers face in helping those who turn to them for advice about employment-related problems.

Around three-quarters of respondents who obtained advice paid none of the cost involved and, in all, two-thirds of advisers provided their services at no cost or only partial cost to respondents. Respondents met the costs of services provided by only around one in ten advisers in full.

Where respondents paid none or only some of the costs of an adviser, legal aid was mentioned in relation to one in twelve advisers. Trade unions and insurance companies were also frequently mentioned. Conditional fee agreements were entered into in around one in twenty of such instances.

Whether advice was 'free' and, if not, who ultimately met the cost varied by adviser and by problem type. Respondents were most likely to pay for advice from solicitors and in relation to family problems, although this did not extend to domestic violence or problems concerning children. Respondents were also prepared to pay the most for advice from solicitors, although solicitors were also associated with the greatest level of assistance with problems.

Legal aid and privately funded advice were more likely than 'free' and otherwise funded advice to be obtained in relation to more serious problems.

Of those respondents who did not pay for advice, just over half indicated that they would have been prepared to pay for it if they had had to. Reflecting levels of assistance and satisfaction, this was more often the case in relation to solicitors and specialist advice agencies than in relation to other advisers. It was least often the case in relation to employers and local councils. Those who indicated that they would not have been prepared to pay for advice most often said either that it would not have been appropriate, or that they could not have afforded it.

Finally, respondents to the temporary accommodation survey reported having taken no action far more often than did respondents to the general population surveys, and they were also significantly more likely to take no action because they thought nothing could be done. Nevertheless, problem types that were associated with higher and lower rates of inaction were similar for temporary accommodation and general population survey respondents. The problem types that were associated with higher and lower rates of advice seeking on the part of respondents who took action were also similar. However, those in temporary accommodation were more likely to obtain advice when they took action to deal with problems. Interestingly, when they did obtain advice, they were more likely to obtain advice from local councils. This may have been because they had more dealings with local councils in general, providing another example of experience dictating behaviour when seeking advice.

4

The End: Objectives, and How and When Justiciable Problems Conclude

This chapter sets out the range of objectives that motivate people to act to resolve justiciable problems. Using information obtained from main interviews, it illustrates the different objectives associated with different problem types, resolution strategies, advisers and population groups. In doing so, it describes how objectives vary along with the consequences of problems, and confirms the triggering effect of some problem types. Using information from screen and main interviews, it then details the ways in which problems conclude, and the extent to which people obtain their objectives. It points to evidence that problems conclude in a more positive manner where people have obtained advice. It also suggests that those who are represented before courts and tribunals fare better than those who are not, and that objectives are more often met in relation to the more important problems. The chapter then explains how the duration of problems varies by problem and adviser type, and also, seemingly, by seriousness. Lastly, it shows that, although people can greatly benefit from taking action to resolve justiciable problems, the resolution process itself can be stressful and can even bring about ill-health.

OBJECTIVES

There are many objectives that motivate people to act to resolve justiciable problems. People can, for example, be motivated by a sense of injustice, a desire to put right something that has gone wrong or a desire to prevent something that has gone wrong from going wrong again.[448] Evidently, also, people can be motivated by money or property. Indeed, in line with earlier findings, in both the 2001 and 2004 surveys the most frequently declared objective in acting to resolve problems was to obtain or preserve money or property,[449] although around one in ten respondents who reported such an objective also had further objectives.

Of course, in the most part objectives are determined by problem type.[450] Binary logistic regression was therefore used to test the influence of problem type, problem resolution strategy and a range of social and demographic predictors on the likelihood of respondents having acted to obtain or preserve money or property.[451]

Problem type was the most influential predictor. Objectives in acting to resolve problems relating to consumer transactions, employment, money/debt, welfare benefits, relationship breakdown and personal injury were most likely to involve obtaining or preserving money or property. In relation to personal injury problems, these findings reflect the general understanding that compensation is payable in relation to negligent accidents.

Objectives in acting to resolve problems concerning neighbours, domestic violence, children, clinical negligence and immigration were least likely to involve obtaining or preserving money or property. As regards clinical negligence, this was despite the fact that such problems are often seen as akin to personal injury problems. As has been reported elsewhere, though, this supports earlier findings that suggest, at least in relation to less serious episodes of clinical negligence, that people are most concerned to understand what has happened to them, to obtain remedial treatment, to prevent recurrences or to obtain recognition of a mistake and an apology.[452] In fact,

---

[448] See, for example, National Consumer Council (1995), above, n.20, Scottish Consumer Council (1997), above, n.20, M. Rosenthal, L. Mulcahy and S. Lloyd-Bostock (eds.) (1999) *Medical Mishaps: Pieces of the Puzzle,* Buckingham: Open University Press, Genn (1999), above, n.3; H. Genn and A. Paterson (2001), above, n.20.

[449] On the face of it the figures were quite different in 2001 and 2004, with 51 per cent of respondents reporting such an objective in 2001, compared to just 39 per cent in 2004. However, this difference was in large part attributable to different problem types being included in the two calculations. Main interviews in 2001 covered consumer problems, but not problems with neighbours. The reverse was the case in 2004. If both these problem types were excluded from calculations, the figures changed to 48 per cent in 2001 and 45 per cent in 2004. These results are similar to the *Paths to Justice* finding that 51 per cent of respondents who took action to resolve a problem described their main objective as being related to money or property: Genn (1999), above, n.3. The corresponding figure reported in *Paths to Justice Scotland* was 50 per cent: p.180, H. Genn and A. Paterson (2001), above, n.20, p.182.

[450] See, for example, Genn (1999), above, n.3, p.83.

[451] Further details are set out at www.lsrc.org.uk.

[452] P. Pleasence, N.J. Balmer, H. Genn, A. Buck and A. O'Grady (2003) The Experience of Clinical Negligence Within the General Population, in 9(6) *Clinical Risk,* p.211. See, also, for example, Chief Medical Officer (2003) *Making Amends: A Consultation Paper Setting Out Proposals for Reforming*

just two of 36 respondents in 2001, and two of 27 in 2004, stated their objective in acting to resolve a problem concerning clinical negligence was to obtain money or property.

When objectives related to money, a lump sum was generally at issue.[453] However, while periodic payments were rare in the case of problems relating to consumer transactions, personal injury and money/debt, they were the norm in the case of welfare benefits problems. They were also the most common form of monetary objective in the case of problems ancillary to relationship breakdown, reflecting frequent disputes relating to maintenance payments.[454]

Although the sums of money at issue were larger in 2004, when problems involved lump sums these frequently amounted to £100 or less.[455] However, 50 per cent of lump sums amounted to £1,000 or more and 23 per cent to £5,000 or more.[456] Unsurprisingly, sums varied by problem type. Thus, whereas consumer and rented housing problems very rarely related to a lump sum of £1,000 or more, personal injuries and problems ancillary to relationship breakdown invariably related to a sum of £1,000 or more.[457]

The fact that a justiciable problem involves a sum of £100 or less does not, of course, mean that the problem is trivial. As well as the lingering sense of injustice or betrayal of trust that can accompany justiciable problems (which can on their own introduce importance to even small value disputes), for those with little disposable

---

the *Approach to Clinical Negligence in the NHS*, London: Department of Health, H. Genn and S. Lloyd-Bostock (1995) *Medical Negligence Research Project: The Operation of the Tort System in Medical Negligence Cases*, London: HMSO, M. Rosenthal, L. Mulcahy and S. Lloyd-Bostock (eds.) (1999), above, n.448, and L. Mulcahy, M. Selwood and A. Netten (2000) *Mediating Medical Negligence Claims: An Option for the Future?* Norwich: The Stationery Office.
[453] Overall, 81 per cent of occasions in 2001 and 66 per cent in 2004. The figures are not directly comparable, owing to the different problem types covered by main interviews in 2001 and 2004. See above, n.449.
[454] In 2001, periodic payments were not sought in relation to a single consumer problem, just 6 per cent of money/debt problems and 8 per cent of personal injuries. In contrast they were sought in respect of 70 per cent of welfare benefits and 51 per cent of family problems: $\chi^2_{28} = 272.48$, $p < 0.001$. Standardised Pearson Residuals = -5.3 (consumer), -2.1 (personal injury), -2.6 (money/debt), 11.3 (welfare benefits), 2.6 (divorce), 3.0 (relationship breakdown), 2.3 (domestic violence) and 3.1 (children). In 2004, the figures for money/debt, personal injury, welfare benefits and family problems were 19, 8, 85 and 80 per cent respectively. Periodic payments were also cited only rarely in the context of rented housing problems: $\chi^2_{11} = 110.44$, $p < 0.001$. Standardised Pearson Residuals = -3.3 (personal injury), -2.9 (money/debt), -1.8 (rented housing), 5.1 (welfare benefits), 4.4 (relationship breakdown) and 0.4 (divorce).
[455] Fourteen per cent of lump sums (where an amount was indicated), compared to 20 per cent in 2001.
[456] This compares to 44 per cent and 17 per cent in 2001.
[457] Where lump sums were at issue, just 12 per cent amounted to £1,000 or more in the context of rented housing problems reported in 2004. This compared to 88 per cent in respect of personal injury problems. The figure in 2001 for consumer problems was 17 per cent.

income even £50 can represent a substantial loss or gain. Consistent with this, it was found that the sum involved in disputes correlated with household income.[458]

Unsurprisingly, housing and consumer problems most often had specific property related objectives, as opposed to or in addition to money related objectives.

The most common stated objectives that did not involve obtaining or retaining money or property included preventing problems from recurring and changing the behaviour of other people. However, such objectives were closely tied to particular problem types, reflecting their often very different consequences.[459] So, for example, respondents who acted to secure employment related objectives (such as preserving or gaining a job) had generally faced employment problems; and those who had not faced employment problems had faced problems relating to discrimination, personal injury and immigration. Respondents who acted to correct information about them held by others had generally faced money/debt problems. Those who acted to show that they were 'in the right' had generally faced problems concerning unfair treatment by the police, employment or divorce. Those who wanted property to be repaired had generally faced consumer problems. Those who acted to prevent problems from recurring had generally faced problems relating to personal injury or clinical negligence. Those who wanted to change the behaviour of other people had generally faced problems concerning neighbours.

As well as those who faced particular types of problem, binary logistic regression also indicated that younger respondents and lone parents were less likely to act to obtain or preserve money or property.

Given the findings concerning problem type, it is not surprising that different types of adviser were also associated with different types of objective. As local councils and the police provided assistance in relation to a disproportionate number of problems concerning neighbours and domestic violence, respondents who ultimately sought advice from them were less likely than others to have had the objective of obtaining or retaining money or property.[460] In contrast, as insurance companies provided assistance in relation to a disproportionate number of problems related to consumer transactions, personal injury and money/debt, respondents who ultimately

---

[458] 2001: Spearman correlation coefficient = 0.173, p < 0.01; 2004: Spearman correlation coefficient = 0.232, p < 0.01.

[459] 2001: $\chi^2_{112} = 534.07$, p < 0.001; 2004: $\chi^2_{154} = 847.59$, p < 0.001.

[460] 2001: $\chi^2_{24} = 77.23$, p < 0.001; Standardised Pearson Residuals = -1.7 (local council) and -0.5 (police). 2004: $\chi^2_{27} = 94.44$, p < 0.001; Standardised Pearson Residuals = -3.2 (local council) and -3.1 (police).

sought advice from them were more likely than others to have had the objective of obtaining or retaining money or property.[461]

MANNERS OF CONCLUSION

In 2004, but not in 2001, respondents were asked in screen interviews about how their problems concluded. This allowed a more detailed picture to emerge of the role of formal processes and advice in the resolution of problems.

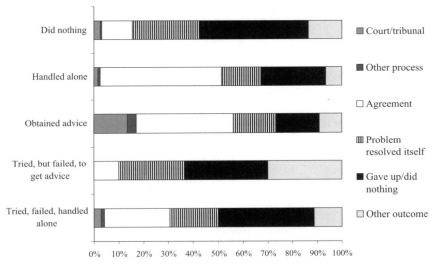

Figure 4.1
Manner of Conclusion by Strategy

Thirty-six per cent of problems reported in 2004 screen interviews were on-going at the time of interview. Respondents also described it as being 'too early to say' whether a further 3 per cent of problems had yet concluded. Of those problems that had (or had 'most likely') concluded, 39 per cent were resolved by agreement between the parties,[462] 8 per cent through a court or tribunal process,[463] 2 per cent

---

[461] Standardised Pearson Residuals = 0.4 (2001) and 2.5 (2004).
[462] Seven per cent of these agreements were arrived at following the issue of court or tribunal proceedings and 1 per cent following mediation.
[463] The resolution of justiciable problems through court processes is relatively rare across jurisdictions. For example, the figure has been put at 9 per cent in Scotland and at 5 per cent in Japan: H. Genn and

through a third party intervention (e.g. police action), 1 per cent through mediation and 1 per cent through an Ombudsman. Eighteen per cent of concluded problems resolved themselves. Finally, respondents reported having 'left behind' 6 per cent, having made no attempt to resolve 6 per cent, and having abandoned attempts to resolve 18 per cent of concluded problems.

Unsurprisingly, different problem resolution strategies were associated with different manners of problem conclusion. So, as can be seen from Figure 4.1, respondents who obtained advice saw their problems conclude through a court or tribunal process far more frequently.[464] They also gave up trying to resolve problems far less often, especially in comparison to respondents who tried, but failed, to obtain advice or, obviously, did nothing.[465]

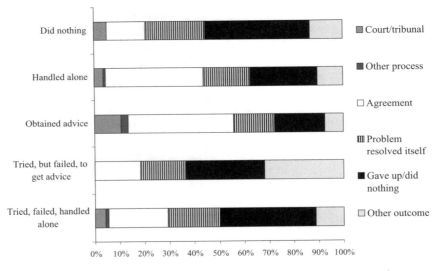

Figure 4.2
Manner of Conclusion by Strategy (Standardised)

Of course, as was illustrated in the previous chapter, different problem types and levels of seriousness of problem were associated with different resolution strategies. Thus, the pattern of conclusion set out in Figure 4.1 might reflect any or all

A. Paterson (2001), above, n.20, p.158; M. Murayama et al (2005), above, n.51, p.9. More generally see, for example, W. Felstiner et al (1981), above, n.286.
[464] $\chi^2_{20} = 211.93$, p < 0.001. Standard Pearson Residual = 5.8.
[465] Standard Pearson Residuals = -3.7 (obtained advice), 2.5 (tried, failed, handled alone).

of these three things. To illustrate the extent to which manners of conclusion were independently influenced by strategy, Figure 4.2 therefore sets out these manners of conclusion after problem resolution strategies were 'standardised' for problem type and seriousness.[466] The picture is very similar, although the proportion of problems about which advice was obtained and which were resolved through a court or tribunal process reduces from 14 to 11 per cent, and the proportion of problems about which advice was obtained and which respondents gave up trying to resolve increases from 18 to 20 per cent. This last percentage compares to 27 per cent for problems which respondents handled alone and 37 per cent for problems about which respondents tried, but failed, to obtain advice (whether or not they were also handled alone). On the face of it, then, it would appear that advice improves the manner of conclusion of justiciable problems.

Figure 4.3 sets out manners of conclusion by problem type. Family problems, most often associated with advice, were naturally more likely than other problem types to conclude through a court or tribunal process.[467] So, 37 per cent of family problems were reported to have concluded through a court or tribunal process, compared to 4 per cent of other problems. Consumer problems were least likely to conclude through a court or tribunal process.[468]

Problems concerning employment or ancillary to relationship breakdown were most often concluded through some other process, such as mediation.[469] The former were also the most likely to involve attempts at resolution being abandoned, along with problems regarding consumer transactions,[470] or problems being 'left behind,' along with problems concerning neighbours.[471] Beside divorce, though, problems with neighbours were the least likely to be abandoned.[472]

---

[466] This means that the problems were weighted to give each strategy a similar distribution of problem types and levels of seriousness.

[467] $\chi^2_{85} = 819.45$, $p < 0.001$; Standardised Pearson Residuals = 15.6 (divorce), 4.8 (relationship breakdown), 3.5 (domestic violence) and 1.7 (children). This pattern is repeated across jurisdictions. See, for example, H. Genn and A. Paterson (2001), above, n.20, p.159 and M. Murayama et al (2005), above, n.51, p.9.

[468] Standard Pearson Residual = -4.6.

[469] Employment problems were the most likely to resolve through mediation: $\chi^2_{136} = 1020.92$, $p < 0.001$, Standardised Pearson Residual = 2.5.

[470] Thus, attempts to resolve consumer and employment problems were abandoned on 27 and 23 per cent of occasions respectively: $\chi^2_{136} = 1020.92$, $p < 0.001$; Standardised Pearson Residuals = 4.1 (consumer) and 1.6 (employment).

[471] Where neighbours were left behind, this involved moving home. Where employment problems were left behind, this involved leaving a job. $\chi^2_{136} = 1020.92$, $p < 0.001$; Standardised Pearson Residuals = 3.1 (neighbours) and 4.8 (employment).

[472] Standardised Pearson Residuals = -3.8 (divorce) and -2.8 (neighbours).

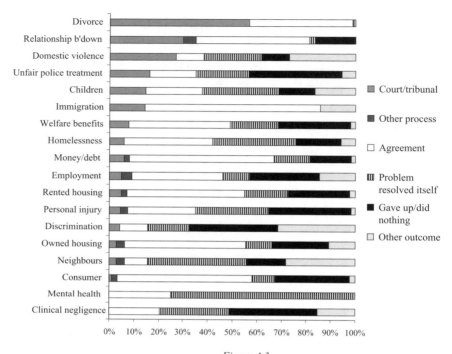

Figure 4.3
Manner of Conclusion by Problem Type

Not all respondents reported whether or not their objectives in acting to resolve problems had been met. Therefore it was not possible to establish conclusively the extent to which this was the case. This was so in respect of both the 2001 and 2004 surveys. At best, more than two-thirds of respondents who took action to deal with justiciable problems secured at least some of their objectives, and more than two-fifths secured all their objectives.[473] However, if it were assumed that those respondents who did not state whether their objectives had been met *and* who reported that their problems concluded without agreement or adjudication were unsuccessful in securing their objectives, then these figures reduced considerably, to

---

[473] In 2001, 73 per cent of respondents who reported whether or not their objectives had been met stated that some of them had been, and 54 per cent stated that all of them had been met. In 2004, the figures were 67 and 42 per cent respectively. As detailed in n. 449, the mix of problems was different in 2001 and 2004.

perhaps as low as two-fifths and one-quarter respectively.[474] However looked at, though, those respondents who reported that their problem concluded without agreement or adjudication were far and away the least likely to secure their objectives.[475]

There was no difference in the rates at which objectives were met between problems resolved by adjudication or agreement.[476] There was evidence from the 2001 survey, though, that those respondents who were represented at a court or tribunal fared better than those who were unrepresented, although this finding was just short of being statistically significant.[477] Whereas 73 per cent of those 2001 survey respondents who were represented at a court or tribunal hearing at which a decision was made reported that they had 'won', only 55 per cent of those respondents who were unrepresented did so. This is in keeping with findings such as those of Genn and Genn in relation to representation before tribunals.[478] However, more recent research has indicated that there may be important differences between problem and tribunal types.[479]

While an analysis of 2001 survey data proved inconclusive,[480] analysis of 2004 survey data indicated significant differences in the rate at which people adopting different problem resolution strategies obtained their objectives.[481] As can be seen from Table 4.1, those respondents who obtained advice were far more successful in obtaining their objectives than those who tried, but failed, to obtain advice.[482] They obtained all of their objectives four times as often and failed to obtain any of their objectives only half as often. This, combined with the above finding that those who obtained advice gave up dealing with problems less often than those who tried, but

---

[474] In 2001, the figures reduced to 52 and 39 per cent respectively, and in 2004 to 43 and 27 per cent respectively. Respondents who did not state their objectives were not asked if their objectives were met.

[475] 2001: $\chi^2_4 = 187.29$, p < 0.001; Standardised Pearson Residual = 10.8. 2004: $\chi^2_{12} = 163.17$, p < 0.001; Standardised Pearson Residual = 8.7.

[476] 2001: $\chi^2_2 = 0.639$, p = 0.726; 2004: $\chi^2_2 = 5.48$, p = 0.065.

[477] $\chi^2_1 = 2.868$, p = 0.090. The dedicated questions on representation during court or tribunal processes were not included in the 2004 survey.

[478] See, for example, H. Genn and Y. Genn (1989) *The Effectiveness of Representation at Tribunals,* London: Lord Chancellor's Department.

[479] H. Genn, B. Lever and L. Gray (2006) *Tribunals for Diverse Users*, London: Department for Constitutional Affairs.

[480] $\chi^2_2 = 0.639$, p < 0.726.

[481] $\chi^2_4 = 11.76$, p = 0.019. The small number of respondents who felt it was 'too early' to say if their objectives were met were excluded from the analysis.

[482] Standard Pearson Residuals = –2.1 (tried but failed, all objectives met) and 2.5 (tried, but failed: no objectives met). See, also, the discussion about advice and satisfaction with the outcome of problems in C. Coumarelos, Z. Wei and A. Zhou (2006), above, n.56.

failed, to obtain advice, provides compelling evidence of the general utility of advice. While respondents who obtained advice also achieved their objectives more often than those who handled problems alone, this difference was not significant. This is hardly surprising, though, as the findings set out in the previous chapter demonstrate clearly that the nature of those problems about which people seek advice is very different from the nature of problems that people deal with themselves. People seek advice in relation to more serious, and most likely more complex, problems. It would seem sensible to maintain that a beneficial impact of advice is necessary simply to maintain levels of success in achieving objectives in respect of such problems. In any event, it seems self-evident that people are better placed to deal with problems if they have an understanding of their position and options for action. Advice is a means through which such an understanding can be arrived at.

Table 4.1

Degree to Which Objectives are Obtained by Problem Resolution Strategy

Strategy	% of respondents who obtained all objectives	% of respondents who obtained some objectives	% of respondents who obtained no objectives
Handled alone	42	25	33
Obtained advice	46	26	28
Tried, but failed	11	26	63

Weighted base = 289

The problem of 'self-selection' in relation to advice makes clear the value of looking closely at the relative success of those who succeed and fail in attempts to obtain advice. Given that both these groups of people set out to adopt the same problem resolution strategy, the differences in the problems they face should be of a smaller magnitude. It was possible to address the problem of self-selection to a small extent by standardising problem resolution strategies for seriousness of problems within analysis. However, the results were little different.[483] Other methodologies,

---

[483] The rate at which all objectives were obtained reduced marginally to 40 per cent for those who handled problems alone and the rate at which no objectives were obtained increased to 34 per cent. Differences with rates for those who obtained advice remained insignificant.

such as random control trials, will need to be adopted in order to address the issue of the impact of advice in detail.[484]

It was not possible to look beyond the provision of advice at issues of quality. Still, there was some evidence that respondents whose advice was funded by legal aid were more likely than others who obtained advice to secure some or all of their objectives, though the finding was not significant in 2004.[485] Numbers were quite small, however.[486] Respondents who described their problem as 'very important' to sort out were also more likely than others to achieve their objectives, perhaps reflecting their greater chance of resolution.[487]

Unsurprisingly, those who 'won' at a court or tribunal were much more likely to have regarded the process as fair (92 per cent compared to 18 per cent).[488] Similarly, in 2001, those who obtained their objectives through an agreement were more likely to regard the process as fair (88 per cent compared to 55 per cent),[489] though there was little difference in 2004 (80 per cent in both cases).[490] Demonstrating that the process of attempting to achieve a resolution of justiciable problems takes 'quite a toll'[491] on people, the most common reason given for respondents having entered into unfair agreements was that they 'just wanted to bring the problem to an end' (51 per cent in 2001 and 54 per cent in 2004). Other common reasons were that they would have found it 'too stressful to go on,' or that they were 'pressured' into agreements. [492] Concerns about the cost of going on were mentioned by a relatively small proportion of respondents.[493]

---

[484] Such a random control trial is currently underway as part of the Impact of Debt Research Project, details of which can be found at www.lsrc.org.uk.

[485] 2001: $\chi^2{}_1 = 4.04$, $p < 0.05$; 2004: $\chi^2{}_1 = 0.65$, $p = 0.42$.

[486] In 2001, only 25 respondents reported receiving legal aid and stated whether their objectives had been met in respect of a problem that had concluded. The number was 12 in 2004.

[487] $\chi^2{}_2 = 18.60$, $p < 0.001$. Standard Pearson Residual = 3.2. This was still significant if those respondents who did not say whether their objectives had been met and who reported that their problems concluded without agreement or adjudication were assumed to be unsuccessful in securing their objectives: $\chi^2{}_2 = 21.39$, $p < 0.001$.

[488] $\chi^2{}_1 = 48.67$, $p < 0.001$. This data was only available for 2001.

[489] $\chi^2{}_1 = 22.95$, $p < 0.001$.

[490] $\chi^2{}_1 = 0.012$, $p = 0.91$.

[491] H. Genn (1999), above, n.3, p.213.

[492] Respondents were free to provide multiple reasons, so these percentages cannot be added together.

[493] Twelve per cent in 2001 and 5 per cent in 2004.

DURATION

While most justiciable problems conclude within a short period of time, some continue over many years. A small number may even conclude only following the death of those involved.[494] So, while 52 per cent of all concluded problems reported through each of the 2001 and 2004 surveys lasted for three months or less, 21 per cent continued for a year or more. Moreover, in 2001, 2 per cent of concluded problems extended for five years or more, and 10 problems ($^1/_2$ per cent) lasted for more than 10 years; the longest running of which – an employment problem concerning equal pay[495] – took 20 years and 8 months to conclude.[496] Slightly fewer problems reported in 2004 lasted for longer than five years (1 per cent), although the longest running – a dispute ancillary to a relationship breakdown – was stated to have surpassed even the length of the equal pay case reported in 2001, running on for 21 years and 3 months. The average concluded problem duration was around eight months and two weeks in 2001, and seven months and two weeks in 2004.

Using information derived from screen interviews, univariate analysis of variance (ANOVA) was employed to test the influence of problem type, problem resolution strategy and the use of formal dispute resolution processes on problem duration.[497]

Family problems, along with problems relating to neighbours, were more likely to last longer than other problem types.[498] So, as can be seen from Table 4.2, concluded relationship breakdown, divorce and domestic violence and neighbours problems lasted, on average, for around a year or more. Problems relating to children and immigration and nationality also lasted on average for around a year, though in

---

[494] Some justiciable problems may continue beyond the death of the person initially involved. For example, the estate or relatives of a deceased person may continue to pursue 'justice' in relation to, for example, an accident or industrial disease.

[495] The respondent was partially successful in her claim against her employer, and was awarded a sum of money by an employment tribunal, at which she was represented by her trade union.

[496] As would be expected, at the time of interview on-going problems had already lasted for an average of seven months longer than concluded problems in 2001 and around 13 months longer in 2004 (15 months compared to eight months in 2001, 20 months compared to seven months in 2004). In 2001, 42 per cent of on-going problems had already lasted for a year or more, 3 per cent for five years or more, and 1 per cent for ten years or more. In 2004, the figures were 53 per cent, 5 per cent and 2 per cent respectively.

[497] Further technical details and output tables are available for download from www.lsrc.org.uk.

[498] Only concluded problems were included in these analyses. In 2001 and 2004, when all problems were included, employment problems were also found to be likely to last longer: $t = 2.413$, $p < 0.05$ (2001); $t = 2.457$, $p < 0.05$ (2004).

the case of immigration, the number of cases was too small for the finding to be significant.

Table 4.2

Average Duration, in Months, of Problems by Type

Problem type	Concluded problems				All problems			
	2001		2004		2001		2004	
	Mean	Median	Mean	Median	Mean	Median	Mean	Median
Discrimination	7	4	5	2	11	4	12	5
Consumer	5	2	4	2	6	3	6	2
Employment	8	3	8	3	12	4	10	5
Neighbours	11	4	12	6	13	4	21	10
Housing (own)	7	3	7	4	11	6	13	6
Housing (rent)	8	4	9	4	10	5	14	6
Money/debt	8	3	8	4	12	6	13	6
Welfare benefits	7	4	5	3	8	5	9	5
Divorce	17	12	12	11	17	12	12	9
Relationship b'down	25	14	17	8	22	14	26	14
Domestic violence	13	4	17	7	15	4	19	13
Children	12	5	11	5	14	6	16	8
Personal injury	7	5	6	2	12	7	13	8
Clinical negligence	6	1	8	4	11	3	20	13
Mental health	2	0	4	3	7	1	27	17
Immigration	16	12	8	9	18	15	25	11
Police treatment	3	1	1	0	5	2	3	1
Homelessness	7	3	10	4	9	3	10	5

The analysis of variance also indicated that problems about which respondents sought advice were likely to have lasted longer than others, particularly if advice was sought from multiple sources.[499] So, when respondents sought advice from multiple sources, problems lasted on average for around one year (12 months in 2001 and 11 months in 2004). When they sought advice from one source, problems lasted for a slightly shorter time (ten months in 2001 and nine months in 2004). When respondents handled problems themselves, those problems lasted for around half a year (six months in 2001 and five months in 2004). Interestingly, though, problems of different duration were associated with different types of adviser. When respondents

---

[499] Problems reported in 2001 where advice had been sought from a trade union, local council, 'other' adviser or from multiple advisers were likely to last longer than others. The same was also true of problems reported in 2004 where advice was sought from local councils or from multiple advisers.

sought advice from only a solicitor or a Citizens Advice Bureau, problems were no different in duration from those that were handled alone or in relation to which nothing was done. However, in 2001, problem duration was significantly greater where advice was sought from any other adviser type, and in 2004 it was significantly greater where advice was sought from a local council. That is not to say that the average duration of problems was around half a year when respondents only sought advice from a solicitor. It was actually closer to one year (11 months in 2001 and ten months in 2004). However, much of the additional duration can be explained by the problem types that solicitors dealt with (e.g. divorce and relationship breakdown), and the common use they made of legal processes, which were also found to be associated with problems that lasted longer (15 months on average in 2001 and 12 months in 2004). When respondents only sought advice from a Citizens Advice Bureau, problems on average lasted around half a year (seven months in 2001 and 6 months in 2004).

In both 2001 and 2004, as with the use of legal processes, the use of an Ombudsman in resolving problems appeared to increase problem duration. When an Ombudsman was used, problems lasted on average for more than one and a half years (20 months in 2001 and 22 months in 2004). However, no increase in duration was observed in relation to mediation or conciliation. Nevertheless, because mediation and conciliation were most frequently used in relation to family problems, mediated or conciliated problems on average lasted for longer than others (14 months in 2001 and 12 months in 2004).

Each of the problem types, resolution strategies and processes associated with problems of longer duration have been identified above as associated with relatively serious problems, and so these links with duration may reflect a more fundamental link between problem seriousness and duration. Consistent with this, an analysis of 2001 main interview data indicated that, when problems concerned money, their duration correlated significantly with the sum involved.[500] Thus, whereas concluded problems that involved a sum of less than £1,000 had an average duration of five months, those that involved a sum of £10,000 had an average duration of 25 months. However, this correlation did not hold with 2004 main interview data. Beyond this, though, while no significant difference was found between the average duration of

---

[500] Pearson correlation coefficient = 0.260, p < 0.001.

problems of different levels of stated importance reported in 2001 main interviews,[501] a far more comprehensive analysis of severity measures incorporated into 2004 screen interviews gave a strong indication of the existence of a link between problem seriousness and duration. The difficulty of carrying on living normally while experiencing problems,[502] the level of importance of resolving problems,[503] the severity of impact of problems on respondents' lives[504] and the amount of time respondents spent worrying about problems[505] were all closely associated with problem duration. Thus, problems lasted for an average of ten months where respondents stated that they spent 'all' or 'most of their time' worrying, compared to eight months where they spent 'some' time worrying, less than five months where they spent only a 'little' time worrying, and less than four months where they spent 'none of their time' worrying.

So, in addition to lasting longer, problems continuing over longer periods also appeared to have a more severe impact on a day-to-day basis.

UNINTENDED CONSEQUENCES

In 2001, respondents were asked about the impact of trying to resolve problems. Fifty-nine per cent of those who had made such an attempt described it as stressful. Furthermore, one-quarter of these respondents also said that their health had suffered as a result. Thus, not only can justiciable problems *directly* bring about ill-health, they can also *indirectly* bring about ill-health through the problem resolution process. Nevertheless, almost half of those respondents who said that acting to resolve problems had been stressful or had brought about ill-health also said that they were glad that they had 'stuck up' for themselves. This was, though, a smaller percentage than for respondents who had not found acting to resolve problems stressful or a cause of ill-health (47 per cent compared to 62 per cent).[506]

---

[501] This finding was limited, though, by the fact that those who reported having taken no action to resolve problems in 2001 were not asked about how important it had been to resolve problems.
[502] Spearman correlation coefficient = 0.265, $p < 0.001$.
[503] Spearman correlation coefficient = 0.204, $p < 0.001$.
[504] Spearman correlation coefficient = 0.294, $p < 0.001$.
[505] Spearman correlation coefficient = 0.275, $p < 0.001$.
[506] $\chi^2_1 = 30.32$, $p < 0.001$.

Respondents were less likely to report having become stressed or ill while attempting to resolve problems they did not regard as 'very important' to sort out.[507] Consequently, they were also less likely to report having become ill while attempting to resolve problems alone.[508] However, they were not significantly less likely to become stressed while attempting to resolve problems alone.[509] This suggests that advisers may alleviate some of the stress of resolving problems by, for example, taking away some of the responsibility for progressing matters, removing the need to deal directly with other parties to disputes, providing emotional support, or by simply allowing those who experience problems to talk about them in an uncritical environment.[510]

Unsurprisingly, respondents were more likely to report that their health suffered through resolving problems that took longer to resolve. So, whereas ill-health was reported in relation to 14 per cent of problems that lasted for more than two years, it was reported in relation to just 7 per cent of problems that lasted for less than a year.[511] Also, respondents who failed to obtain their objectives in acting to resolve justiciable problems were more likely to report that their health suffered.[512] Lastly, respondents whose objectives in acting to resolve problems had been non-monetary were more likely to report that their health suffered.[513]

SUMMARY

There are many objectives that motivate people to act to resolve justiciable problems. Often, though, objectives have a monetary dimension. Thus, just over half of those respondents to the 2001 and 2004 surveys who took action to resolve a problem stated that their objective had been to obtain or preserve money or property. Although monetary objectives often involved relatively small sums, this did not mean they were

---

[507] $\chi^2_6 = 179.73$, p < 0.001. Standard Pearson Residuals = -2.4 (stress), -2.9 (ill-health). They were also less likely to have regarded the resolution process in beneficial terms (-2.4).
[508] $\chi^2_6 = 121.10$, p < 0.001. Standard Pearson Residual = -4.2.
[509] Standard Pearson Residual = -1.3.
[510] See, for example, G. Davis, S. Cretney and J. Collins (1995) *Simple Quarrels*, Oxford: Oxford University Press, and J. Eekelaar, M. Maclean and S. Beinart (2000) *Family Lawyers: The Divorce Work of Solicitors*, Oxford: Hart.
[511] $\chi^2_{12} = 32.91$, p < 0.01. Standard Pearson Residual = 2.5.
[512] $\chi^2_1 = 5.81$, p < 0.05.
[513] $\chi^2_6 = 28.83$, p < 0.001. Standard Pearson Residual = 2.2.

unimportant. Sums correlated with household income. They also varied by problem type, as did the nature of objectives in general.

Objectives in acting to resolve problems relating to consumer transactions, employment, money/debt, welfare benefits, relationship breakdown and personal injury were most likely to involve obtaining or preserving money or property. Objectives in acting to resolve problems concerning neighbours, domestic violence, children, clinical negligence and immigration were least likely to do so. Linked to this, objectives relating to problems about which advice had been sought from local councils and the police were also less likely to involve obtaining or preserving money or property.

Just over one-third of problems reported in 2004 were on-going at the time of interview, although respondents were sometimes no longer trying to resolve them. Of those problems that had concluded, around two-fifths were resolved by agreement between the parties and one-fifth resolved themselves. Slightly less than one in ten were resolved through a court or tribunal process. For most of the remainder, it appeared that either no attempt had been made to resolve them, or an attempt had been abandoned. However, there was evidence that respondents who obtained advice were less likely to give up trying to resolve problems than others.

At best, more than two-thirds of those who took action to deal with justiciable problems secured at least some of their objectives, and more than two-fifths secured their objectives in full. There was no difference in the rates at which objectives were met between problems resolved by adjudication or agreement. However, there was evidence in 2001 that those who were represented at a court or tribunal hearing fared better than those who were unrepresented.

Overall, there was no significant difference in the rate at which objectives were met between those who obtained advice and those who handled problems themselves. However, data from the 2004 survey indicated that those who obtained advice were more successful in obtaining their objectives than those who tried, but failed, to obtain advice. This, combined with the finding that those who obtained advice gave up dealing with problems less often than others, provides compelling evidence of the general utility of advice. Moreover, this is without the quality of advice being taken into account.

There was also some evidence that advice funded by legal aid was more frequently associated with the securing of some or all of respondents' objectives.

Demonstrating that the process of attempting to achieve a resolution of justiciable problems takes a toll on people, many respondents entered into agreements that they regarded as unfair; often because they would have found it too stressful to go on. This was in a context of one-fifth of problems continuing for a year or more, and the duration of problems appearing to reflect, at least in part, their seriousness.

More generally, over half of those who attempted to resolve justiciable problems said that their attempt had been stressful. A significant minority of these respondents also said that their health had suffered as a result. Thus, it is clear that not only can justiciable problems directly bring about ill-health, but that they can also indirectly bring about ill-health through the problem resolution process.

Unsurprisingly, respondents were less likely to report having become stressed or ill while attempting to resolve problems they did not regard as 'very important' to sort out. Consequently, they were also less likely to report having become ill while attempting to resolve problems alone. However, they were not less likely to become stressed while attempting to resolve problems alone, suggesting that advisers may alleviate some of the stress of resolving problems. Also, respondents were more likely to report that their health suffered through trying to secure non-monetary objectives and through acting to resolve problems that took longer to resolve.

Importantly, almost half of those respondents who said that acting to resolve problems had been stressful or had brought about ill-health also said that they were glad that they had 'stuck up' for themselves – demonstrating the importance to individuals of acting to secure justice.

5

An Integrated Approach to Social Justice

This chapter summarises the principal findings detailed in the preceding three chapters and sets out their implications. It suggests that the nature and impact of justiciable problems require that they should be of general concern. It highlights the role of education and information in raising awareness of the civic context of justiciable problems and the methods that can be used to resolve them. It suggests that dedicated advice services should mirror the needs and behaviour of those who wish to use them. It also underscores the importance of equipping those from whom people initially seek advice with the means to quickly and effectively refer them on when necessary, and the importance of accessible general advice services that act as gateways to formal advice and legal services. More broadly, it recognises the important role to be played by those who have routine professional contact with individuals vulnerable to justiciable problems in 'problem noticing' and signposting people to such gateways. The chapter then underlines the importance of development and co-ordination of advice and other services so that problems are not just dealt with in isolation, but in the context of their causes and consequences. It notes that the 2001 and 2004 survey findings indicate how resources might be targeted to these ends. Finally, it asks where investment should come from to develop the methods and services that will enable more people to benefit from early and effective advice, and suggests the key role of the government.

A GENERAL CONCERN

Findings from the 2001 and 2004 English and Welsh Civil and Social Justice Surveys illustrate clearly that justiciable problems are ubiquitous. They affect many people and many aspects of people's lives. They are not problems that should concern only lawyers and those charged with civil law policy development. They are problems that should be of general concern since they relate to and impact on health, education, housing, welfare, commerce, citizenship, policing and communities. They are, in sum, problems that should not be associated narrowly with civil law, but broadly with social justice.

While there was a decrease in problem incidence between 2001 and 2004, which can be explained at least in part by differences in the social and demographic profile of the survey samples, around one-third of 2004 survey respondents still reported having experienced one or more problems during the three-and-a-half year survey reference period. More than one-third of these respondents reported having experienced multiple problems.

Common problems, such as those relating to consumer transactions, were frequently reported by people from all walks of life. However, the 2001 and 2004 findings demonstrate clearly that differences in life circumstances entail differences in exposure to the 'defining circumstances' of problems and, consequently, differences in vulnerability to problems. As a result, the experience of problems was far from randomly distributed across the survey populations. For example, consumer problems tended to affect people on higher incomes; problems relating to relationship breakdown and children tended to affect people at distinct stages of life; problems relating to discrimination tended to affect black and minority ethnic people or people with a long-term illness or disability; and problems concerning unfair treatment by the police tended to affect young men.

Overall, those who reported long-standing ill-health or disability, lone parents, those living in the rented housing sector, those living in high density housing, those aged between 25 and 44, the unemployed, those on means tested benefits and those on very low incomes were found to be most likely to experience problems. Therefore, although there was also a tendency for those on very high incomes, those who had regular use of a motor vehicle and those with academic qualifications to report problems at a higher than average rate, it appears that people who are vulnerable to 'social exclusion' are also particularly vulnerable to justiciable problems. This was emphasised by the finding from the 2004 survey that there is a substantial commonality between patterns of crime and civil justice problems. Just under half of those respondents who reported having been victims of crime also reported having experienced one or more civil justiciable problems, and an even greater proportion of offenders did so.

However, reporting rates did not only reflect vulnerability. Justiciable problems can have a dramatic impact on people's lives and this, in turn, can be reflected in the profile of those who report them. Of particular concern, problems can sometimes constitute or lead to elements of social exclusion, and can, as the American Consortium on Legal Services and the Public have argued, undermine people's 'self-sufficiency,' and consequently also their capacity to improve their own position and contribute to broader society.[514] For example, the findings of the 2001 and 2004 surveys indicate that problems concerning employment, welfare benefits, rented housing, homelessness, domestic violence, relationship breakdown, personal injury, clinical negligence and mental health can not only follow on from, but can also lead on to ill-health or disability. Indeed, over one-third of all justiciable problems identified in 2004 were reported to have resulted in ill-health. Also, problems ancillary to relationship breakdown can lead to downward mobility in the housing market, loss of income and unemployment, and can adversely affect children's education. In addition, problems relating to employment and personal injury can bring about loss of income or unemployment.

Vulnerability to problems is not static, but cumulative. Each time a person experiences a problem, the likelihood of experiencing an additional problem increases. This is not just as a consequence of initial vulnerability, but also as a consequence of the increased vulnerability brought about by the impact of initial problems. Some 'trigger' problems, such as domestic violence and divorce, naturally bring about other problems, and these can be key elements of problem clusters, such as the three that are identified in Chapter 2.

One implication of this is that, as well as socially excluded groups being particularly vulnerable to justiciable problems, some justiciable problems can reinforce and bring about social exclusion. Promoting access to justice is therefore an important route to tackling social exclusion.

Of course, the findings set out in this book also demonstrate that policies concerning access to justice need to be set out in a broader context than that of social exclusion.[515] Justiciable problems are frequently encountered by people from all

---

[514] Consortium on Legal Services and the Public (1996), above, n.1, p.ix.
[515] This is particularly so as the government's interpretation of social exclusion appears narrower than that advanced in other countries. As Ardill has observed, 'unlike most European versions, the [Social Exclusion Unit definition] omits any reference to rights, participation in decision making or social justice': N. Ardill (2005) The Social Exclusion Trap, in *Legal Action,* August 2005.

walks of life and can have a great impact on their lives. Access to justice policy must therefore be broadly directed towards enabling all citizens to make effective use of the law and dispute resolution processes, so as to ensure that the framework of civil justice instituted in their name has legitimacy and meaning.

EDUCATION AND ENABLING PEOPLE TO ACT

The 2001 and 2004 survey findings confirm the diversity of people's responses to justiciable problems. Although fewer respondents to the 2004 survey reported that they took no action to resolve problems, it remains the case that inaction is relatively common. Furthermore, the problem types most closely associated with inaction – such as those concerning clinical negligence, unfair police treatment, mental health and domestic violence – are striking in how far they consist of problems associated with a substantial imbalance of knowledge, standing and institutional support and, also, with inter-personal conflict.

Reflecting the importance of personal capacity and experience to people's ability to resolve problems,[516] it is evident that those with qualifications, those who have acted to resolve problems in the past or live in households where people have done so, those who have the experience of age and (despite it rarely being mentioned as a reason for inaction) those who are aware of help that is locally available are all more likely to act to resolve problems than others. This last factor is of particular importance given how many people are unaware of local advice and legal services.

Coupled with the general finding that people's choices of advisers can be uncertain and unpromising, the apparent inability of many people to even start to act to resolve sometimes serious problems demonstrates the need for continued

[516] Building personal capacity recently emerged as one of the six key themes of the Social Exclusion Unit's report on the effective use of public services by disadvantaged groups: Social Exclusion Unit (2005) *Improving Services, Improving Lives*, London: Office of the Deputy Prime Minister. The report set out those vulnerable groups within society that are least able to make effective use of public services (such as people with low levels of literacy, people with long-standing illness or disability and people from certain ethnic minority groups). Interestingly, in the context of access to the courts, it has been argued that, as well as the most disadvantaged sections of the community, 'middle class' people also face particular difficulties. Those who are too poor to pay for effective legal assistance, but too well off to be eligible for legal aid, have been described as the losers in an 'access to justice j-curve': H. Kritzer (2005) Access to Justice for the Middle Class, in J. Bass, W.A. Bogart and F. Zemans (eds.) *Access to Justice for a New Century: The Way Forward*, Toronto: Law Society of Upper Canada. The recent Clementi review, recognising the barrier of cost to access to the courts, thus observed that 'high quality legal services [while] important to society, [are] of limited value if available only to the very rich or those paid for by the state': D. Clementi (2004) *Review of the Regulatory Framework for Legal Services in England and Wales: Final Report*, London: Department for Constitutional Affairs.

development of education and information strategies regarding rights, obligations, sources of help and methods for resolving justiciable problems. This is important both to equip people with an understanding of their responsibilities and to enable them to enforce their rights, factors that are both critical to the effective promotion of social justice. To adapt Cappelletti and Garth's famous pronouncement on the utility of rights, the possession of rights is meaningless if people are unaware of their existence or of the means through which they can be effected.[517]

Schemes of work for Citizenship within the National Curriculum set out a basic framework for understanding rights and obligations.[518] Further development could see this extend beyond human rights, rights of protection against discrimination, consumer rights and employment rights, and provide more of an emphasis on sources of information and advice about rights, and methods of dispute resolution. Of course, developments within the National Curriculum will only translate to improvements in understanding if properly implemented,[519] and in the main, they can only lead to improvements in the understanding of those who have not yet left school. More generally, therefore, the use and development of methods to raise levels of understanding among adults is also important. As Macdonald has indicated, basic methods of increasing awareness, such as distributing information through leaflets, videotapes, radio-spots and other (both fact and fiction based) media outlets 'can be very effective.'[520] Targeted distribution of information is also possible through organisations and individuals that routinely engage with the public, such as community groups or church leaders,[521] or services that are made available to the public at specific points in their lives. Macdonald provides the example of 'adding a

---

[517] 'The possession of rights is meaningless without mechanisms for their effective vindication': M. Cappelletti and B. Garth (1981) Introduction: Access to Justice and the Welfare State, in M. Cappelletti and B. Garth (eds.) *Access to Justice and the Welfare State,* Alphen aan den Rijn, Netherlands: Sijthoff and Noordhoff.

[518] See Units 7 and 8 of Key Stages 1 and 2, Units 3 and 16 of Key Stage 3, and Units 1, 3, 9 and 10 of Key Stage 4.

[519] See, for example, Office for Standards in Education (2003) *National Curriculum Citizenship: Planning and Implementation 2002/03: An Inspection Report of 25 Schools*, available for download at www.ofsted.gov.uk/publications.

[520] R.A. Macdonald (2004) Access to Justice in Canada Today: Scope, Scale and Ambitions, in J. Bass, W.A. Bogart and F. Zemans (eds.) *Access to Justice for a New Century: The Way Forward,* Toronto: Law Society of Upper Canada.

[521] As the Department for Constitutional Affairs and Law Centres Federation have noted, informal advisers such as these play a particularly important role in reaching those people, who because of 'language barriers or lack of confidence ... would otherwise be unlikely to access formal sources of advice': Department for Constitutional Affairs and Law Centres Federation (2004), above, n.12, p.40.

legal dimension to pre-natal classes.'[522] Thus, the current five-year strategy of the Department of Constitutional Affairs has 'front-line sources of first contact' and 'popular programming' among the 'priority channels' for delivering a new education, information and advice strategy.[523]

However, as Genn and Paterson have argued, methods of improving public knowledge and understanding such as those set out above will need to overcome the often inaccurate impression regarding rights and processes that people receive 'through the haphazard and selective reports of journalists, whose primary interest is in selling newspapers, and via televised representations of legal proceedings in which the principal objective is entertainment.'[524] Also, the success of any methods used will rely, to a great extent, on the commitment of those who promote them and the resources that are made available to implement them. The development of the Department for Constitutional Affairs' education, information and advice strategy, in so far as it seeks to operate across government departments and agencies, could play an important role in this regard. Importantly, also, the Legal Services Commission has greater scope and authority to promote knowledge and awareness of the civil law, dispute resolution processes and sources of help than the Legal Aid Board it replaced.[525] It now produces a broad range of general information leaflets,[526] hosts an information based website, and has funded a broad range of education initiatives – most notably through the second round of the Partnership Innovation Budget.[527] The development of information about people's rights is also one of three 'priority' areas

---

[522] R.A. Macdonald (2003) *Foundation Paper: Access to Justice in 2003 – Scope, Scale and Ambitions*, paper prepared for the Law Society of Upper Canada.
[523] These priority channels also include the education system in England and Wales, Community Legal Service Direct and limited web products.
[524] H. Genn and A. Paterson (2001), above, n.20, p.261.
[525] See, s.4 of the Legal Aid Act 1988 and s.4(2)(a) of the Access to Justice Act 1999.
[526] The Legal Services Commission produces 31 information leaflets, mostly covering specific areas of law. Specific leaflets, though, have been produced for veterans and for people who are living together. More information is available at www.clsdirect.org.uk.
[527] Legal education was one of two key themes of the second round of the Partnership Innovation Budget, leading to a number of projects being set up. For example, the Tamil Relief Centre was awarded a grant to employ an Information Officer to liaise with statutory, voluntary and community organisations to raise awareness of local advice services among refugees and people from minority ethnic groups in North London. Also, the Benefits Information Project enabled Hull City Council Welfare Rights Service to work with local organisations to improve the quality of legal information they provide: L. Macmillen and A. Walters (2005) Local Support for the Advice and Information Sector, in Legal Services Commission (ed.) *Innovation in the Community Legal Service*, London: Legal Services Commission, p.63, and Department for Constitutional Affairs and Law Centres Federation (2004), above, n.12, p.40. It has, though, been observed that, with the current pressure on its expenditure, the LSC does not in any event have resources for a legal education programme: A. Hannah (2004), above, n.7.

set out in the Legal Services Commission's consultation paper on its strategy for the Community Legal Service.[528] However, reflecting the use of the word *information*, rather than *education*, in s.4 of the Access to Justice Act 1999, the Legal Services Commission does not have a stated education strategy or dedicated education department or post; as does, for example, the New Zealand Legal Services Agency.[529,530]

However information and education is delivered, it is important that it stresses the many methods by which problems can be resolved, and states that legal process should generally be regarded as a rare and last resort. As Macdonald has cautioned, information and education must not 'co-opt citizens into thinking that they cannot obtain justice without the aid of lawyers, judges and official law.'[531] Such co-opting is, though, a possible consequence of information and education that sets out rights, obligations and processes in an overtly legal and/or technical framework.

Evidently, raising awareness of rights, responsibilities and options to enforce them is not all that is required to enable people to take effective action to resolve justiciable problems. As Genn and Paterson have also argued, drawing on Galanter's work of the 1970s,[532] individuals must have a broader 'capability' to act to resolve problems than simple understanding provides. They must, for example, be able to recognise problems, recognise when advice and assistance is necessary, and communicate effectively, whether in taking action on their own behalf, obtaining advice, or instructing others to act for them. Information and education are therefore necessary to enable people to take effective action to resolve problems, but not always sufficient. Those with language difficulties, poor verbal skills, or facing complex,

---

[528] Legal Services Commission (2005) *Making Legal Rights a Reality: The Legal Services Commission's Strategy for the Community Legal Service, Volume 1,* London: Legal Services Commission, p.37. The paper also, though, sets out an intention not 'to increase the amount of information provided.' Instead, the Legal Services Commission intends to support and facilitate access to 'trusted sources' of information (p.44).

[529] The distinction between information and education is an important one. As the National Consumer Council stated in its response to the consultation paper for the Review of the Regulatory Framework for Legal Services, 'education is concerned with knowledge, understanding, values, skills and attitudes.' It is concerned with empowering, rather than just informing.

[530] While the Legal Services Agency provides information services to the public in similar fashion to the Legal Services Commission – such as LawAccess, an on-line gateway to information on legal rights and responsibilities – it also creates 'standardised training packages for the delivery of education sessions on priority law-related topics': Legal Services Agency (2005) *Statement of Intent,* Wellington: Legal Services Agency. See also Legal Services Agency (2004) *Annual Report 2003-4,* Wellington: Legal Services Agency.

[531] R.A. Macdonald (2004), above, n.520, p.97.

[532] M. Galanter (1974) Why the 'Haves' Come Out Ahead, in 9 *Law and Society Review*, p.95.

intransigent or serious problems will often also require advice and assistance in order to act effectively. Also, as was noted in *Paths to Justice,* even 'the most self-reliant and confident people will, for certain types of problems, almost automatically obtain legal advice.'[533] Thus, as Giddings and Robertson have warned, information and education should not be regarded as cheap alternatives to advice and assistance.[534]

Furthermore, as indicated by the finding that many people take no action to deal with domestic violence because they are too scared to act, people facing certain types of problem may require not just advice and representation, but also broader support if they are to be able to act effectively.[535] This may require substantial co-ordination of advice and non-advice services. Those facing domestic violence may, for example, require emergency housing or shelter, perhaps arranged by a local council, as well as counselling, perhaps arranged through social or health services, if they are to be able to have confidence to act. However, as the recent World Health Organisation report on women's health and domestic violence indicated, such support can be difficult to provide (for example, in rural areas) and requires substantial commitment from all responsible agencies.[536] Also, if there are children involved, co-ordination of advice with education and social services, as envisaged by Part 2 of the Children Act 2004, is vital if the impact of violence on educational development and children's general well-being is to be minimised.

Also, to maximise the ability of people to act to resolve the justiciable problems they face requires that laws and legal instruments be framed in the clearest language possible. The results of three recent experiments conducted in Australia, comparing the use of a relatively simple model Australian Contract Code with a more complex code and with case law, indicated that clear and broadly framed laws are easier to understand and implement, and therefore improve the 'accessibility' of

[533] H. Genn (1999), above, n.3, p.253.
[534] J. Giddings and M. Robertson (2003) Large Scale map or the A-Z? The Place of Self-Help Services in Legal Aid, in 30(1) *Journal of Law and Society,* p.102.
[535] The same may also be true for particular population groups. See, for example, the discussions concerning co-ordination of services aimed at younger people in J. Kenrick (2002), above, n.323, p.24, and, more recently, Social Exclusion Unit (2005) *Transitions – Young Adults with Complex Needs,* London: Office of the Deputy Prime Minister, Chapter 5.
[536] World Health Organisation (2005), above, n.119, p.26. For details of the many recent government initiatives in this area see, for example, Home Office (2003), above, n.110 and Home Office (2005), above, n.110. For an example of a recent specific multi-agency initiative, set up in line with the Home Office's 'Break The Chain Multi-Agency Guidance for Addressing Domestic Violence,' see www.cheshire.gov.uk/domesticabuse. See, also, A. Griffith (2005), above, n.340, p.16, and M. Hester and N. Westmarland (2005) *Tackling Domestic Violence: Effective Interventions and Approaches,* London: Home Office (Home Office Research Study 290).

law.[537] However, as Moorhead and Pleasence have recently observed, the extent to which general simplification of the law is likely is unclear.[538]

BARRIERS TO ADVICE

The findings set out in Chapter 3 indicate that between one in six and one in seven people who seek advice to help resolve justiciable problems fail to obtain any. This is in part because the demand for particular advice services, and the manner in which they operate, can make it difficult for some people to access them. Findings from both the 2001 and 2004 surveys indicate, for example, that people frequently encounter difficulties in getting through to advisers on the telephone. This was, however, seemingly less of a problem for 2004 respondents, reflecting growth in the capacity of legal helplines and efforts by advice organisations (many of which routinely experience more demand than they have capacity to cope with)[539] to improve levels of access to advice over the telephone and other forms of advice. However, difficulties accessing advice organisations remain, and are often compounded by the hours during which services tend to operate. The findings in Chapter 3 suggest, for example, that people who work full-time can face real difficulties in accessing the many services that operate mainly during normal working hours.

---

[537] Interestingly, there appears to be an interaction between simplicity of law and consistency of decision making. Overall, the consistency of decision making did not vary between occasions on which the model code, alternative code and case law were applied. However, the model code appeared to lead to increased consistency in 'easier' decisions and decreased consistency in 'harder' decisions. Nevertheless, the researchers concluded that 'if anything' broad principles of law make decisions more predictable and more transparently fair. They also observed that 'detailed rules have a tendency to complicate even easier cases': M.P. Ellinghaus and E.W. Wright (2005) The Common Law of Contracts: Are Broad Principles Better than Detailed Rules? An Empirical Investigation, in 11(2) *Texas Wesleyan Law Review*, p.399, at pp.412-413. See, further, M.P. Ellinghaus, E.W. Wright and M. Karras (2005) *Models of Contract Law: An Empirical Evaluation of their Utility*, New South Wales: The Federation Press. The importance of clear laws and clear explanation of laws was also a key factor identified in a study of gateways to the law in New South Wales: S. Scott and C. Sage (2001) *Gateways to the Law: An Exploratory Study of How Community Agencies Assist Clients with Legal Problems*, New South Wales: Law and Justice Foundation of New South Wales.

[538] R. Moorhead and P. Pleasence (2003) Access to Justice after Universalism: Introduction, in 30(1) *Journal of Law and Society*, p.1.

[539] Nevertheless, Citizens Advice recently estimated that, each year, they 'have to turn away hundreds of thousands of individuals due to insufficient time and resources.' See Citizens Advice (2004) *Manifesto for Advice: The Role of Independent Advice and the Citizens Advice Service in Shaping Public Policy*, London: Citizens Advice, p.6. Citizens Advice do not as yet, though, operate a national telephone service. A mismatch of demand and supply has also been noted recently in relation to the solicitors' profession: House of Commons Constitutional Affairs Select Committee (2004) *Civil Legal Aid: Adequacy of Provision*, London: The Stationery Office, p.12.

While the resources that are currently available to advice organisations limit the extent to which they can develop their operations to mirror the behaviour of those who wish to use them, the findings in this book demonstrate the importance of continued efforts to do so.

The benefits of extended hours access to general advice services – the most common route into advice and legal services – and of the expansion of 'cost-efficient' telephone advice services are evident. Greater choice of times and methods of accessing advice should only increase the accessibility of advice.

In fact, already, as the findings from the 2004 survey demonstrate, although face-to-face advice remains dominant, the telephone has come to play a central role in people's efforts to obtain help in resolving problems. Initial contact with advisers was reported to have occurred more frequently by telephone than by any other means, and on more than one occasion in ten all the advice a respondent had received had been obtained via the telephone.

The Legal Services Commission's recent telephone advice pilot indicated that such advice, as well as evidently being preferred by some, is also valuable for those who face particular difficulties accessing other forms of advice service. Thirty per cent of reasons for using the pilot telephone advice service related to distance, disability or mobility problems.[540] It was also suggested that the pilot telephone advice delivered equivalent outcomes to face-to-face advice;[541] although the veracity of this claim could only be effectively tested through an experimental methodology,[542] for the reasons of self-selection of problem resolution strategies set out in the previous chapter.

However, as the Legal Services Commission's pilot report and the Constitutional Affairs Select Committee report on the adequacy of civil legal aid provision both warned, telephone advice should not be seen simply as a cheap alternative to face-to-face advice:

---

[540] J. Hobson and P. Jones (2004) Telephone Advice Pilot, in Legal Services Commission (ed.) *Improving Access to Advice in the Community Legal Service: Report on Evaluation Research on Alternative Methods of Delivery*, London: Legal Services Commission, p.9.
[541] *Ibid.*, pp.16-31.
[542] Some further evidence that telephone advice services can match face-to-face services in outcome terms was provided by a recent study of legal hotlines conducted in the United States: J. Pearson and L. Davis (2002) *The Hotline Outcomes Assessment Study: Final Report – Phase III: Full-Scale Telephone Survey*, Denver: Center for Policy Research. It found that those who met face-to-face with advisers following initial telephone contact fared no better than others. Again, though, the methodology was not of an experimental design. Also, for discussion of the role telephone advice can play in relation to specific client groups see, for example, R. Moorhead, M. Sefton and G. Douglas (2004), above, n.67.

'Telephone advice is not suitable for all clients and all problems. Clients need to be able to fully understand the advice that is given over the telephone; and the adviser needs to be able to discern the facts of the case and take proper instructions over the telephone or by correspondence ... The capabilities of the client influence the complexity of problem that can be dealt with.'[543]

People with complex problems or people with learning difficulties, language problems or similar difficulties are therefore unlikely to benefit from telephone advice. Likewise, they will be unlikely to benefit from expansion of other new methods of advice delivery, such as those employing personal computer technology.[544] In fact, as the Legal Services Commission has recognised, for people such as this, the ready availability of telephone advice may lead to an increase in demand for face-to-face advice.

The warning just stated is echoed also in the evidence of a recent large-scale study of legal hotlines conducted in the United States.[545] It found that there were clear differences in the capacities of different types of people to benefit from telephone advice. Those least likely to benefit had lower levels of educational attainment, did not speak English as a first language, had low incomes and had suffered a relationship breakdown. In European terms, they were the socially excluded. Furthermore, the study found that, on more than one in five occasions, those who obtained telephone advice had not acted upon it three to six months afterwards.[546] This was attributed primarily to a failure to understand the advice that had been given.[547]

The importance of face-to-face advice in relation to serious and complex problems and for people who are unsuited to other forms of communication is

---

[543] J. Hobson and P. Jones (2004), above, n.540, p.10; House of Commons Constitutional Affairs Select Committee (2004), above, n.539.

[544] Internet and e-mail based advice systems are being developed around the world. For example, the Illinois Joint Simplified Dissolution of Marriage Pilot saw the creation of a virtual advice process delivered via the internet. It employed a simple graphical interface in which an adviser asks simple questions that lead to progress down a virtual road towards a court building. See, for example, R.W. Stadt (2003) *Technology, the Courts and Self-Represented Litigants*, paper presented at the International Legal Aid Group Conference, Harvard University, 18-20 June 2003. Details of further development of this system can be found at www.judgelink.org. Expert systems can also be used to develop off-line systems, such as the Legal Guidedog series of self-help CD-Roms.

[545] J. Pearson and L. Davis (2002), above, n.542.

[546] *Ibid.*, p.32. A recommendation was therefore made that hotlines should 'institute or improve follow-up procedures' (p.78).

[547] *Ibid.*, p.76.

164

therefore clear. Moreover, the benefits of *readily accessible* physical locations where services can be obtained are evident. Only rarely did 2001 or 2004 survey respondents complain that they had been unable to obtain advice because an adviser had been too far away.[548] This is likely to have been at least in part because around one-third of respondents who obtained advice had visited a solicitor at some stage, and solicitors' firms are geographically well distributed across England and Wales. However, it will also have been due to the broad availability of telephone, internet and other forms of remote advice delivery. Thus, as people become more and more used to obtaining services via the telephone and internet, and as new technologies such as remote video-linking are perfected and become commonly used,[549] the need for local face-to-face advice may diminish. For the reasons set out above, though, the need is unlikely to diminish substantially or quickly in relation to socially excluded groups. Also, it should not be forgotten, as Holdsworth has pointed out, that people who experience the multiple deprivation of social exclusion rarely have ready access to new information technologies.[550] Indeed, for some of the most socially excluded people within the community, more active forms of face-to-face advice, involving different forms of physical 'outreach,' may be necessary if advice is to reach and be effective

---

[548] This sits in tension with recent suggestions that there exist 'advice deserts' in parts of England and Wales, in which there is little or no legal aid solicitor capacity: Citizens Advice (2004) *Geography of Advice: An Overview of the Challenges Facing the Community Legal Service,* London: Citizens Advice. Similar evidence was also presented to the Constitutional Affairs Select Committee enquiry into the adequacy of civil legal aid, including a claim from the Legal Aid Practitioners Group that 36 per cent of legal aid solicitors' firms had turned clients away 'in the current year' because they had 'run out of matter starts': House of Commons Constitutional Affairs Select Committee (2004), above, n.539, p.12. It should be noted, though, that the issue of geographical adequacy of supply is extremely complex. As the Advice Services Alliance's evidence to the enquiry recognised, geographical access is not simply a function of distance. They noted, for example, that 'many rural areas ... contain no legal aid suppliers, but people are used to travelling significant distances [maybe 20 or 30 miles] to access various services, or indeed do their shopping ... [Conversely] many people in large cities are unable or unwilling to travel a few miles to obtain the advice they need' (p.19). Moreover, there have always been areas of the country, particularly rural areas, where there are few (or indeed any) legal aid solicitors' firms. The geography of access is discussed further in P. Pleasence et al (2001), above, n.19, pp.58-70. However, the evidence of the 2001 and 2004 surveys certainly does not discount the possibility that there are problems of geographical access to advice and legal services. For one thing, the questions in the English and Welsh Civil and Social Justice Survey are concerned primarily with initial attempts to access advice. The question of geography was not explored in the context of referrals.
[549] See, for example, the use of remote advice kiosks in the East Ridings: R. O'Brien and R. Seymour (2005) Videolink Projects, in Legal Services Commission (ed.) *Innovation in the Community Legal Service,* London: Legal Services Commission. For an overseas example, see the video link operated by Legal Aid Queensland. Details available at www.legalaid.qld.gov.au/services.
[550] M. Holdsworth (1999) *Social Exclusion: Is Advice a Solution?* London: Advice Services Alliance.

for all those who may need it.[551] As indicated in the previous section, not all people who need advice will seek it. Advisers could therefore play a useful role if they placed themselves in environments where such people are frequently found.[552]

It is important that advice services mirror the behaviour and capacity of those people who wish to use them, and in doing so are physically and intellectually accessible. It is also important that they exhibit cultural empathy towards those people who may need to use them. In addition, it is important that services can be provided in the languages of those who may wish to use them. As suggested in Chapter 3, some minority ethnic groups appear less likely to act or seek advice about problems. Findings relating to the provision of both legal and health services suggest that culturally rigid services and the unavailability of multiple language service provision or translation facilities can present significant barriers to the obtaining of advice.

SIGNPOSTING AND THE CO-ORDINATION OF ADVICE SERVICES

The findings in Chapter 3 also indicate that, although barriers such as those described above commonly prevent people from obtaining advice, it is people's choices of adviser that most often undermine their efforts to do so. The most common reason reported by respondents to both the 2001 and 2004 surveys for attempts to obtain advice having failed was that a chosen adviser was unable to provide any help. In many cases this was because respondents had simply sought advice from the wrong place.

It is apparent that people seek advice from a wide range of types of adviser, and while choices of adviser are generally logical and apposite, they are sometimes, as noted above, uncertain and unpromising. There were also indications that some respondents who found an adviser was unable to help had been offered advice that failed to recognise their circumstances, was irrelevant or was otherwise defective. This emphasises the need for public legal education to extend to sources of advice, and for education and support to be provided to less qualified advisers, to ensure that

---

[551] The Department for Constitutional Affairs has recently indicated that 'active outreach' is an important advice delivery method for the socially excluded: Department for Constitutional Affairs (2005), above, n.294, p.34.

[552] For developments in this area see, for example, the Financial Inclusion Fund money advice outreach projects being developed by the Legal Services Commission: Department of Trade and Industry (2005), above, n.119, p.30. Given their lesser likelihood of seeking advice from mainstream advice services, outreach may serve a particularly important role in delivering advice to younger people. See, for example, J. Kenrick (2002), above, n.323, pp.17-20.

those who *do* provide assistance *can* provide appropriate assistance, even if this amounts to simply signposting people elsewhere.[553]

It also makes evident the need for clear and simple gateways to good quality advice. Some generally recognised routes for people to take to obtain help (across all aspects of life) would be of enormous help in this regard; perhaps along the lines of the 2-1-1 and 3-1-1 telephone information and referral access numbers being developed in North America.[554]

In circumstances where people seek advice from the wrong place, it is important that they are quickly and effectively referred on to an appropriate adviser. It is also important that the advisers people are referred to are as accessible as possible. If people are not referred on quickly and effectively, they will often give up trying to resolve problems without attempting to obtain advice elsewhere – a matter of particular concern given the possibility that problem resolution strategies can become entrenched. Alternatively, people may speculatively approach other advisers, who may or may not be able to help them. It is also of particular importance that people who may require *specialist* help are quickly directed to the *most* appropriate adviser, as the evident phenomenon of referral fatigue means that the more times people are referred on by advisers for further advice, the less likely they become to act on referrals.

Of course, developing the means to facilitate quick and effective referrals is far from easy. The Independent Review of the Community Legal Service, the Constitutional Affairs Select Committee report on the adequacy of civil legal aid and the Legal Services Commission's consultation paper on its strategy for the Community Legal Service have all drawn attention to the disappointing rate of

---

[553] This was recognised, for example, in Scott and Sage's study of how community agencies assist clients with legal problems: S. Scott and C. Sage (2001), above, n.537. They also pointed to the utility of expert systems to assist less qualified advisers in navigating legal issues. For an early discussion of the role of lay advisers, see, for example, G. Bellow (1968) The Extension of Legal Services to the Poor: New Approaches to the Bar's Responsibility, in A.E. Sutherland (ed.) The Path of the Law from 1967, Cambridge, Mass.: Harvard University Press.

[554] A recent cost-benefit analysis of the 2-1-1 information and referral network for health and human services estimated that it could contribute $1.1 billion of value to American society over ten years: D. O'Shea, C.T. King, S. Greenfield, E. Shelton, L. Sullivan, E. Taber and J.A. Olsen (2004) *National Benefit/Cost Analysis of Three Digit-Accessed Telephone Information and Referral Services*, Austin, Texas: Ray Marshall Center for the Study of Human Resources. In the United Kingdom the Directgov digital service already acts as a broad portal to web-based public service information: www.direct.gov.uk.

progress in developing (particularly active)[555] referral systems within the Community Legal Service, although improvements are recognised as having been made.[556]

As a matter of general principle, it seems that the effectiveness of referral systems depends upon the extent to which they are simple, active and reflect the behaviours of both people with problems and service providers. In a referral system that is largely passive and in which clients are 'signposted' (i.e. a system where the individual or organisation making referrals simply provides people with details of appropriate services), simplicity can be promoted by providing single, rather than multiple, options of appropriate services. As Pleasence, Maclean and Morley have noted, commenting on earlier work by Sherr, Moorhead and Paterson,[557] options can be something of a chimera when people have no knowledge or experience upon which to gauge their relative benefits.[558] From an adviser's perspective, simplicity can be achieved by making details of services readily available. This, for example, was a principal reason behind the production of the Community Legal Service Directory.[559]

In an active referral system, integrated booking systems – such as *Choose and Book*, the National Health Service's £196 million electronic booking system – provide greatest simplicity.[560] They also provide a means to audit the operation of referrals, which in this context means tracking whether the referral was successful. The resources necessary to develop and implement a system such as *Choose and Book* could be prohibitive. However, the electronic storage and exchange of data does offer the potential for the development of less expensive referral technology. For example, data on providers can be stored on web servers and standard software can be used to

---

[555] That is, systems where the individual or organisation making referrals makes arrangements for those they are referring to attend an appropriate service.

[556] Matrix Research and Consultancy (2004) *The Independent Review of the Community Legal Service*, London: Department for Constitutional Affairs, p.43; House of Commons Constitutional Affairs Select Committee (2004), above, n.539, p. 32; Legal Services Commission (2005) *Making Legal Rights a Reality: The Legal Services Commission's Strategy for the Community Legal Service, Volume 2*, London: Legal Services Commission, p.45.

[557] A. Sherr, R. Moorhead and A. Paterson (1993) *Franchising Legal Aid: Final Report*, London: Legal Aid Board, p.23.

[558] P. Pleasence, S. Maclean and A. Morley (1996) *Profiling Civil Litigation: The Case for Research*, London: LABRU.

[559] See for example, R. Moorhead and A. Sherr (2003) *An Anatomy of Access: Evaluating Entry and Initial Advice and Signposting Using Model Clients*, London: Legal Services Commission, who found little evidence that the Directory was being used by Specialist Quality Mark holders to signpost clients that the advice provider was unable to assist.

[560] See, for example, Department of Health (2003) *NHS Plan Booking Systems: Electronic Booking Systems: Scoping paper for the Strategic Outline Case for Information Systems for Health Community-Wide Booking*, London: Department of Health; and National Audit Office (2005) *Patient Choice at the Point of GP Referral*, London: The Stationery Office.

make bookings via advice services' websites. The National Health Service also provides examples of relatively low-cost web-based solutions, such as that adopted by the Countess of Chester Hospital NHS Foundation Trust, which allows general practitioners at 33 local surgeries in both England and Wales to transmit and receive referral information electronically.[561] It is also used to update patients' electronic records, so mitigating one of the principal concerns levelled at referral systems: that they can be administratively burdensome. A few electronic referral projects have also been set up in the advice and legal services context, and it is the intention that the CLS Direct telephone service should operate along these lines.[562]

The Independent Review of the Community Legal Service identified a number of concerns about the burden that referral protocols developed within Community Legal Service Partnerships were sometimes perceived to place on advisers:

> 'Some [advice suppliers] regarded the system as too complicated and overly bureaucratic; some identified problems with the time associated with complying with the systems ... [and] maintaining the database and information was cited as resource heavy.'[563]

A survey of general practitioners conducted for the National Audit Office to inform its recent review of *Choose and Book* also found referral processes to be generally perceived as adding to administrative workload.[564] Furthermore, in the context of active referrals, the report of the review went on to suggest that the administrative burden of referrals can be compounded, when choice is offered to those being referred, by that choice being exercised in 'unexpected ways.' People may ask for multiple referrals, referrals to organisations not provided as options, and may

---

[561] Reported in *E-Health Insider*, 8th September 2005.

[562] Legal Services Commission (2005), above, n.528, p.39. Elsewhere, the 'Wirral Wired' project run by Bebington Citizens Advice Bureau, for example, was set up to research and develop, among other things, an electronic referral system, including a directory and electronic diary. The South East Regional Partnership and Planning team of the Legal Services Commission has also been developing a system. Details are available at www.referralnetwork.org.uk.

[563] Matrix Research and Consultancy (2004), above, n.556, p.43. The report of the review went on to state that 'these problems have led to many of the referral systems [set up by Community Legal Service Partnerships] falling into disuse, with basic signposting likely to be a more common occurrence.'

[564] National Audit Office (2005) *Knowledge of the Choose and Book Programme Amongst GPs in England,* London: National Audit Office.

introduce additional considerations, such as the cost of transport, that act to complicate the decision-making process.[565]

Ultimately, of course, the success of a referral system depends on knowledge and trust. Those individuals approached by people with problems must, in the first instance, be able to recognise their many dimensions, as well as have an understanding of what is the best gateway into, or route through, the plethora of advice and legal services available. For those outside the recognised advice sector, the most appropriate referring action may often, at present, be to provide the telephone number of Community Legal Service Direct.[566] Where a dedicated advice service is the first organisation approached, the most appropriate action may most often be to direct people to specialist services that are already known about. Trust is also essential, as the extent to which service providers think *broadly* about appropriate services will depend on their belief in the competence of other providers. There is evidence to suggest that barriers may persist in this regard. For example, the findings of the 2001 and 2004 surveys confirm findings from other studies that solicitors tend to refer within sector to other solicitors.[567] Also, clients must have confidence that an organisation they approach is indeed acting to meet their need in making a referral, and not simply moving them on elsewhere. In this regard, as the National Audit Office report on referrals in the health sector argued, sufficient capacity should exist to ensure that referrals are not accompanied by unreasonable delay, and those making referrals should provide people with an explanation of the whole process that lies before them.[568]

In illustrating the wide range of types of adviser from which 2001 and 2004 survey respondents sought advice, the mixed success they had in obtaining advice and the apparent importance of advice in the successful resolution of problems, the findings set out in Chapters 3 and 4 indicate clearly the need for effective supervision and control of advice related activities. Of course, as the report of the Clementi review of the regulatory framework for legal services in England and Wales suggested, it would be unwarranted and impossible to impose a regulatory framework upon all

---

[565] National Audit Office (2005), above, n.560, p.19.

[566] This is a local rate number, 0845 345 4 345.

[567] See, for example, R. Moorhead and A. Sherr (2003), above, n.559. Also of interest here is Scott and Sage's finding that advice agencies in New South Wales often exhibit confusion about the nature and extent of services provided by different organisations. Tools to assist referral need to go substantially beyond just listing potential service providers: S. Scott and C. Sage (2001), above, n.537.

[568] National Audit Office (2005), above, n.560, p. 9 and p.19.

170

those organisations and people that engage in the provision of advice concerning legal rights, responsibilities and processes – i.e. those advisers making up Clementi's 'inner' and 'outer' circles of provision.[569] The problem of defining comprehensively what constitutes an advice service alone precludes such an all-encompassing framework.[570] Nevertheless, regulation and quality assurance – such as through the proposed Legal Services Board,[571] Professional Panel Schemes, Legal Services Commission's Quality Mark and peer-review system, etc. – is clearly fundamental to the proper working and integrity of the infrastructure of civil justice.

It is also important that *all* advice provided within Clementi's outer circle of advice services is acknowledged and integrated into broad civil justice policy. Moreover, the findings set out in Chapter 3 suggest an additional role should be acknowledged and supported for some individuals beyond the outer circle who currently act as occasional signposters. The findings suggest that those who have routine professional contact with people vulnerable to justiciable problems could have a far reaching role in actively looking out for the signs of problems and providing people with basic literature about these problems and/or signposting them to appropriate advisers. Some professionals, such as those in the health sector, are uniquely placed to view aspects of people's lives that might raise the suspicion of their facing justiciable problems,[572] although the skills of problem noticing would need to be developed through training or awareness raising.

Evidently, the problems that professionals might look out for should generally relate to their field. The utility of the role would otherwise be diminished, especially as there would be resource implications if professionals needed to be trained to spot

---

[569] D. Clementi (2004), above, n.516, p.94.

[570] As the 1988 report of the Committee on the Future of the Legal Profession observed, '"Legal Services" is not a phrase which is susceptible of a precise definition': R.M. Marre (1988) *A Time for Change: Report of a Committee on the Future of the Legal Profession,* London: Bar Council and Law Society. A study by Matrix Research and Consultancy recently set out thirteen types of people and organisations that might be classed as 'civil legal advice providers', along with a further twenty-five types of referrers and signposters: Matrix Research and Consultancy (2005), above, n.382, p.17 *et seq.*. In Germany, as noted above, the provision of legal advice was, until late 2005, restricted by law to lawyers. Nevertheless, if a survey such as the 2001 and 2004 surveys were to have been conducted in Germany prior to the change in law, it would no doubt also have found a broad range of informal advice providers. See, further, Kilian (2003), above, n.400.

[571] Department for Constitutional Affairs (2005) *The Future of Legal Services: Putting Consumers First,* Norwich: HMSO, p.12. See, also, D. Clementi (2004), above, n.516, and the new Legal Services Bill, currently awaiting Parliamentary passage.

[572] In Ontario, for example, the ability to respond to the broad range of legal and other problems that frequently accompany drug dependency has been recognised as an important aspect of treatment programmes: M. Erdelyan (2000) *Methodone Maintenance Treatment: A Community Planning Guide,* Toronto: Centre for Addiction and Mental Health.

problems and signpost those affected to appropriate advisers. Nevertheless, the benefits of increasing the likelihood of problems being resolved, or addressed at a point before they have had the chance to escalate or bring about further problems, could contribute enormously to efforts to reduce their impact and extend the jurisdiction of social justice. In fact, there are already examples of training being provided to enable professionals to spot justiciable problems on the part of those they serve. At least a proportion of doctors in England and Wales have received training in identifying domestic violence,[573] and the British Medical Association has published advice on good practice in identifying and dealing with the same issue.[574] Also, with effect from April 2004, the Police Reform Act 2002 amended Section 5(1) of the Crime and Disorder Act 1998 to make Primary Care Trusts responsible authorities within crime and disorder partnerships, in recognition that 'the NHS may be first contact point with professionals who can recognise and intervene in [cases of domestic violence].'[575]

In the early 1990s, the Legal Action Group asserted that 'a comprehensive view of legal services must include all legal advice, assistance, and representation, ranging from preliminary advice with a legal component provided by agencies like Citizens Advice Bureaux to the specialised advocacy services of Queen's Council.'[576] Today, it could be asserted that a comprehensive view of legal services must include even more than this. It must extend beyond the generalist gatekeepers to formal advice and legal services to all those types of individual or organisation to whom people routinely turn for advice, and even to those who might act simply as lookouts for problems. Clearly, though, this view gives rise to issues of responsibility, co-ordination and the control of the quality of such a broad range of legal services, and therefore presents considerable challenges to policymakers.

---

[573] P. Abbott and E. Williamson (1997) *Women, Health and Domestic Violence.* Paper presented at the BSA Medical Conference, 1997, reported in British Medical Association (1998) *Domestic Violence: A Health Care Issue?* London: British Medical Association.
[574] British Medical Association (1998), above, n.573.
[575] See, further, www.womenandequalityunit.gov.uk/domestic_violence. Also, see A. Tacket (2004) *Tackling Domestic Violence: The Role of Health Professionals,* London: Home Office (Development and Practice Report 32).
[576] Legal Action Group (1992) *A Strategy for Justice,* London: Legal Action Group.

JOINED UP SOLUTIONS TO JOINED UP PROBLEMS[577]

The findings set out in this book demonstrate the importance of dealing with justiciable problems not in isolation, but in the context of their causes and consequences. It has been shown how people's life circumstances can bring about justiciable problems, how justiciable problems can alter life circumstances, and how justiciable problems can thereby contribute to downward spirals in quality of life, health, economic circumstances, personal capacity and self-sufficiency. Justiciable problems frequently occur in combination. They frequently link to serious economic, social and health problems. In setting out patterns of experience of justiciable problems and the links between justiciable problems and problems of other types, this book therefore points to the additional considerations and areas of advice and assistance that those who provide advice should bear in mind and deliver. It also points to the broader roles that those who deal with linked problems could usefully take on to promote social justice more effectively.

In the context of legal advice, there are now many examples across the country of co-ordination of services between advice providers. This represents a significant change from the situation just a few years ago. Prior to the development of Community Legal Service Partnerships, as the Independent Review of the Community Legal Service noted, 'co-ordination between [advice] suppliers was either non-existent or ad hoc.'[578] The introduction of Community Legal Service Partnerships in 1998 by the Lord Chancellor's Department therefore represented a critical change in civil justice policy, as such partnerships constitute 'the first nationally co-ordinated attempt to develop a more seamless [advice] service.'[579] However, Community Legal Service Partnerships have not been as successful as was originally hoped, and have struggled to get off the ground in some areas of the country and failed to maintain themselves in others.[580]

---

[577] The phrase 'joined up solutions to joined up problems' was used to describe the purpose of the Social Exclusion Unit. See the 10 Downing Street press release of 25th September 2000, downloadable from www.number-10.gov.uk.
[578] Matrix Research and Consultancy (2004), above, n.556, p.14. For an account of the early development of Community Legal Service Partnerships, see R. Moorhead (2000) *Pioneers in Practice*, London: Lord Chancellor's Department.
[579] *Ibid.*
[580] See, for example, Legal Services Commission (2005), above, n.556, p.37. In terms of partnership activities directed towards particular populations, see, for example, J. Kenrick (2005) Young People Need Advice Too, in *Legal Action,* July 2005.

Effective partnership working is, of course, as the Treasury's *Working Together* report declared, 'very difficult to achieve.'[581] This is especially so in a context of constantly evolving policy and competing objectives,[582] and even more so in a context of limited resources. As Huxham has observed, 'effective collaboration is highly resource intensive.'[583] That does not, though, lessen the value of attempting to 'actively change the landscape of legal and advice services in order to improve access' and make services more reflective of people's lives.[584]

The report of the Independent Review of the Community Legal Service listed a number of problems lying behind the limited success of Community Legal Service Partnerships. These problems included, for example, uncertainty regarding the aims and functions of partnerships, as well as regarding accountability and control. It was also said to be a problem that while partnerships 'have been charged with identifying need and developing strategies to address need, [they] have not been able to access any significant new funding for unmet or unprioritised need.'[585] The Legal Services Commission's recent consultation paper on the Community Legal Service's strategy also noted resourcing problems within the context of Community Legal Service Partnerships, and further noted that conflicts of interest exist within their structure.[586] As a consequence of the various problems, the Legal Services Commission has therefore proposed withdrawing direct support for Community Legal Service Partnerships,[587] and refocusing its resources instead on the development of strategic partnerships with other funders of advice services and direct engagement with other public partnership structures.[588] It also intends to promote co-ordination of advice services through contracting arrangements, which will see the development of

---

[581] M. Frye and A. Webb (2002) *Working Together: Effective Partnership Working on the Ground,* London: H.M. Treasury, p.4.
[582] See, for example, P. Banks (2002) *Partnerships Under Pressure,* London: King's Fund. Also, M. Frye and A. Webb (2002), above, n.581.
[583] C. Huxham (1996) Advantage or Inertia? Making Collaboration Work, in R. Paton, G. Clark, G. Jones, J.M. Lewis and P. Quintas (eds.) *The New Management Reader,* London: Routledge, cited in A. Griffith (2002) *Partnerships and the Community Legal Service: A Discussion Paper,* London: Advice Services Alliance.
[584] Legal Services Commission (2002) *Post-Implementation Review of the Community Legal Service,* London: Legal Services Commission, cited in A. Griffith (2002), above, n.583.
[585] Matrix Research and Consultancy (2004), above, n.556, p.8.
[586] Legal Services Commission (2005) above, n.528, p.25 and p.31.
[587] Rather than bolstering them as the Independent Review of the Community Legal Service recommended.
[588] The Community Legal Service strategy consultation paper, for example, stated that 'whilst Community Legal Service Partnerships may remain as service provider forums they are likely to continue without direct input or support from the Legal Services Commission.' See Legal Services Commission, above, n.528, pp.31-32.

Community Legal Advice Centres and Community Legal Advice Networks.[589] The former are not dissimilar to the legal advice centres proposed by the Rushcliffe Committee in 1945,[590] and the proposals are evocative of neighbourhood law firms and Legal Services Centers in the United States, Community Legal Clinics in Canada, Law Centres in the United Kingdom, Community Law Centres in Australia and New Zealand, Bureaus Rechtshulp in the Netherlands, etc..[591] The Legal Services Commission's proposals are also, effectively, an extension of the approach adopted by Family Advice and Information Services launched in 2002.[592] The findings set out above indicate clearly that a further logical extension would be to adapt a similar approach in the context of criminal defence services.

Furthermore, the findings set out in Chapter 2 that illustrate the substantial concurrence of the experience of civil justice problems and criminality, suggest that co-ordination between civil and criminal justice services should extend to the National Offender Management System. The factors set out as 'key factors that influence re-offending' by the Social Exclusion Unit overlap considerably with the factors of vulnerability set out in Chapter 2 of this book.[593] If effective co-ordination of civil legal advice services with criminal defence services and the National Offender Management System were to have even a small impact on the ability of offenders to avoid criminal activity, this could have a great impact within communities and on the estimated £11 billion cost of re-offending by released prisoners every year.[594]

---

[589] *Ibid.*, p.70. The former is intended to offer a one-stop shop for advice on a range of connected problem types. The latter is intended to offer access to advice on connected problems through a network of advisers. The proposals tie-up with broader government proposals to allow for alternative business structures within the regulated legal services market: Department for Constitutional Affairs (2005) *The Future of Legal Services: Putting Consumers First,* Norwich: HMSO, p.21. See, also, D. Clementi (2004), above, n.516, and the new Legal Services Bill, currently awaiting Parliamentary passage.

[590] Rushcliffe Committee (1945) *Report of the Committee on Legal Aid and Legal Advice in England and Wales,* London: HMSO.

[591] The last of these have recently been replaced by *Juridisch Loket* offices, perhaps more akin to the gateway that might front a Community Legal Advice Partnership: P.J.M. van den Biggelaar (2005) *The Value-Added of a Good Gateway to the Legal Aid System,* paper presented at the International Legal Aid Group Conference, Killarney, Ireland, 8-10 June 2005. In general see, for example, Legal Action Group (1992), above, n.576. See, also, the discussion of methods of clinic organisation in R.A. Macdonald (2004), above, n.520, pp.41-42.

[592] J. Walker (2004) FAInS – A New Approach for Family Lawyers? in 34 *Family Law,* p.436.

[593] *Ibid.*, p.6.

[594] Social Exclusion Unit (2002) *Reducing Re-Offending by Ex-Prisoners,* London: Office of the Deputy Prime Minister, p.5. In the foreword to this report the Prime Minster, Tony Blair, stressed the need for 'improvements and innovations' targeted at reducing re-offending to '[carry] through into the community.' Also, on page 9 the report calls for a 'co-ordinated multi-agency response' to be 'sustained long after [prisoner] release.' See also, for example, Home Office (2001) *Through the Prison Gate: A Joint Thematic Review by H.M. Inspectorates of Prisons and Probation,* London: Home

Initiatives such as the Reducing Offending Through Advice project set up in the North East of England in 2004 and the placing of electronic information kiosks in local prisons in the East Midlands, represent important developments in this area. Furthermore, given the substantial overlap between the experience of civil justice problems and crime victimisation, victim organisations have a potentially important role as signposters in the civil justice system. The possible impact this could have is suggested by the fact that community-based Victim Support services assist 1.3 million people a year, and Witness Services help a further 400,000 people.[595]

Away from crime, as reported elsewhere, the relationship between justiciable problems and ill-health and disability requires that the identification, prevention, amelioration and resolution of these problems should be regarded as policy objectives for both public health and civil justice.[596] To some extent, the coincidence of health and justice policy objectives has already been manifested. At a strategic level, a number of Community Legal Service Partnerships and Health Action Zones have worked together to integrate aspects of service delivery that are mutually beneficial.[597] The setting up of Patient Advice and Liaison Services within National Health Service Trusts and Primary Care Trusts,[598] the creation of Independent Complaints Advocacy Services to assist those wishing to make complaints about NHS services,[599] the development of partnerships between Primary Care Trusts and advice agencies (enabling general and legal advice to be provided on-site in, say, general practitioner

---

Office. Interestingly, while the National Offender Management System Action Plan recognises a role for housing advice in successful rehabilitation, neither the current Business Plan nor Corporate Plan make any mention of advice: Home Office (2004) *NOMS Action Plan*, London: Home Office; Home Office (2005) *NOMS Business Plan 2005-06*, London: Home Office; and Home Office (2005) *Corporate Plan 2005-06 to 2007-08*, London: Home Office.

[595] Victim Support (2005) *Victim Support Annual Report and Accounts 2005*, London: Victim Support, p.5.

[596] P. Pleasence, N.J. Balmer, A. Buck, A. O'Grady and H. Genn (2004) Civil Law Problems and Morbidity, in 58(7) *Journal of Epidemiology and Community Health*, p.552.

[597] For example, the Leicester Community Legal Services Partnership, along with Leicester City Council, secured funding from the Leicester Health Action Zone to provide welfare benefits advice in general practitioner surgeries: Lord Chancellor's Department (2003) *Departmental Report 2002-2003*, Norwich: The Stationery Office, p.50. See also, for example, Legal Services Commission (2001) Joining Up With the Health Sector, in *CLSP News*.

[598] See, for example, Department of Health (2002) *Supporting the Implementation of Patient Advice and Liaison Services*, London: Department of Health.

[599] Department of Health (2003) *NHS Complaints: Making Things Right*, London: Department of Health, p.12. These Independent Complaints Advocacy Services would be commissioned or provided by Primary Care Trust Patient Care Forums, and delivered according to standards identified and disseminated by a new Commission for Healthcare Audit and Inspection.

176

surgeries),[600] and the training of health professionals in problem identification all provide examples of how this is possible.

However, integration of health and justice policy and operations is still at an early stage. The strategic development of Patient Advice and Liaison Services and the Independent Complaints Advocacy Services are only loosely integrated with the Community Legal Service.[601] The benefits of further integration and strategic co-ordination could be substantial. As the findings in Chapter 2 have highlighted, the National Health Service incurs substantial costs as a result of people experiencing justiciable problems. Furthermore, those who experience problems tend to be among the most vulnerable in society, and thus problems act to increase health inequalities, the tackling of which is 'a top priority' for the current government.[602]

Aside from integration of advice and health services, similar arguments can be made in relation to advice and social services, including SureStart, Children's Centres, Jobcentre Plus, education services, and many other government services.[603] Thus, a joint publication by the government and Law Centres Federation spoke of a commitment 'to see further links formed between legal and advice services and initiatives such as Jobcentre Plus, Connexions, New Deal, New Deal for Communities, Care Direct, SureStart, Crime and Disorder Partnerships, Education Action Zones and Health Action Zones.'[604] The findings in Chapters 2 and 3 indicate how and where further links might be developed.

More generally, the findings in this book should allow for a better understanding of social exclusion, and so help in the development of more effective

---

[600] In the last few years, a whole range of advice agencies have started to provide outreach advice, often relating to welfare benefits and debt, in primary health care settings. Details of outreach projects involving Barnsley, Chiltern, Hull, Nottingham, Oxford, Powys and other Citizens Advice Bureaux are set out in H. Perkins and L. Macmillen (2005) Primary Health Care Projects, in Legal Services Commission (ed.) *Innovation in the Community Legal Service,* London: Legal Services Commission. Citizens Advice Bureaux also provide outreach services in many hospitals across the country, such as Addenbrooke's Hospital in Cambridge. Also see, for example, Lord Chancellor's Department (2003), above, n.597; Legal Services Commission (2001), above, n.597; and S. Abbot and L. Hobby (2003) Who Uses Welfare Benefits Advice Services in Primary Care? in 11(2) *Health and Social Care in the Community*, pp.168-174.
[601] Indeed, the report of the first year of activities of the Independent Complaints Advocacy Service did not mention the Community Legal Service, although reference was made to the Legal Service Commission's *Quality Mark:* Department of Health (2004) *The First Year of ICAS: 1 September 2003 to 31 August 2004,* London: Department of Health.
[602] Department of Health (2002) *Tackling Health Inequalities,* London: Department of Health, p.i.
[603] Examples of integration can also be found in relation to such services. In the East of England, for example, a joint protocol between the Legal Services Commission and Jobcentre Plus was developed to facilitate access to advice: Legal Services Commission (2005), above, n.528, p.56.
[604] Lord Chancellor's Department and Law Centres Federation (2001), above, n.11.

policy to address it. As Hills has argued, the causes and processes of social exclusion are complex and multi-dimensional, and the chances of developing effective policy to combat them are therefore greater the more that is understood about them.[605]

CHANGE, AND CO-ORDINATING AND TARGETING RESOURCES

In this book it has been shown that justiciable problems are a matter of general concern, that they impinge on the business of and substantially contribute to the expenditure of many government departments,[606] and that they play a significant role as a cause, and in the processes, of social exclusion. The findings set out in this book therefore suggest that investment to develop the methods and services that will enable more people to benefit from early and effective advice should come from across government. Advice about justiciable problems is already funded by a range of government departments and agencies and local authorities, and resource intensive initiatives such as Patient Advice and Liaison Services, Independent Complaints Advocacy Services, Consumer Direct,[607] Consumer Support Networks,[608] the National Domestic Violence Helpline[609] and Financial Inclusion Fund debt advice projects[610] are evidence of a real interest in and commitment to assisting people to deal with justiciable problems across government. Evidence such as that presented in this book can only serve to heighten that interest and commitment. However, as with services (and 'solutions' more generally), public investment needs to be co-ordinated to reduce duplicity of effort, to prevent initiatives being at odds and to best bring about government objectives.

If the objective is to promote social justice and combat social exclusion, then the findings in Chapters 2 and 3 provide much in the way of guidance as regards decisions about where limited public resources should be targeted. Investment in education and awareness could, for example, be targeted towards those population groups most likely not to act because they do not think anything can be done about their problems. Investment in support services could be targeted towards those people

---

[605] J. Hills (2002) 'Does a Focus on 'Social Exclusion' Change the Policy Response', in J. Hills, J. Le Grand and D. Piachaud (eds.) *Understanding Social Exclusion*, Oxford: Oxford University Press.
[606] The cost of domestic violence alone has been estimated at over £3.1 billion per annum: S. Walby (2004) *The Cost of Domestic Violence,* London: National Statistics and the Women and Equality Unit.
[607] Details are available at www.consumerdirect.gov.uk.
[608] Details are available at www.csnconnect.org.uk.
[609] Details are available at www.womensaid.org.uk.
[610] Department of Trade and Industry (2004), above, n.119.

who are most likely not to act because they are scared or lack capacity to do so. Investment in advice services and problem noticing could be targeted towards those people most vulnerable to problems and those problems that are the most serious and have the greatest impact on people's lives. Again, investment in referral and quality assurance systems could be targeted towards those advisers to whom people naturally gravitate.

Of course, there is no reason for investment to emanate only from the public sector. In demonstrating the use of and potential demand for generalist gateways to advice and legal services, and the benefit that is gained from referrals from these gateways by advice services operating on a commercial basis, the above findings also suggest that investment could come from the private sector. For example, the market for legal expenses insurance has developed relatively slowly in England and Wales since its introduction in the 1970s and seemingly has potential to expand to provide easy access to general advice to a greater number of people than at present.[611] Also, the solicitors' profession, which is the beneficiary of a substantial proportion of referrals to specialist legal services from generalist advisers, could potentially benefit greatly from contributing to the development of a comprehensive networked referral system, as could other advice providers operating on a commercial basis.

The development of the infrastructure of civil justice could, then, be resourced from both the private and the public sector. However, the effective co-ordination and targeting of all resources is ultimately the responsibility of government. Thus, the key role for government over the years ahead will be a co-ordinating one. Just as the findings set out in the first edition of this book evidently assisted the development of Community Legal Service policy, it is hoped that the many new insights in this second edition will assist in further advancing civil justice and broader policy to enable the government to fulfil this key role.

---

[611] See, for example, M. Kilian (2003), above, n.400.

Appendix A

Overview

Chapter 1 explains that the problems to which the principles of civil law apply are not abstract legal problems, but for the most part problems of everyday life. It observes that legal process does not always provide the best means, or even a sensible means, through which to resolve such problems, as many alternative means of resolution exist. However, it asserts that the existence of a defining framework of civil law applicable to many problems of everyday social life and social well-being, and the possibilities for utilising legal services and process to reach solutions to such 'justiciable' problems when necessary, mean that the infrastructure of civil justice today plays an important role in realising social justice. It also plays an important role in tackling social exclusion. The chapter then introduces the English and Welsh Civil and Social Justice Survey, along with a survey of people living in temporary accommodation conducted in parallel with the 2001 survey. These surveys have allowed a comprehensive and unique analysis to be undertaken of the experience and impact of 18 categories of 'justiciable' problem (discrimination, consumer, employment, neighbours, owned housing, rented housing, homelessness, money/debt, welfare benefits, divorce, relationship breakdown, domestic violence, children, personal injury, clinical negligence, mental health, immigration and unfair police treatment), the difficulties people face in resolving them, and the degree to which advice, legal services and formal processes facilitate problem resolution.

Chapter 2 sets out the pattern of experience of justiciable problems across England and Wales, by describing the 36 per cent of 2001 survey, 33 per cent of 2004 survey and 84 per cent of temporary accommodation survey respondents who reported having experienced one or more problems in the three-and-a-half year survey reference periods. It provides a detailed analysis of how differences in life circumstances entail differences in vulnerability to problems, and why different rates of problem incidence are therefore associated with differently constituted population groups, both in general terms and within individual problem categories. As part of this, it describes the vulnerability of certain population groups to problems that can be constituent elements of social exclusion, and the particular vulnerability of socially excluded groups to the experience of justiciable problems. It also illustrates how vulnerability to justiciable problems is linked to geography and crime. The chapter then describes the distribution of problems among those respondents who reported having experienced one or more of them. It shows how the experience of problems has an additive effect; meaning that each time a person experiences one problem, they become increasingly likely to experience another. It illustrates how this additive effect can act to reinforce social exclusion. It also explains how certain justiciable problems are more likely to lead to others, and then demonstrates the extent to which justiciable problems also lead to broader social, economic and health problems. These broader problems are extensive and entail substantial public expenditure. Lastly, the chapter details how some problems tend to occur together or in sequence in problem clusters. Three distinct clusters are identified. These are characterised as family, homelessness and economic clusters.

Chapter 3 sets out the ways in which people deal with justiciable problems. It highlights the sense of powerlessness and helplessness often experienced by those who face them, and confirms there is a general lack of knowledge about obligations, rights and procedures on the part of the general public. It reports that no action was taken to resolve 19 per cent of problems reported through the 2001 survey, 10 per cent of problems reported through the 2004 survey and 28 per cent of problems reported through the temporary accommodation survey. It explains that inaction is particularly common in relation to some serious problem types (such as mental health and domestic violence), and also, apparently, more likely among some disadvantaged population groups (such as minority ethnic groups). It also reports that inaction owing to fear is common in relation to some problem types (such as neighbours and domestic violence). When action is taken to resolve problems, formal advice is sought on just under two-thirds of occasions, although it is actually obtained on fewer occasions. In describing the problems in relation to which people most often seek advice, the chapter demonstrates that advice is more likely to be sought in relation to more serious problems. It also explains, though, that awareness of advice services and previous strategies employed to resolve problems, including those of other household members, influence the manner in which problems are resolved. The chapter then details the many sources from which people attempt to obtain formal 'rights-based' and 'personal' advice (from solicitors to social workers, trade unions to politicians, and the police to the media), the difficulties they experience in doing so, and the nature of the advice and additional help received by those who are successful in doing so. Through this, it illustrates how people's choices of advisers, although often logical and apposite, can be uncertain and unpromising and, also, how people's choices can be undermined by the provision of services in manners that do not fit with their lives. In doing this, it reveals the extent to which the telephone is now used as a means to obtain advice. In addition, it exposes the phenomenon of referral fatigue, whereby the more times people are referred on to another advice service by an adviser, the less likely they become to act on a referral. The chapter also demonstrates the relative infrequency of court, tribunal and alternative dispute resolution processes being used as part of problem resolution process. Lastly, it details the people and organisations that pay for advice. It confirms that most advice is provided free at the point of delivery and, where advice is paid for, it is commonly paid for by legal aid, trade unions, legal expenses insurance and private individuals. It also observes that legal aid appears to be targeted towards more serious problems, in large part because it is focused on a relatively narrow range of problems and advice services.

Chapter 4 sets out the range of objectives that motivate people to act to resolve justiciable problems (such as obtaining an apology for a wrongdoing, obtaining or retaining money or property, obtaining or retaining a job, improving working conditions or securing access to children). It illustrates the different objectives associated with different problem types, problem resolution strategies, advisers and population groups. As part of this, it describes how objectives vary along with the consequences of problems, and confirms that certain problems are more likely to lead to others. It then details the ways in which problems conclude, and the extent to which people obtain their objectives. It points to evidence that resolutions are more favourable for those who obtain advice. It also suggests that those who are represented before courts and tribunals fare better than those who are not, and also that objectives are more often met in relation to more important problems. It also observes that those who obtain advice that is funded by legal aid appear to fare better than others who obtain advice. The chapter then explains how the duration of problems varies by problem and adviser type, and also, seemingly, by seriousness. Lastly, it shows that although people can benefit greatly from taking action to resolve justiciable problems, the resolution process can be stressful and even bring about ill-health.

Chapter 5 draws together the findings detailed in earlier chapters and sets out their implications. It suggests that the nature of justiciable problems requires that they should be of general concern, and that their prevention and resolution should be seen as a central part of efforts to tackle social exclusion. It also argues, though, that policies concerning access to justice need to be set out in a broader context than just that of social exclusion. Justiciable problems are frequently encountered by people from all walks of life and can have great impact on their lives. Access to justice policy must therefore be broadly directed towards enabling all citizens to make effective use of the law and dispute resolution processes, so as to ensure that the framework of civil justice instituted in their name has legitimacy and meaning. The chapter then highlights the role of education and information in raising awareness of the civic context of justiciable problems and the methods that can be used to resolve them, and stresses the importance of framing laws and legal instruments in the clearest language possible. While recognising the great difficulties involved, it underlines the importance of development and co-ordination of advice and other services so that people are able to obtain the help they need to resolve problems and to ensure that problems are not just dealt with in isolation once they have arisen, but also that their likelihood of occurring or leading to further problems is lessened through holistic and preventative action. It notes that the findings set out in this book indicate usefully how resources might be targeted towards problem prevention. The chapter then suggests that dedicated advice services should mirror the needs and behaviour of those who wish to use them. Noting the phenomenon of referral fatigue, the chapter highlights the importance of equipping those from whom people initially seek advice with the means to quickly and effectively refer them on to the most appropriate adviser, and the importance of accessible and good quality general advice services that act as formal gateways to the great array of advice and legal services. It suggests general access numbers, along the lines of the 2-1-1 and 3-1-1 information and referral numbers being developed in North America, would be a great help in this regard. More broadly, the chapter recognises the important role to be played by those who have routine professional contact with individuals vulnerable to justiciable problems in 'problem noticing' and signposting people to such gateways.

Finally, Chapter 5 discusses where investment should come from to develop the methods and services that will enable more people to benefit from early and effective advice. Given that advice on the resolution of justiciable problems is already provided under the remit of a range of government departments and local authorities, and that a range of government departments and local authorities can benefit greatly from the timely resolution of justiciable problems, it suggests that public investment should come from across government. It also suggests that public sector investment could be complemented by private sector investment. The development of initial advice and referral services will, for example, inevitably generate demand for commercial advice services. The chapter warns, though, that investment, as well as the development of the broad infrastructure of civil justice, must be properly co-ordinated and targeted to maximise the public benefit they deliver, and suggests that this is a key challenge for government.

Appendix B

Bibliography

Abbot, S. and Hobby, L. (2003) Who Uses Welfare Benefits Advice Services in Primary Care? in 11(2) *Health and Social Care in the Community.*

Abbott, P. and Williamson, E. (1997) *Women, Health and Domestic Violence.* Paper presented at the BSA Medical Conference, 1997, reported in British Medical Association (1998) *Domestic Violence: A Health Care Issue?* London: British Medical Association.

Abel-Smith, B., Zander, M. and Brooke, R. (1973) *Legal Problems and the Citizen: A Study in Three London Boroughs,* London: Heinemann.

Agresti, A. (2002) *Categorical Data Analysis* (second edition), Hoboken, NJ: Wiley.

Allan, G. and Crow, G. (2001) *Families, Households and Society,* Basingstoke: Palgrave.

Allan, G., Hawker, S. and Crow, G. (2001) Family Diversity and Change in Britain and Western Europe, in 22(7) *Journal of Family Issues.*

Allin, S. and Mossialos, E. (2005) *Inequity and Inequality in Health Care Use Among Older People in the United Kingdom,* paper presented at the British Household Panel Survey 2005 Conference, Colchester, 1st July 2005.

Amato, P. R. (2000) The Consequences of Divorce for Adults and Children, in 62 *Journal of Marriage and the Family.*

Amato, P. R. and Keith, B. (1991) Parental Divorce and the Well-Being of Children: A Meta-analysis, in 110 *Psychological Bulletin.*

American Bar Association (1994) *Legal Needs and Civil Justice: A Survey of Americans – Major Findings from the Comprehensive Legal Needs Study,* Chicago: American Bar Association.

American Bar Association (1994) *Report on the Legal Needs of the Low- and Moderate-Income Public: Findings of the Comprehensive Legal Needs Study,* Chicago: American Bar Association.

Ardill, N. (2005) The Social Exclusion Trap, in *Legal Action,* August 2005.

Ashton, C. M., Haidet, P., Paterniti, D. A., Collins, T. C., Gordon, H. S., O'Malley, K., Petersen, L. A., Sharf, B. F., Suarez-Almazor, M. E., Wray, N. P. and Street, R. L. (2003) Racial and Ethnic Disparities in the Use of Health Services - Bias, Preference, or Poor Communication? in 18(2) *Journal Of General Internal Medicine.*

Asian and Pacific Islander Institute on Domestic Violence (2002) *Fact Sheet: Domestic Violence in Asian and Pacific Islander Communities,* San Francisco: Asian and Pacific Islander Institute on Domestic Violence

Baddeley, A., Lewis, A. J. and Nemo-Smith, I. (1978) 'When Did You Last ...?' in Gruneberg, M. M., Morris, P. E. and Sykes, R. N. (eds.) *Practical Aspects of Memory. Volume 1: Memory in Everyday Life,* New York: Wiley.

Banks, P. (2002) *Partnerships Under Pressure,* London: King's Fund.

Bed and Breakfast Unit (2001) *Targets and Action for Reducing B&B – The Way Forward,* London: Department for Transport, Local Government and the Regions.

Bellow, G. (1968) 'The Extension of Legal Services to the Poor: New Approaches to the Bar's Responsibility' in Sutherland, A. E. (ed.) *The Path of the Law from 1967,* Cambridge, Mass.: Harvard University Press.

Bertakis, K. D., Azari, R., Helms, L. J., Callahan, E. J. and Robbins, J. A. (2000) Gender Differences In The Utilization Of Health Care Services, in 49(2) *Journal Of Family Practice.*

Bevan, G. (1996) Has There Been Supplier-Induced Demand for Legal Aid? in 15 *Civil Justice Quarterly.*

Bevan, G., Clisby, S., Cumming, Z., Davis, G., Dingwall, R., Fenn, P., Finch, S., Fitzgerald, R., Goldie, S., Greatbatch, D., James, A. and Pearce, J. (2000) *Monitoring Publicly Funded Family Mediation: Report to the Legal Services Commission,* London: Legal Services Commission.

Bevan, G., Davis, G. and Pearce, J. (1999) Piloting a Quasi-Market for Family Mediation Amongst Clients Eligible for Legal Aid, in 18 *Civil Justice Quarterly.*

Bindel, J. (1994) *The Hidden Figure: Domestic Violence in North London,* report prepared for Islington Council, London.

Bird, L. (1999) *Fundamental Facts: All the Latest Facts and Figures on Mental Illness,* London: The Mental Health Foundation.

Blackburn, R. M., Dale, A. and Jarman, J. (1997) 'Ethnic Differences in Attainment in Education, Occupation and Lifestyle' in Karn, V. (ed.) *Employment, Education and Housing among Ethnic Minorities in Britain,* London: HMSO.

Blacksell, M., Economides, K. and Watkins, C. (1991) *Justice Outside the City: Access to Legal Services in Rural Britain,* Harlow: Longman.

Bowen, E., Heron, J., Waylen, A. and Wolke, D. (2005) Domestic Violence Risk During and After Pregnancy: Findings from a British Longitudinal Study, in *BJOG: An International Journal of Obstetrics and Gynaecology,* Vol.112, No.8.

Bradshaw, J., Kemp, P., Baldwin S. and Rowe, A. (2004) *The Drivers of Social Exclusion: A Review of the Literature for the Social Exclusion Unit in the Breaking the Cycle Series,* London: Office of the Deputy Prime Minister.

British Medical Association (1998) *Domestic Violence: A Health Care Issue?* London: British Medical Association.

British Medical Association (2003) *Housing and Health: Building for the Future,* London: British Medical Association.

Bryson, A. (1994) *Information and Advice about Benefits,* London: Policy Studies Institute.

Buck, A., Pleasence, P., Balmer, N. J., O'Grady A. and Genn, H. (2004) Lone Parents and Civil Law: Their Experience of Problems and Their Advice Seeking Behaviour, in *Social Policy and Administration,* Vol.38, No.3.

Burrows, R. (1997) 'The Social Distribution of the Experience of Homelessness' in Burrows, R., Pleace, N. and Quilgars, D. (eds.) *Homelessness and Social Policy,* London: Routledge.

Cappelletti, M. and Garth, B. (1981) 'Introduction: Access to Justice and the Welfare State' in Cappelletti, M. and Garth, B. (eds.) *Access to Justice and the Welfare State,* Alphen aan den Rijn, Netherlands: Sijthoff and Noordhoff.

Casebourne, J. et al. *Findings from the Individuals' Awareness Knowledge and Exercise of Employment Rights Second Benchmark Survey.* London: Department of Trade and Industry Employment Relations Research Series Number 51, forthcoming.

186

Casey, B. and Creigh, S. (1988) Self-employment in Great Britain: Its definition in the Labour Force Survey, in tax and social security law, and in labour law, in 2 *Work, Employment and Society.*

Cass, M. and Sackville, R. (1975) *Legal Needs for the Poor,* Canberra: Australian Government Publishing Service.

Chambaz, C. (2001) Lone Parent Families in Europe: A Variety of Economic and Social Circumstances, in 35(6) *Journal of Social Policy and Administration.*

Chapman, P. and Underwood, G. (2000) Forgetting Near-Accidents: The Roles of Severity, Culpability and Experience in the Poor Recall of Dangerous Driving Situations, in 14(1) *Applied Cognitive Psychology.*

Chief Medical Officer (2003) *Making Amends: A Consultation Paper Setting Out Proposals for Reforming the Approach to Clinical Negligence in the NHS,* London: Department of Health.

Chung, R., Donaldson, D., Herring, I., McColl, H., Snow, J., Cockerham, J., Ellerd-Elliott, S., Hirani, B. and Shome, J. (2004) *Family Resources Survey,* London: Department for Work and Pensions.

Citizens Advice (2002) *Annual Report,* London: Citizens Advice.

Citizens Advice (2004) *Geography of Advice - An Overview of the Challenges Facing the Community Legal Service,* London: Citizens Advice.

Citizens Advice (2004) *Manifesto for Advice: The Role of Independent Advice and the Citizens Advice Service in Shaping Public Policy,* London: Citizens Advice.

Citizens Advice (2005) *Annual Report,* London: Citizens Advice.

Clark, C. and Corstvet, E. (1938) The Lawyer and the Public: An A.A.L.S. Survey, in 47 *Yale Law Journal.*

Clementi, D. (2004) *Review of the Regulatory Framework for Legal Services in England and Wales: Final Report,* London: Department for Constitutional Affairs.

Cole, B. (2002) *Law Society Annual Statistical Report,* London: Law Society.

Cole, B. (2005) *Law Society Annual Statistical Report,* London: Law Society.

Consortium on Legal Services and the Public (1996) *Agenda for Access: The American People and Civil Justice,* Chicago: American Bar Association.

Consumers' Association (2000) *The Community Legal Service: Access for All?* London: Consumers' Association.

Coumarelos, C., Wei, Z. and Zhou, A. (2006) *Multiple Pathways to Justice in Disadvantaged Communities: NSW Legal Needs Survey 2003,* Sydney: Law and Justice Foundation of New South Wales.

Craig, G., Dornan, P., Bradshaw, J., Garbutt, R., Mumtaz, S., Syed, A. and Ward, A. (2002) *Understanding Citizenship for Older People: The Impact of Additional Benefit Income for Older People,* London: National Audit Office.

Crane, M. and Warnes, A. (2000) Evictions and Prolonged Homelessness, in *Housing Studies,* Vol.15, No.5.

Crane, M. and Warnes, A. M. (2000) Policy and Service Responses to Rough Sleeping Among Older People, in 29 *Journal of Social Policy.*

Curran, B. (1977) *The Legal Needs of the Public,* Chicago: American Bar Foundation.

Currie, A. (2005) *A National Survey of the Civil Justice Problems of Low And Moderate Income Canadians: Incidence and Patterns*, paper presented at the ILAG conference, Killarney, Ireland, 8-10 June 2005.

Dale, A. (1986) Social Class and the Self-Employed, in 20 *Sociology.*

Datamonitor (2005) *UK Personal Injury Litigation 2004*, London: Datamonitor.

Davis, G., Bevan, G., Clisby, S., Cumming, Z., Dingwall, R., Fenn, P., Finch, S., Fitzgerald, R., Goldie, S., Greatbach, D., James, D. and Pearce, J. (2000)

Monitoring Publicly Funded Family Mediation, London: Legal Services Commission.

Davis, G., Cretney, S. and Collins, J. (1994) *Simple Quarrels: Negotiations and Adjudications in Divorce,* Oxford: Clarendon Press.

Deadman, D. and MacDonald, Z. (2004) Offenders as victims of crime?: an investigation into the relationship between criminal behaviour and victimization, in the *Journal of the Royal Statistical Society,* Vol. 167, Part 1.

Department for Constitutional Affairs (2005) *A Fairer Deal For Legal Aid,* Norwich: HMSO.

Department for Constitutional Affairs (2005) *The Future of Legal Services: Putting Consumers First,* Norwich: HMSO.

Department for Constitutional Affairs and Law Centres Federation (2004) *Legal and Advice Services: A Pathway to Regeneration,* London: Lord Chancellor's Department.

Department of Health (2002) *Supporting the Implementation of Patient Advice and Liaison Services,* London: Department of Health.

Department of Health (2002) *Tackling Health Inequalities,* London: Department of Health.

Department of Health (2003) *NHS Complaints: Making Things Right,* London: Department of Health.

Department of Health (2003) *NHS Plan Booking Systems: Electronic Booking Systems: Scoping Paper for the Strategic Outline Case for Information Systems for Health Community-Wide Booking,* London: Department of Health.

Department of Health (2004) *The First Year of ICAS: 1 September 2003 to 31 August 2004,* London: Department of Health.

Department of Trade and Industry (2004) *Over-Indebtedness in Britain: A DTI Report on the MORI Financial Services Survey 2004,* London: Department of Trade and Industry.

Department of Trade and Industry (2005) *Tackling Over-Indebtedness: Annual Report 2005,* London: HMSO.

Dignan, T. (2004) *Legal Need in Northern Ireland: Literature Review,* Belfast: Northern Ireland Legal Services Commission.

Dixon, A., Le Grand, J., Henderson, J., Murray, R. and Poteliakhoff, E. (2003) *Is the NHS Equitable? A Review of the Evidence,* London: London School of Economics (Health and Social Care Discussion Paper Number 11).

Dodd, T., Nicholas, S., Povey, D. and Walker, A. (2004) *Crime in England and Wales 2003/2004,* London: Home Office (Home Office Statistical Bulletin 10/04).

Donovan, N., Brown, J. and Bellulo, L. (2001) *Satisfaction with Public Services: A Discussion Paper,* London: Cabinet Office.

Down, D. (2002) *Family Spending: A Report on the 2000-01 Family Expenditure Survey,* London: The Stationery Office.

Dozier, A. M., Kitzman, H. J., Ingersoll, G. L., Holmberg, S. and Schultz, A. W. (2001) Development of an Instrument to Measure Patient Perception of the Quality of Nursing Care, in 24 *Research in Nursing and Health.*

Easterlow, D., Smith, S. J. and Mallinson, S. (2000) Housing for Health: The Role of Owner Occupation, in 15 *Housing Studies.*

Edwards, S. (2003) *In Too Deep: CAB Clients' Experience of Debt,* London: Citizens Advice Bureaux.

Eekelaar, J., Maclean, M. and Beinart, S. (2000) *Family Lawyers: The Divorce Work of Solicitors,* Oxford: Hart Publications.

188

Ellinghaus, M. P. and Wright, E. W. (2005) The Common Law of Contracts: Are Broad Principles Better than Detailed Rules? An Empirical Investigation, in 11(2) *Texas Wesleyan Law Review.*

Ellinghaus, M. P., Wright, E. W. and Karras, M. (2005) *Models of Contract Law: An Empirical Evaluation of their Utility,* New South Wales: The Federation Press.

Ellison, S., Schetzer, L., Mullins, J., Perry, J. and Wong, K. (2004) *Access to Justice and Legal Needs: The Legal Needs of Older People in New South Wales,* Sydney: Law and Justice Foundation of New South Wales.

Ellsberg, M., Winkvist, A., Heise, L., Peña, R. and Agurto, S. (2001) Researching Domestic Violence Against Women: Methodological and Ethical Considerations, in 32(1) *Studies In Family Planning.*

Erdelyan, M. (2000) *Methodone Maintenance Treatment: A Community Planning Guide,* Toronto: Centre for Addiction and Mental Health.

Everitt, B. S., Landau, S. and Leese, M. (2001) *Cluster Analysis,* London: Arnold.

Felstiner, W., Abel, R. and Sarat, A. (1981) The Emergence and Transformation of Disputes: Naming, Blaming, Claiming …, in 15 *Law and Society Review.*

Fenn, P., Gray, A., Rickman, N. and Carrier, H. (2002) *The Impact of Conditional Fees on the Selection, Handling and Outcome of Personal Injury Cases,* London: Lord Chancellor's Department.

Frye, M. and Webb, A. (2002) *Working Together: Effective Partnership Working on the Ground,* London: H.M. Treasury.

Gadd, D., Farrall, S., Dallimore, D. and Lombard, N. (2002) *Domestic Abuse Against Men in Scotland,* Edinburgh: Scottish Office Central Research Unit.

Galanter, M. (1974) Why the 'Haves' Come Out Ahead, in 9 *Law and Society Review.*

Gee, G. C. (2002) A Multilevel Analysis of the Relationship Between Institutional and Individual Racial Discrimination and Health Status, in 92 *American Journal of Public Health.*

Genn, H. (1988) 'Multiple Victimisation' in Maguire, M. (ed.) *Victims of Crime: A New Deal?,* Milton Keynes: Open University Press.

Genn, H. (1999) *Paths to Justice: What People Do and Think About Going to Law,* Oxford: Hart Publishing.

Genn, H., Lever, B. and Gray, L. (2006) *Tribunals for Diverse Users,* London: Department for Constitutional Affairs.

Genn, H. and Lloyd-Bostock, S. (1995) *Medical Negligence Research Project: The Operation of the Tort System in Medical Negligence Cases,* London: HMSO.

Genn, H. and Paterson, A. (2001) *Paths to Justice Scotland: What People in Scotland Do and Think About Going to Law,* Oxford: Hart Publishing.

Gibbins, C. (2004) *Family Spending: A Report on the 2003-04 Expenditure and Food Survey,* London: The Stationery Office.

Gibbons, S. and Machin, S. (2003) Valuing English Primary Schools, in 53 *Journal of Urban Economics.*

Giddings, J. and Robertson, M. (2003) Large Scale Map or the A-Z? The Place of Self-Help Services in Legal Aid, in 30(1) *Journal of Law and Society.*

Goriely, T. (1997) *Resolving Civil Disputes: Choosing Between Out of Court Schemes and Litigation,* London: Lord Chancellor's Department.

Goriely, T. (1998) 'Making the Welfare State Work' in Regan, F., Paterson, A., Goriely, T., and Fleming, D. (eds.) *The Transformation of Legal Aid,* Oxford: Oxford University Press.

Griffith, A. (2002) *Partnerships and the Community Legal Service: A Discussion Paper,* London: Advice Services Alliance.

Griffith, A. (2005) *Regional Planning and Its Limitations*, London: Advice Services Alliance.

H.M. Government (2005) *Opportunity Age - Meeting the Challenges of Ageing in the 21st Century*, London: The Stationery Office.

Hannah, A. (2004) 'Exercising Rights as the Way to Social Inclusion' in Grieve, J., and Howard, R. (eds.) *Communities, Social Inclusion and Crime*, London: Smith Institute.

Harris, D., Maclean, M., Genn, H., Lloyd-Bostock, S., Fenn, P., Corfield, P. and Brittan, Y. (1984) *Compensation and Support for Illness and Injury*, Oxford: Clarendon Press.

Haskey, J. (1998) One Parent Families and their Dependent Children in Great Britain, in 91 *Population Trends*.

Hester, M. and Westmarland, N. (2005) *Tackling Domestic Violence: Effective Interventions and Approaches*, London: Home Office (Home Office Research Study 290).

Hills, J. (2002) 'Does a Focus on 'Social Exclusion' Change the Policy Response' in Hills, J., Le Grand, J. and Piachaud, D. (eds.) *Understanding Social Exclusion*, Oxford: Oxford University Press.

Hobson, J. and Jones, P. (2003) *Methods of Delivery: Telephone Advice Pilot: Evaluation Report*, London: Legal Services Commission.

Hobson, J. and Jones, P. (2004) 'Telephone Advice Pilot' in Legal Services Commission (ed.) *Improving Access to Advice in the Community Legal Service: Report on Evaluation Research on Alternative Methods of Delivery*, London: Legal Services Commission.

Holdsworth, M. (1999) *Social Exclusion: Is Advice a Solution?* London: Advice Services Alliance.

Home Office (2001) *Through the Prison Gate: A Joint Thematic Review by H.M. Inspectorates of Prisons and Probation*, London: Home Office.

Home Office (2003) *Safety and Justice: The Government's Proposals on Domestic Violence*, London: The Stationery Office.

Home Office (2004) *NOMS Action Plan*, London: Home Office.

Home Office (2005) *Corporate Plan 2005-06 to 2007-08*, London: Home Office.

Home Office (2005) *Domestic Violence: A National Report*, London: Home Office.

Home Office (2005) *NOMS Business Plan 2005-06*, London: Home Office.

House of Commons Constitutional Affairs Select Committee (2004) *Civil Legal Aid: Adequacy of Provision*, London: The Stationery Office.

Howard, M. (1999) *Enabling Government: Joined up Policies for a National Disability Strategy*, London: Fabian Society.

Howard, M., Garnham, A., Fimister, G. and Veit-Wilson, J. (2001) *Poverty: The Facts*, London: CPAB.

Hughes Commission (1980) *Report of the Royal Commission on Legal Services in Scotland*, Edinburgh: HMSO (Cmd. 7846).

Hughes, B. (2002) Bauman's Strangers: Impairment and the Invalidation of Disabled People in Modern and Post-Modern Cultures, in 17 *Disability and Society*.

Hughes, S. (2002) *Addressing the Advice Needs of Black and Minority Ethnic Communities*, Brighton: Brighton and Hove Community Legal Service Partnership.

Hunt, S. (1997) 'Housing Related Disorders' in Charlton, J., and Murphy, M. (eds.) *The Health of Adult Britain 1841-1994*, London: The Stationery Office.

Huxham, C. (1996) 'Advantage or Inertia? Making Collaboration Work' in Paton, R., Clark, G., Jones, G., Lewis, J. M. and Quintas, P. (eds.) *The New Management Reader,* London: Routledge.

Jones, J. R., Huxtable, C. S. and Hodgson, J. T. (2001) *Self-Reported Work-Related Illness in 1998/99: Results from EUROSTAT Ill-Health Module in the 1999 Labour Force Summer Quarter,* London: Health and Safety Executive.

Kenrick, J. (2002) *Rights to Access: Meeting Young People's Needs for Advice,* London: Youth Access.

Kenrick, J. (2005) Young People Need Advice Too, in *Legal Action,* July 2005.

Kershaw, C., Budd, T., Kinshott, G., Mattinson, J., Mayhew, P. and Myhill, A. (2000) *The 2000 British Crime Survey,* London: Home Office (Home Office Statistical Bulletin 18/00).

Kilian, M. (2003) Alternatives to Public Provision: The Role of Legal Expenses Insurance in Broadening Access to Justice: The German Experience, in 30(1) *Journal of Law and Society.*

Kitson, G. R. and Morgan, L. A. (1990) The Multiple Consequences of Divorce: A Decade Review, in 52 *Journal of Marriage and the Family.*

Kritzer, H. (2005) 'Access to Justice for the Middle Class' in Bass, J., Bogart, W. A. and Zemans, F. (eds.) *Access to Justice for a New Century: The Way Forward,* Toronto: Law Society of Upper Canada.

Kyambi, S. (2005) *Beyond Black and White: Mapping New Immigrant Communities,* London: Institute for Public Policy Research.

Kyriacou, D. N., Anglin, D., Taliaferro, E., Stone, S., Tubb, T., Linden, J.A., Muelleman, R., Barton, E. and Kraus, J. F. (1999) Risk Factors For Injury To Women From Domestic Violence, in 341(25) *New England Journal Of Medicine.*

Law Commission (1994) *Personal Injury Compensation: How Much is Enough?* London: Law Commission (Report No. 225).

Law, J., Assenti, S., Barton, G., McKissock, K., Baker, D., Ballow, S. and Cookson, D. (2004) *Community Legal Service: Assessing Need for Legal Advice in Scotland,* Edinburgh: The Stationery Office.

Legal Action Group (1992) *A Strategy for Justice,* London: Legal Action Group.

Legal Services Agency (2004) *Annual Report 2003-4,* Wellington: Legal Services Agency.

Legal Services Agency (2005) *Statement of Intent,* Wellington: Legal Services Agency.

Legal Services Commission (2001) Joining Up With the Health Sector, in *CLSP News.*

Legal Services Commission (2002) *Corporate Plan 2002/3-2003/4,* London: Legal Services Commission.

Legal Services Commission (2002) *Post-Implementation Review of the Community Legal Service,* London: Legal Services Commission.

Legal Services Commission (2003) *Community Legal Services Directory* (fifth edition), London: Legal Services Commission.

Legal Services Commission (2005) *Annual Report 2004/5,* London: The Stationery Office.

Legal Services Commission (2005) *Corporate Plan 2005/6-2007/8,* London: Legal Services Commission.

Legal Services Commission (2005) *Making Legal Rights a Reality: The Legal Services Commission's Strategy for the Community Legal Service, Volume 1,* London: Legal Services Commission.

Legal Services Commission (2005) *Making Legal Rights a Reality: The Legal Services Commission's Strategy for the Community Legal Service, Volume 2*, London: Legal Services Commission.

Legal Services Research Centre (2002) *Summary Technical and Baseline Report on the Lord Chancellor's Department's SR2000 PSA Targets 5 and 6*, London: Legal Services Research Centre.

Legal Services Research Centre (2005) *Summary Technical Report on Measures for the LCD/DCA SR2000 PSA Targets 5 and 6 / SR2002 PSA Target 6 / SR2004 PSA Target 5*, London: Legal Services Research Centre.

Lewis, P. (1973) 'Unmet Legal Needs' in Morris, P., White R., and Lewis, P. (eds.) *Social Needs and Legal Action*, Oxford: Martin Robertson.

Lord Chancellor's Department (1998) *Modernising Justice*, London: HMSO.

Lord Chancellor's Department (2003) *Departmental Report 2002-2003*, Norwich: The Stationery Office.

Lord Chancellor's Department and Law Centres Federation (2001) *Legal and Advice Services: A Pathway Out of Social Exclusion*, London: Lord Chancellor's Department.

Macdonald, R. A. (2003) *Foundation Paper: Access to Justice in 2003 – Scope, Scale and Ambitions*, paper prepared for the Law Society of Upper Canada.

Macdonald, R. A. (2004) 'Access to Justice in Canada Today: Scope, Scale and Ambitions' in Bass, J., Bogart, W. A., and Zemans, F. (eds.) *Access to Justice for a New Century: The Way Forward*, Toronto: Law Society of Upper Canada.

Macmillen, L. and Walters, A. (2005) 'Local Support for the Advice and Information Sector' in Legal Services Commission (ed.) *Innovation in the Community Legal Service*, London: Legal Services Commission.

Maguire, M., Morgan, R. and Reiner, R. (eds.) *The Oxford Handbook of Criminology*, third edition, Oxford: Oxford University Press.

Maher, J. and Green, H. (2002) *Carers 2000*, London: The Stationery Office.

Marcell, A. V., Klein, J. D., Fischer, I., Allan, M. K. and Kokotailo, P. K. (2002) Male Adolescent Use Of Health Care Services: Where Are The Boys? in 30(1) *Journal Of Adolescent Health*.

Marre, R. M. (1988) *A Time for Change: Report of a Committee on the Future of the Legal Profession*, London: Bar Council and Law Society.

Marsh, A. and Perry, J. (2003) *Family Change 1999-2001*, London: Department for Work and Pensions.

Matrix Research and Consultancy (2004) *The Independent Review of the Community Legal Service*, London: Department for Constitutional Affairs.

Matrix Research and Consultancy (2005) *Estimating the Size and Nature of the Civil Legal Advice Sector in England and Wales*, London: Matrix.

Maxwell, G., Smith, C., Shepherd, P. and Morris, A. (1999) *Meeting Legal Service Needs: Research Report Prepared for the Legal Services Board*, Wellington: Legal Services Board.

McCullagh, P. (1980) Ordinal Regression Models, in 42(2) *Journal of the Royal Statistical Society, Series B (Methodological)*.

Means, B. and Loftus, E. (1991) When Personal History Repeats Itself: Decomposing Memories for Recurring Events, in 5 *Applied Cognitive Psychology*.

Meltzer, D., Fryers, T. and Jenkins, R. (2002) *Social Inequalities and the Distribution of Common Mental Disorders*, Cambridge: Institute of Public Health.

Messier, C. (1975) *Les Mains de la Loi* (In the Hands of the Law), Montreal: Commission des Services Jurisdiques.

Millar, C. (1999) *Referrals Between Advice Agencies and Solicitors*, Edinburgh: Scottish Office Central Research Unit.

Millar, J. and Ridge, T. (2001) *Families, Poverty, Work and Care – A Review of the Literature on Lone Parents and Low Income Couple Families with Children*, London: Department for Work and Pensions (Research Report No.153).

Mirrlees-Black, C. (1999) *Domestic Violence: Findings From a New British Crime Survey Self-Completion Questionnaire*, London: Home Office (Home Office Research Study 191).

Mnookin, R. H. and Kornhauser, L. (1979) Bargaining in the Shadow of the Law: The Case of Divorce, in 88 *Yale Law Journal* 950.

Money Advice Trust (2005) *Annual Report and Accounts*, London: Money Advice Trust.

Moorhead, R. (2000) Conditional Fee Agreements, Legal Aid and Access to Justice, in 33 *University of British Columbia Law Review*.

Moorhead, R. (2000) *Pioneers in Practice*, London: Lord Chancellor's Department.

Moorhead, R. and Pleasence, P. (2003) Access to Justice after Universalism: Introduction, in 30(1) *Journal of Law and Society*.

Moorhead, R., Sefton, M. and Douglas, G. (2004) *The Advice Needs of Lone Parents*, London: National Council for One Parent Families.

Moorhead, R. and Sherr, A. (2003) *An Anatomy of Access*: *Evaluating Entry and Initial Advice and Signposting Using Model Clients*, London: Legal Services Commission.

Moorhead, R., Sherr, A., Webley, L., Rogers, S., Sherr, L., Paterson, A. and Domberger, S. (2001) *Quality and Cost: Final Report on the Contracting of Civil, Non-Family Advice and Assistance Pilot*, London: The Stationery Office.

MORI (2004) *Unmet Demand for Citizens Advice Bureaux*, London: Citizens Advice.

Morris, S., Sutton, M. and Gravelle, H. (2005) Inequity and Inequality in the Use of Health Care in England: An Empirical Investigation, in 60 *Social Science and Medicine*.

Mulcahy, L., Selwood, M. and Netten, A. (2000) *Mediating Medical Negligence Claims: An Option for the Future?* Norwich: The Stationery Office.

Murayama, M., Minamikata, S., Hamano, R., Ageishi, K., Ozaki, I. and Sugino, I. (2005) *Legal Problems and their Resolution – Disputing Behaviour in Japan*, paper presented at the Annual Meeting of the Research Committee of Sociology of Law, International Sociological Association, Paris, France, 11-13 July 2005.

National Association of Citizens Advice Bureaux (1998) *The CAB Service and Community Legal Services: A Paper for the Lord Chancellor*, London: NACAB.

National Audit Office (2005) *Knowledge of the Choose and Book Programme Amongst GPs in England*, London: National Audit Office.

National Audit Office (2005) *Patient Choice at the Point of GP Referral*, London: The Stationery Office.

National Consumer Council (1995) *Seeking Civil Justice: A Survey of People's Needs and Experiences*, London: National Consumer Council.

National Council for One Parent Families (2001) *One Parent Families Today: The Facts*, London: National Council for One Parent Families.

National Council for One Parent Families, Crisis, Health Action for Homeless People (2001) *A Secure Start for Young Families: the housing and support needs of young lone mothers*, London: NCOPF.

Neisser, U. (1986) 'Nested Structure in Autobiographical Memory' in Rubin, D. C. (ed.) *Autobiographical Memory*, Cambridge: Cambridge University Press.

Nettleton, S. and Burrows, R. (1998) Mortgage Debt, Insecure Home Ownership and Health: An Exploratory Analysis, in 20 *Sociology of Health and Illness*.

Nettleton, S. and Burrows, R. (2000) When a Capital Investment Becomes an Emotional Loss: The Health Consequences of the Experience of Mortgage Possession in England, in 15 *Housing Studies*.

Netto, G., Arshad, R., de Lima, P., Diniz, F. A., MacEwen, M., Patel, V. and Syed, R. (2001) *Audit of Research on Minority Ethnic Issues in Scotland from a 'Race' Perspective*, Edinburgh: Scottish Executive Central Research Unit.

Newburn, T. (2002) 'Young People, Crime and Youth Justice' in Maguire, M., Morgan, R. and Reiner, R. (eds.) *The Oxford Handbook of Criminology* (third edition), Oxford: Oxford University Press.

Ngo-Metzger, Q., Massagli, M. P., Clarridge, B. R., Manocchia, M., Davis, R. B., Iezzoni, L. I. and Phillips, R. S. (2003) Linguistic And Cultural Barriers To Care, in 18(1) *Journal Of General Internal Medicine*.

Nicholas, S., Povey, D., Walker, A. and Kershaw, C. (2005) *Crime in England and Wales 2004/2005,* London: Home Office (Home Office Statistical Bulletin 11/05).

Noble, M., Lloyd, M., Sigala, M., Wright, G., Cox, M., Dibben, C., Perkins, H. and Strudwick, N. (2002) *Predictive Legal Needs Models Development Project: Report to the Legal Services Research Centre,* Oxford: Social Disadvantage Research Centre, Department of Social Policy and Social Work, University of Oxford.

O'Brien, R. and Seymour, R. (2005) 'Videolink Projects' in Legal Services Commission (ed.) *Innovation in the Community Legal Service,* London: Legal Services Commission.

O'Grady, A., Balmer, N. J., Carter, B., Pleasence, P., Buck, A. and Genn, H. (2005) Institutional Racism and Civil Justice, in 28(4) *Ethnic and Racial Studies*.

O'Shea, D., King, C. T., Greenfield, S., Shelton, E., Sullivan, L., Taber, E. and Olsen, J. A. (2004) *National Benefit/Cost Analysis of Three Digit-Accessed Telephone Information and Referral Services,* Austin, Texas: Ray Marshall Center for the Study of Human Resources.

Office for Standards in Education (2003) *National Curriculum Citizenship: Planning and Implementation 2002/03: An Inspection Report of 25 Schools*, London: OFSTED.

Office of the Deputy Prime Minister (1996) *More than a Roof: A Report into Tackling Homelessness,* London: Office of the Deputy Prime Minister.

Office of the Deputy Prime Minister (2002) *The Provision of Accommodation and Support for Households Experiencing Domestic Violence in England,* London: Office of the Deputy Prime Minister.

Office of the Deputy Prime Minister (2003) *English House Condition Survey*, London: HMSO.

Office for National Statistics (2001) *Social Trends 31*, London: The Stationery Office.

Office for National Statistics (2003) *Social Trends 33*, London: The Stationery Office.

Office for National Statistics (2004) *General Household Survey 2003 Technical Appendix B*, London: Office for National Statistics.

Palmer, C. and Monoghan, C. (2001) *The Public Perspective on Accessing Legal Advice and Information: Key Findings from a Microcosm Study*, Edinburgh: Scottish Executive Central Research Unit.

Parker, S., Limbers, L. and McKeon, E. (2002) *Homelessness and Accommodation Models for People Living with Mental Health Problems,* Rozelle, New South Wales: Mental Health Coordinating Council.

Pearson, J. and Davis, L. (2002) *The Hotline Outcomes Assessment Study: Final Report – Phase III: Full-Scale Telephone Survey*, Denver: Center for Policy Research.

Pease, K. (1998) *Repeat Victimisation: Taking Stock,* London: Home Office, Crime Detection and Prevention Paper 90.

Perkins, H. and Macmillen, L. (2005) 'Primary Health Care Projects' in Legal Services Commission (ed.) *Innovation in the Community Legal Service*, London: Legal Services Commission.

Petterson, G., Sissons, P. and Wann, M. (1995) *Users' Views of CAB Services*, London: NACAB.

Peysner, J. and Seneviratne, M. (2005) *The Management of Civil Cases: The Courts and the Post-Woolf Landscape,* London: Department for Constitutional Affairs.

Phelps, A., Hayward, B. and Hanson, T. (2005) *2004 English and Welsh Civil and Social Justice Survey: Technical Report*, London: BMRB.

Pleasence, P. (1998) *Personal Injury Litigation in Practice*, London: LABRU.

Pleasence, P., Balmer, N. J., Buck, A., O'Grady, A. and Genn, H. (2003) Family Problems: Who Does What and When: Further Findings from the LSRC Survey of Justiciable Problems, in 33 *Family Law.*

Pleasence, P., Balmer, N. J., Buck, A., O'Grady, A. and Genn, H. (2004) Multiple Justiciable Problems: Common Clusters and their Social and Demographic Indicators, in *Journal of Empirical Legal Studies,* Vol.1, No.2.

Pleasence, P., Balmer, N. J., Buck, A., O'Grady, A. and Genn, H. (2004) Civil Law Problems and Morbidity, in 58(7) *Journal of Epidemiology and Community Health.*

Pleasence, P., Balmer, N. J., Buck, A., O'Grady, A., Maclean, M. and Genn, H. (2003) Family Problems – What Happens and to Whom, in 33 *Family Law.*

Pleasence, P., Balmer, N. J., Genn, H., Buck, A. and O'Grady, A. (2003) The Experience of Clinical Negligence Within the General Population, in 9(6) *Clinical Risk.*

Pleasence, P., Buck, A., Balmer, N. J., O'Grady, A., Genn, H. and Smith, M. (2004) *Causes of Action: Civil Law and Social Justice* (first edition), Norwich: The Stationery Office.

Pleasence, P., Buck, A., Goriely, T., Taylor, J., Perkins, H. and Quirk, H. (2001) *Local Legal Need,* London: Legal Services Research Centre.

Pleasence, P., Genn, H., Balmer, N. J., Buck, A. and O'Grady, A. (2003) Causes of Action: First Findings of the LSRC Periodic Survey, in 30(1) *Journal of Law and Society.*

Pleasence, P., Maclean, S. and Morley, A. (1996) *Profiling Civil Litigation: The Case for Research,* London: LABRU.

Popay, J. and Jones, G. (1990) Patterns of Health and Illness Amongst Lone Parents, in 19(4) *Journal of Social Policy.*

Reiser, B. J. (1988) 'Predictive Inferencing in Autobiographical Memory Retrieval' in Gruneberg, M. M., Morris, P. E. and Sykes, R. N. (eds.) *Practical Aspects of Memory. Volume 1: Memory in Everyday Life,* New York: Wiley.

Ritchie, J., Morrisey, C. and Ward, K. (1988) *Keeping in Touch with the Talking: The Community Care Needs of People with Mental Illness,* London: SCPR.

Rosenthal, M., Mulcahy, L. and Lloyd-Bostock, S. (eds.) (1999) *Medical Mishaps: Pieces of the Puzzle,* Buckingham: Open University Press

Rowland, M. (2002) *Family Resources Survey: Annual Technical Report: 2000-01,* London: Office for National Statistics.

Royal Commission on Legal Services (1979) *Final Report,* London: HMSO.

Rubin, D. C. and Kozin, M. (1984) Vivid Memories, in 16 *Cognition*.

Rushcliffe Committee (1945) *Report of the Committee on Legal Aid and Legal Advice in England and Wales,* London: HMSO.

Rutter, M., Giller, H. and Hagell, A. (1998) *Antisocial Behaviour by Young People,* Cambridge: Cambridge University Press.

Schuyt, K., Groenendijk, K. and Sloot, B. (1976) *De Weg naar Het Recht* (The Road to Justice), Deventer: Klewer.

Scott, S. and Sage, C. (2001) *Gateways to the Law: An Exploratory Study of How Community Agencies Assist Clients with Legal Problems,* New South Wales: Law and Justice Foundation of New South Wales.

Scottish Consumer Council (1997) *Civil Disputes in Scotland,* Glasgow: Scottish Consumer Council.

Scottish Executive Justice Department (2005) *Advice for All: Public Funded Legal Assistance in Scotland – The Way Forward,* Edinburgh: Scottish Executive.

Sharpe, J. and Bostock, J. (2002) *Supporting People with Debt and Mental Health Problems: Research With Psychological Therapists in Northumberland,* Newcastle: Department of Psychological Services and Research, North Tyneside and Northumberland NHS Mental Health Trust.

Sherr, A., Moorhead, R. and Paterson, A. (1993) *Franchising Legal Aid: Final Report,* London: Legal Aid Board.

Sherr, A., Moorhead, R. and Paterson, A. (1994) *Lawyers – The Quality Agenda, Volume 1: Assessing and Developing Competence and Quality in Legal Aid; The Report of the Birmingham Franchising Pilot,* London: HMSO.

Smith, D. J. (1997) 'Ethnic Origins, Crime and Criminal Justice in England and Wales' in Tonry, M. (ed.) *Ethnicity, Crime and Immigration: Comparative and Cross-National Perspectives,* Chicago: University of Chicago Press.

Snijders, T. A. B. and Boskers, R. J. (1999) *Multilevel Analysis,* Newbury Park, California: Sage.

Social Exclusion Unit (2000) *National Strategy for Neighbourhood Renewal: Report of Policy Action Team 8: Anti-Social Behaviour,* London: The Stationery Office.

Social Exclusion Unit (2001) *Preventing Social Exclusion,* London: Cabinet Office.

Social Exclusion Unit (2002) *Reducing Re-Offending by Ex-Prisoners,* London: Office of the Deputy Prime Minister.

Social Exclusion Unit (2005) *Improving Services, Improving Lives,* London: Office of the Deputy Prime Minister.

Social Exclusion Unit (2005) *Transitions - Young Adults with Complex Needs,* London: Office of the Deputy Prime Minister.

Social Market Foundation (1994) *Organising Cost-Effective Access to Justice,* Social Market Foundation Memorandum Number 7.

Sommerlad, H. (1999) English Perspectives on Quality: The Client-Led Model of Quality – A Third Way, in 33(2) *University of British Columbia Law Review*.

Sparkes, J. and Glennerster, H. (2002) 'Preventing Social Exclusion: Education's Contribution' in Hills, J., Le Grand, J. and Piachaud, D. (eds.) *Understanding Social Exclusion,* Oxford: Oxford University Press.

Sproston, K. A., Pitson, L. B. and Walker, E. (2001) The Use of Primary Care Services by the Chinese Population Living in England: Examining Inequalities, in 6(3-4) *Ethnicity & Health*.

Stadt, R. W. (2003) *Technology, the Courts and Self-Represented Litigants,* paper presented at the International Legal Aid Group Conference, Harvard University, 18-20 June 2003.

196

Statistics New Zealand (1998) *Young New Zealanders,* Wellington: Statistics New Zealand.

Stein, J. (2001) *The Future of Social Justice in Britain: A New Mission for the Community Legal Service,* London: Centre for Analysis of Social Exclusion, London School of Economics.

Straus, M., Gelles, R. and Steinmetz, S. (1980) *Behind Closed Doors,* New York: Anchor.

Sullivan, G., Burnam A. and Koegel, P. (2000) Pathways To Homelessness Among The Mentally Ill, in 35(10) *Social Psychiatry And Psychiatric Epidemiology.*

Swales, K. (2001) *Measuring Legal Needs: Technical Report,* London: National Centre for Social Research.

Tacket, A. (2004) *Tackling Domestic Violence: The Role of Health Professionals,* London: Home Office (Development and Practice Report 32).

Trinder, L., Connolly, J., Kellett, J. and Notley, C. (2005) *A Profile of Applicants and Respondents in Contact Cases in Essex,* London: Department for Constitutional Affairs.

Tsushima, T. and Gecas, V. (2001) Role Taking and Socialisation in Single Parent Families, in 22(3) *Journal of Family Issues.*

Turner, A. G. (1982) 'What Subjects of Survey Research Believe About Confidentiality' in Sieber, J. E. (ed.) *The Ethics of Social Research: Surveys and Experiments,* New York: Springer Verlag.

Van den Biggelaar, P. J. M. (2005) *The Value-Added of a Good Gateway to the Legal Aid System,* paper presented at the International Legal Aid Group Conference, Killarney, Ireland, 8-10 June 2005.

Van Velthoven, B. C. J. and ter Voert, M. (2005) *Paths to Justice in the Netherlands,* paper presented at the ILAG conference, Killarney, Ireland, 8-10 June 2005.

Victim Support (2005) *Victim Support Annual Report and Accounts 2005,* London: Victim Support.

Wagenaar, W. A. (1986) My Memory: A Study of Autobiographical Memory Over Six Years, in 18 *Cognitive Psychology.*

Walby, S. (2004) *The Cost of Domestic Violence,* London: National Statistics and Women and Equality Unit.

Walby, S. and Allen, J. (2004) *Domestic Violence, Sexual Assault and Stalking: Findings from the British Crime Survey,* London: Home Office (Home Office Research Study 276).

Walker, A., Maher, J., Coulthard, M., Goddard, E. and Thomas, M. (2001) *Living in Britain: Results from the 2000-01 General Household Survey,* London: The Stationery Office.

Walker, J. (2004) FAInS – A New Approach for Family Lawyers? in 34 *Family Law.*

Walker, L. (1979) *The Battered Woman,* New York: Harper and Row.

Weitzman, L. J. and Maclean, M. (eds.) (1992) *Economic Consequences of Divorce,* Oxford: Clarendon Press.

Welsh Assembly (2003) *The Housing and Socio-Economic Circumstances of Black and Minority Ethnic People Living in Wales,* Cardiff: Welsh Assembly (Housing Research Report HR 1/03).

White, R. (1976) *Report to the Lord Chancellor: The Unmet Need for Legal Services,* London: Lord Chancellor's Office.

Wilcox, P. (2000) Lone Motherhood: The Impact on Living Standards of Leaving a Violent Relationship, in 34(2) *Journal of Social Policy and Administration.*

Williams, B. (1999) *Working with Victims of Crime: Policies, Politics and Practice,* London: Jessica Kingsley Publishers.

Wilson, S. H. and Walker, G. M. (1993) Unemployment and Health, in 107 *Public Health.*

World Health Organisation (2005) *WHO Multi-Country Study on Women's Health and Domestic Violence Against Women: Initial Report on Prevalence, Health Outcomes and Women's Responses,* Geneva: World Health Organisation.

Yang, J. A. and Jackson, C. L. (1998) Overcoming Obstacles in Providing Mental Health Treatment to Older Adults: Getting in the Door, in 35(4) *Psychotherapy.*

Yarrow, S. (2000) *Just Rewards? The Outcome of Conditional Fee Cases,* London: University of Westminster.

Yarrow, S. and Abrams, P. (1999) *Nothing to Lose? Clients' Experiences of Using Conditional Fees,* London: University of Westminster.

Young, J. (1994) 'Recent Paradigms in Criminology' in Maguire, M., Morgan, R. and Reiner, R. (eds.) *The Oxford Handbook of Criminology* (first edition), Oxford: Clarendon Press.

Zedner, L. (2002) 'Victims' in Maguire, M., Morgan, R. and Reiner, R. (eds.) *The Oxford Handbook of Criminology* (third edition), Oxford: Clarendon Press.